ISBN 978-1-326-46349-6

THE EXPERIENCED

English House-keeper,
For the Use and Ease of
Ladies, Housekeepers, Cooks, &c.
Wrote purely from PRACTICE,
And dedicated to the

Hon. Lady Elizabeth Warburton,
Whom the Author lately served as Housekeeper.
Consisting of near Nine Hundred Original Receipts,
most of which never appeared in Print.

PART I, Lemon Pickle, Browning for all Sorts of made Dishes, Soups, Fish, Plain Meat, Game, Made Dishes both hot and cold, Pyes, Puddings, &c.

PART II. All Kinds of Confectionary, particularly the Gold and Silver Web for covering of Sweet meats, and a Dessert of Spun Sugar with Directions to set out a Table, in the most elegant Manner, and in the modern Taste ; Floating Islands, Fish-Ponds, Transparent Puddings, Trifles, Whips, &c.

PART III-. Pickling, Potting, and Collaring, Wines, Vinegars, Catch ups, Distilling, with two most valuable Receipts, one for refining Malt Liquors, the other for curing Acid Wines, and a correct List of every Thing in Season for every Month in the Year:

THE TENTH EDITION.
WITH AN ENGRAVED HEAD OF THE AUTHOR;
Also Two Plans of a Grand Table of Two Covers;
and
A curious new invented Fire Stove, wherein any common Fuel may be burnt instead of Charcoal.

By ELIZABETH RAFFALD.
LONDON:
PRINTED FOR R, BALDWIN NO. 47, IN PATER-NOSTER-ROW.
MDCCLXXXVI.

Table of Contents

Page
9   Introduction
11   Dedication
13   Preface
15   Description of the plate

    Part I
17   I Soups
29   II Dressing fish
59   III Roasting and boiling
81   IV On made dishes
129   V Pies
147   VI puddings

    Part II
161   VII Decorations for a table
181   VIII Preserving
203   IX Drying and candying
213   X On creams, custards and cheesecakes
227   XI Cakes
239   XII little savoury dishes (no observations)

    Part III
249   XIII Potting and collaring
261   XIV possets and gruel
269   XV wines, catchup and vinegar
289   XVI pickling
303   XVII Keeping garden stuff and fruit
309   XVIII Distilling
313   List of seasons
329   Directions for a grand table
333   Index

Introduction

Thank you for buying this reproduction of Elizabeth Raffald's cookbook from the tenth edition, published in 1786. The original was first published in 1769 and went on to have 13 genuine reprints and over 23 pirate versions.

I have reproduced the cookbook exactly as Elizabeth wrote it, apart from this introduction and the list of contents. I have also begun each chapter on a new page, as we would expect to see now. The original index is included although I'm afraid it does not relate as closely as it should to this edition. Something to improve for future editions, I hope.

Elizabeth was an amazing woman, achieving a great many things in a short time. She was an author, innovator, benefactor and entrepreneur as well as a mother and a wife. From the age of 15 she was in service as a housekeeper to great families such as the Warburtons of Arley Hall, Cheshire, before marrying their head gardener and at the age of 30 beginning her career in business. She began with catering, included a school and employment office before writing this cookbook which contains her own original, innovative recipes, giving us wedding cake, stock cubes, Eccles cakes and much more that we take for granted. She went on to gain a huge reputation for her confectionery skills, while running shops and a coaching inn, giving financial aid to the only newspaper in Manchester at the time, producing the town's first ever directory in 1772, (only the second after London), supporting several poor widows of the area, collaborating on a book of midwifery, and having 9 children.

In 2014 I came across her story by accident, having lived in Manchester virtually all my life and I began to wonder why I had never heard of her. The more I looked the more interested I became. First I began to give talks about her, then realized there was too much information to take in on a 30 minute hearing, so I produced a short summary of her story, 'Elizabeth Raffald, The Experienced English Housekeeper of Manchester'. Shortly afterwards I heard about the campaign for Manchester to have a new female statue and I nominated her for that, which gave more impetus to my passion to tell more people about her.

I also felt that it was a shame that her cookbook was inaccessible to most people. The only versions I could find were expensive originals or cheap digitized copies, neither of which satisfied me as accessible. I must mention a predecessor of mine, Roy Shipperbottom, who spent 20 years researching Elizabeth before me who also retyped her recipes in hardback form but which is now also difficult to find.

My next book about her will be one to draw together all my research to provide a reference work for future studies, for she surely should be studied and celebrated. After that I intend to return to my fiction roots and produce a novel of her story, one that does justice to the character I have found in her writing. I will continue telling anyone who will listen how amazing Elizabeth was and I hope that soon when I ask a group 'Has anyone heard of her before?' most people will say yes.

Thank you and I hope you enjoy some, if not all, of Elizabeth's recipes.

Suze Appleton

To The HONOURABLE
Lady Elizabeth Warburton.

PERMIT me, honoured Madam, to lay before you a work, for which I am ambitious of obtaining your Lady ship's approbation, as much as to oblige a great number of my friends, who are well acquainted with the practice I have had in the art of Cookery, ever since left your Ladyship's family, and have often sollicited me to publish for the instruction of their housekeepers. As I flatter myself I had the happiness of giving satisfaction, during my service, Madam, in your family, it would be a still greater encouragement, should my endeavours for the service of my sex be honoured with the favourable opinion of so good a judge of propriety and elegance as your Ladyship. I am not vain enough to propose adding any thing to the Experienced Housekeeper, but hope these receipts (written purely from practice) may be of use to young persons who are willing to improve themselves. I rely on your Ladyship's candour, and whatever Ladies favour this book with reading it, to excuse the plainness of the style ; as, in compliance with the desire of my friends, I have studied to express myself so as to be understood by the meanest capacity, and think myself happy in being allowed the honour of subscribing,

MADAM,

    Your Ladyship's

        Most dutiful,

            Most obedient,

                And most humble Servant,

                      ELIZABETH RAFFALD.

Preface to the First Edition

WHEN I reflect upon the number of books already in print upon this subject, and with what contempt they are read I cannot but be apprehensive that this may meet the same fate from- some, who will censure before they either see it or try its value. Therefore the only favour I have to beg the publick is, not to censure my work before they have made trial of some one receipt, which I am persuaded, if carefully followed, will answer their expectations; as I can faithfully assure my friends, that they are truly written from my own experience, and not borrowed from any other author, nor glossed over with hard names, or words of high stile, but written in my own plain language, and every sheet care fully perused as it came from the press, having an opportunity of having it printed by a neighbour, whom I can rely on doing it the strictest justice, without the least alteration. The whole work being now completed to my wishes, I think it my duty to render my most sincere and grateful thanks to my most noble and worthy friends, who have already shown their good opinion of my endeavours to serve my sex, by raising me so large a subscription, which far exceeds my expectations. I have not only been honoured by having above eight- hundred of their names inserted in my subscription, but also have had all their interest in this laborious undertaking, which I have at last arrived to the happiness of completing, though at the expence of my health, by being too studious, and giving too close application. The only anxious wish I have left is, that my worthy friends may find it useful in their families, and bean instructor to the young and ignorant as it has been my chiefest Care to write in as plain a stile as possible, so as to be under stood by the weakest capacity. I am not afraid of being called extravagant, if my reader does not think that I have erred on the frugal hand. I have made it my study to please both the eye and the palate, without using pernicious things for the sake of beauty. And though

I have given some of my dishes French names as they are only known by those names, yet they will not be found very expensive, nor add compositions but as plain as the nature of the dish will admit of. The receipts for the confectionary are such as I daily sell in my own shop, which any Lady may examine at pleasure, as I still continue my best endeavours to give satisfaction to all who are pleased to favour me with their custom. It may be necessary to inform my readers, that I have spent fifteen years in great and worthy families, in the capacity of a house keeper, and had an opportunity of travelling with them ; but finding the common servants generally so ignorant in dressing meat, and a good cook so hard to be met with, put me upon studying the art of cookery, more than perhaps I otherwise should have done : always endeavouring to join œconomy with neatness and elegance, being sensible what valuable qualifications these are in a housekeeper or cook ; for of what use is their skill, if they put their master or lady to an immoderate expence in dressing a dinner for a small company, when at the same time a prudent manager would have dressed twice the number of dishes for a much greater company, at half the cost. I have given no directions for cullis, as I have found by experience, that lemon pickle and browning answers both for beauty and taste (at a trifling expence) better than cullis, which is extravagant: for had I known the use and value of those two receipts when I first took upon me the part and duty of a house-keeper, it would have saved me a great deal of trouble in making gravy, and those I served a deal of expence. The number of receipts in this book are not so numerous as in some others, but they are what will be found useful and sufficient for any gentleman's family — neither have I meddled with physical receipts, leaving them to the physicians' superior judgment, whose proper province they are.

Description of the PLATE.

THE Plate is the design of three stove-fires for the kitchen that will burn coals or embers instead of char coal (which I always found expensive, as well as pernicious to the cooks) and will carry off the smoke of the coals and steam, and smell of the pots and stew pans ; the coals are burnt in cast iron pots, flat at the bottom, with bars, A A, Fronts of the stove. BB, Top of the stove, which is covered all over with cast iron. CC, Stove-pots, in which the fire is made. D, The form of the pot, with two vents cast in them, six inches deep at the top, and three wide, as expressed at HH in the pot, and to let the smoke through at HH in the flues. EE, Carried from there through the back wall to the kitchen chimney, as expressed in the lower plan. FF, Back wall G, The chimney breast, betwixt which and the back wall the steam rises, and goes, off into the kitchen chimney by a vent made into it. HH, Vents in the pot. II, Draughts for the fires, and to receive the allies. The scale will give the dimensions.

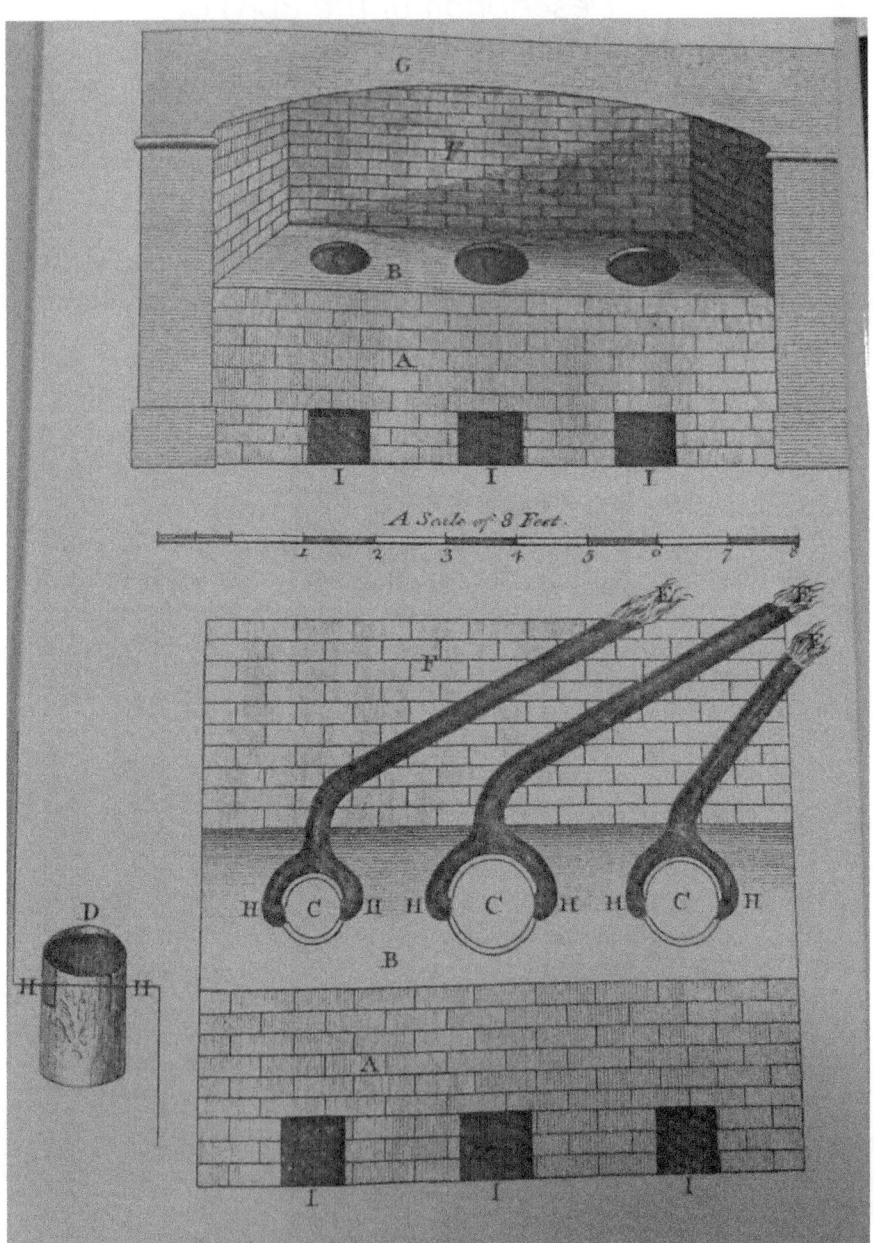

THE EXPERIENCED

English House-keeper,

CHAP. I

Observations on SOUPS

WHEN you make any kind of soups, particularly portable, vermicelli, or brown gravy soup, or any other that has roots or herbs in, always observe to lay your meat in the bottom of your pan with a good lump of butter; cut the herbs and roots small, lay them over your meat, cover it close, set it over a very slow fire, it will draw all the virtue out of the roots or herbs, and turn it to a good gravy, and give the soup a very different flavour from putting water in at the first: when your gravy is almost dried up fill your pan with water, when it begins to boil take off the fat, and follow the directions of your receipt for what sort of soup you are making: when you make old peas soup take soft water, for green peas hard is the best, it keeps the peas a better colour: when you make any white soup don't put in cream till you take it off the fire: always dish up your soups the last thing; if it be a gravy soup will skin over if you let it stand; if it be a peas soup it often settles, and the top looks thin.

To make PORTABLE SOUP *for Travellers.*
TAKE three large legs of veal, and one of beef, the lean part of half a ham, cut them in small pieces, put a quarter of a pound of butter at the bottom of a large cauldron, then lay in the meat and bones, with four ounces of anchovies, two ounces of mace, cut off the green leaves of five or six heads of celery, wash the heads quite clean, cut them small, put them in with three large carrots cut thin, cover

the cauldron close, and set it over a moderate fire ; when you find the gravy begins to draw, keep taking it up till you have got it all out, then put water in to cover the meat, set it on the fire again and let it boil slowly for four hours, then strain it through a hair sieve into a clean pan, and let it boil three parts away, then strain the gravy that you drew from the meat into the pan, let it boil gently (and keep scumming the fat off very clean as it rises) till it looks thick like glue; you must take great care when it is near enough that it don't burn; put in Chyan pepper to your taste, then pour it on flat earthen dishes, a quarter of an inch thick, and let it stand till the next day, and cut it out with round tins a little larger than a crown piece; lay the cakes on dishes, and let them in the sun to dry; this soup will answer best to be made in frosty weather; when the cakes are dry, put them in a tin box with writing paper betwixt every cake, and keep them in a dry place; this is a very useful soup to be kept in gentle men's families, for by pouring a pint of boiling water on one cake, and a little salt, it will make a good basin of broth. A little boiling water poured on it will make gravy for a turkey or fowls, the longer it is kept the better.- N.B. Be careful to keep turning the cakes as they dry.

To make a TRANSPARENT SOUP.

TAKE a leg of veal, and cut off the meat as thin as you can; when you have cut off all the meat clean from the bone, break the bone in small pieces, put the meat in a large jug, and the bones at top, with a bunch of sweet herbs, a quarter of an ounce of mace, half a pound of Jordan almonds blanched and beat fine, pour on it four quarts of boiling water, let it stand all night by the fire covered close, the next day put it into a well tinned saucepan, and let it boil slowly till it is reduced to two quarts; be sure you take the scum and fat off as it rises, all the time it is boiling; strain it into a punch bowl, let it settle for two hours, pour it into a clean sauce-pan clear from the sediments, if any at the bottom; have ready three ounces of rice boiled in water; if you like vermicelli better, boil two ounces, when enough, put it in and serve it up.

To make a HARE SOUP.

CUT a large old hare in small pieces, and put it in a mug. with three blades of mace, a little salt, two large onions, one red herring, six morels, half a pint of red wine, three quarts of water, bake it in a quick oven three hours, than strain it into a tossing-pan, have ready boiled three ounces of French barley, or sago, in water; scald the liver of the hare in boiling water two minutes; rub it through a hair sieve with the back of a wooden spoon, put it into the soup with the barley or sago, and a quarter of a pound of butter, set it over the fire, keep stirring it but don't let it boil; if you don't like liver, put in crisped bread steeped in red wine. This is a rich soup, and proper for a large entertainment; and where two soups are required, almond or onion soup for the top, and the hare soup for the bottom.

To make a RICH VERMICELLI SOUP.

INTO a large tossing-pan put four ounces of butter, cut a knuckle of veal, and a scrag of mutton into small pieces, about the size of walnuts; slice in the meat of a shank of ham, with three or four blades of mace, two or three carrots, two parsnips, two large onions, with a clove stuck in at each end, cut in four or five heads of celery washed clean, a bunch of sweet herbs, eight or ten morels, and an anchovy; cover the pan close up, and set it over a flow fire, without any water, till the gravy is drawn out of the meat, then pour the gravy out into a pot or bason, let the meat brown in the same pan, and take care it don't burn, then pour in four quarts of water, let it boil gently till it is wasted to three pints, then strain it, and put the other gravy to it, set it on the fire, add to it two ounces of vermicelli, cut the nicest part of ahead of celery, Chyan pepper and salt, to your taste, and let it boil for four minutes } if not a good colour, put in a little browning, lay a small French roll in the soup dish, pour in the soup upon it, and lay some of, the vermicelli over it.

To make an OX CHEEK SOUP.

FIRST break the bones of an ox cheek, and wash it in many waters, then lay it in warm water, throw in a little salt to fetch out the lime, wash it out very well, than take a large stew-pan, put two ounces of butter at the bottom of the pan, and lay the flesh side of the cheek down, add to it half a pound of a shank of ham cut in slices, and four heads of celery, pull off the leaves, wash the heads clean, and cut them in with three large onions, two car rots, and one parsnip sliced, a few beets cut small, and three blades of mace, set it over a moderate fire a quarter of an hour; this draws the virtue from the roots, which gives a pleasant strength to the gravy. I have made a good gravy by this method, with roots and butter, only adding a little browning to give it a pretty colour: when the head has simmered a quarter of an hour, put to it six quarts of water, and let it stew till it is reduced to two quarts: if you would have it eat like soup, strain and take out the meat and other ingredients, and put in the white part of a head of celery cut in small pieces, with a little browning to make it a fine colour, take two ounces of vermicelli, give it a scald in the soup, and put the top of a French roll in the middle of a tureen, and serve it up. If you would have it eat like stew, take up the face as whole as possible, and have ready cut in square pieces, a boiled turnip and carrot, a slice of bread toasted and cut in small dices, put in a little Chyan pepper, and strain the soup through a hair sieve upon the meat, carrot, turnip, and bread, to serve it up.

To make ALMOND SOUP.

TAKE a neck of veal, and the scrag end of a neck of mutton, chop them in small pieces, put them in a large tossing pan, cut in a turnip, with a blade or two of mace, and five quarts of water, set it ever the fire, and let it boil gently till it is reduced to two quarts, strain it through a hair sieve into a clear pot, then put in six ounces of almonds blanched and beat fine, half a pint of thick cream, and Chyan pepper to your taste, have ready three small French rolls, made for that purpose, the size of a small teacup; if they are larger they will not look well, and drink up too much of the soup; blanch a few Jordan almonds, and cut them lengthways, stick them round the edge of the rolls slant- ways, then stick them all over the top of the rolls, and put them in the tureen ; when dished up pour the soup upon the rolls : these rolls look like a hedge-hog: some French cooks give this soup the name of hedge- hog soup.

To make SOUP A-LA-REINE.

TAKE a knuckle of veal, and three or four pounds of lean beef, put to it six quarts of water with a little salt, when it boils scum it well, then put in six large onions, two large carrots, a head or two of celery, a parsnip, one leek, and a little thyme, boil them all together till the meat is boiled quite down, then strain it through a hair sieve, and let it stand about half an hour, then scum it well, and clear it off gently from the settlings into a clear pan boil half a pint of cream, and pour it on the crumbs of a half-penny loaf, and let it soak well; take half a pound of almonds, blanch and beat them as fine as possible, putting in now and then a little cream to pre vent them from oiling, then take the yolks of six hard eggs, and the roll that is soaked in the cream, and beat them all together quite fine, then make your broth hot and pour it to your almonds, strain it through a fine hair sieve, rubbing it with a spoon till all the goodness is gone through into a stew-pan, and add more cream to make it white; set it over the fire, keep stirring it till it boils, scum off the froth as it rises, soak the tops of two French rolls in melted butter in a stew-pan till they are crisp, but not brown, then take them out of the butter, and lay them on a plate before the fire; and, a quarter of an hour before you send it to the table take a little of the soup hot, and put it to the roll in the bottom of the tureen, put your soup on the fire, keep stirring it till ready to boil, then pour it into your tureen, and serve it up hot; be sure you take all the fat off the broth before you put it to the almonds, or it will spoil it, and take care it does not curdle.

To make ONION SOUP.

BOIL eight or ten large Spanish onions in milk and water, change it three times, when they are quite soft, rub them through a hair sieve, cut an old cock in pieces, and boil it for gravy with one blade of mace, strain it, and pour it upon the pulp of the onions, boil it gently with, the crumb of an old penny loaf, grated into half a pint of cream; add Chyan pepper and salt to your taste: a few heads of asparagus or stewed spinage, both make it eat well and look very pretty: grate a crust of brown bread round the edge of the dish.

To make WHITE ONION SOUP.

TAKE thirty large onions, boil them in five quarts of water with a knuckle of veal, a blade or two of mace, and a little whole pepper; when your onions are quite soft take them up, and rub them through a hair sieve, and work half a pound of butter with flour in them when the meat is boiled so as to leave the bone, strain the liquor to the onions, and boil it gently for half an hour, serve it up with a coffee cup full of cream and a little salt, be sure you stir it when you put in the flour and butter, for fear of its burning,

To make BROWN ONION SOUP.

SKIN and cut round ways in slices six large Spanish onions, fry them in butter till they are a nice brown, and very tender, then take them out and lay them on a hair sieve to drain out the butter, when drained put them in a pot with five quarts of boiling water, boil them one hour and stir them often, then add pepper and salt to your taste, rub the crumbs of a penny loaf through a cullender, put it to the soup, stir it well to keep it from being in lumps, and boil it two hours more; ten minutes before you send it up beat the yolks of two eggs, with two spoonfuls of vinegar, and a little of the soup, pour it in by degrees, and keep stirring it all the time one way, put in a few cloves if you choose it. — N. B. It is a fine soup, and will keep three or four days.

To make GREEN PEAS SOUP.

SHELL a peck of peas, and boil them in spring water till they are soft, then work them through a hair sieve, take the water that your peas were boiled in, and put in a knuckle of veal, three slices of ham, and cut two carrots, a turnip, and a few beet leaves shred small, add a little more water to the meat, set it over the fire, and let it boil one hour and a half; then strain the gravy into a bowl and mix it with the pulp, and put in a little juice of spinage, which must be beat and squeezed through a cloth, put in as much as will make it look a pretty colour, then give it a gentle boil, which will take off the taste of the spinage, slice in the whitest part of a head of celery, put in a lump of sugar the size of a walnut, take a slice of bread and cut it in little square pieces, cut a little bacon the same way, fry them a light brown in fresh butter, cut a large cabbage lettuce in slices, fry it after the other, put it in the tureen with the fried bread and bacon: have ready boiled as for eating a pint of young peas, and put them in the soup, with a little chopped mint if you like it, and pour it into your tureen.

To make a COMMON PEAS SOUP.

TO one quart of split peas put four quarts of soft water, a little lean bacon, or roast beef bones, wash one head of celery, cut it and put it in with a turnip, boil it till reduced to two quarts, then work it through a cullendar, with a wooden spoon, mix a little flour and water, and boil it well in the soup, and slice in another head of celery, chyan pepper and salt to your taste; cut a slice of bread in small dice, fry them a light brown, and put them in your dish, then pour the soup upon it.

To make a PEAS SOUP FOR LENT.

PUT three pints of blue boiling peas into five quarts of soft cold water, three anchovies, three red herrings, and two large onions, stick in a clove at each end, a carrot and a parsnip sliced in, with a bunch of sweet herbs, boil them all together, till the soup is thick, strain it through a cullendar, then slice in the white part of a head of celery, a good lump of butter, a little pepper and salt, a slice of bread toasted and buttered well, and cut in little diamonds, put it into the dish, and pour the soup upon it, and a little dried mint if you choose it.

To Make a GRAVY SOUP *thickened with Yellow Peas,*

PUT a shin of beef to six quarts of water, with a pint of peas and six onions, set them over the fire, and let them boil gently till all the juice be out of the meat, then strain it through a sieve, add to the strained liquor one quart of strong gravy to make it brown, put in pepper and salt to your taste, then put in a little celery, and beet leaves, and boil it till they are tender.

To make a WHITE PEAS SOUP.

TO four or five pounds of lean beef and six quarts of water put in a little salt, when it boils scum it, and put in two carrots, three whole onions, a little thyme, and two heads of celery, with three quarts of old green peas, boil them till the meat is quite tender, then strain it through a hair sieve, and rub the pulp of the peas through the sieve, split the blanched part of three goss lettuces into four quarters, and cut them about one inch long, with a little mint cut small, then put half a pound of butter in a stew pan that will hold your soup, and put the lettuce and mint into the butter with a leek sliced very thin, and a pint of green peas, stew them a quarter of an hour, and keep shaking them often about, then put in a little of the soup, and stew them a quarter of an hour longer; then put in your soup and as much thick cream as will make it white, keep stirring it till it boils; fry a French roll in butter a little crisp, put it in the bottom of the tureen, and pour your soup over it.

To make GREEN PEAS SOUP *without Meat.*

IN shelling your peas separate the old ones from the young, and boil the old ones soft enough to strain through a cullendar, then put the liquor and what you strained through to the young peas, which must be whole, and some whole pepper, mint, a little onion shred small, put them in a large sauce-pan, with near a pound of butter, as they boil up shake in some flour, then put in a French roll fried in butter, to the soup; you must season it to your taste with salt, and herbs, when you have done so, add the young peas to it, which must be half boiled first you may leave out the flour if you don't like it, and instead of it put in a little spinage, and cabbage lettuce, cut small, which must be first fried in butter, and well mixed with the broth.
,

To make an *excellent* WHITE SOUP,

TO six quarts of water put in a knuckle of veal, a large fowl, and a pound of lean bacon, and half a pound of rice, with two anchovies, a few pepper corns, two or three onions, a bundle of sweet herbs, three or four heads of celery in slices, stew all together, till your soup is as strong as you choose it, then strain it through a hair sieve into a clean earthen pot, let it stand all night, then take off the scum, and pour it clear off into a tossing pan, put in half a pound of Jordan almonds beat fine, boil it a little and run it through a lawn sieve, then put in a pint of cream and the yolk of an egg. Make it hot, and send it to the table.

To make WHITE SOUP a second Way.

BOIL a knuckle of veal and a fowl, with a little mace, two onions, a little pepper and salt, to a strong jelly, then strain it and scum off all the fat, have ready the yolks of six eggs well beat, put them in and keep stirring it or it will curdle, put it in your dish with boiled chickens and toasted bread cut in pieces; if you do not like the eggs, you may put in a large handful of vermicelli half an hour before you take it off the fire.

To make CRAW-FISH SOUP.

BOIL half a hundred of fresh craw-fish, pick out all the meat, which you must save, take a fresh lobster and pick out all the meat, which you must likewise save, pound the shells of the craw-fish and lobster fine in a marble mortar, and boil them in four quarts of water with four pounds of mutton, a pint of green split peas, nicely picked and washed, a large turnip, carrot, onion, mace, cloves, anchovy, a little thyme, pepper, and salt. Stew them on a low fire till all the goodness is out of the mutton and shells, then strain it through a sieve, and put in the tails of your craw-fish and the lobster meat, but in very small pieces, with the red coral of the lobster, if it has any ; boil it half an hour, and just before you serve it up, add a little butter melted thick and smooth, stir it round several times, when you put it in, send it up very hot, but don't put too much spice in it. N. B. Pick out all the bags and the woolly part of your craw-fish before you pound them.

To make PARTRIDGE SOUP.

TAKE off the skins of two old partridges, cut them into small pieces with three slices of ham, two or three onions sliced and some celery, fry them in butter till they are as brown as they can be made without burning, then put them into three quarts of water with a few pepper corns, boil it slowly till a little more than a pint is consumed, then strain it, put in some stewed celery and fried bread.

CHAP. II

Observations on DRESSING FISH

WHEN you fry any kind of fish, wash them clean, dry them well with a cloth, and dust them with flour, or rub them with egg and bread crumbs; be sure your dripping, hog's-lard, or beef suet, is boiling before you put in your fish, they will fry hard and clear, butter is apt to burn them black, and make them soft; when you have fried your fish, always lay them in a dish or hair sieve to drain, before you dish them up; boiled fish should always be washed and rubbed carefully with a little vinegar, before they are put into the water; boil all kinds of fish very slowly, and when they will leave the bone they are enough; when you take them up set your fish plate over a pan of hot water to drain, and cover it with a cloth or close cover, to prevent it from turning their colour; set your fish-plate in the inside of your dish, and send it up, and when you fry parsley, be sure you pick it nicely, wash it well, then dip it in cold water, and throw it into a pan of boiling fat, take it out immediately, it will be very crisp and a fine green.

To dress a TURTLE *of a hundred Weight.*

CUT off the head, take care of the blood, and take off all the fins, lay them in salt and water, cut off the bottom shell, then cut off the meat that grows to it, (which is the callepee or fowl) take out the hearts, livers, and lights, and put them by themselves, take out the bones and the flesh out of the back shell (which is the callepash) cut the fleshy part into pieces, about two inches square, but leave the fat part, which looks green, (it is called the monfieur) rub it first with salt, and wash it in several waters to make it come clean, then put in the pieces that you took out, with three bottles of Madeira wine, and four quarts of strong veal gravy, a lemon cut in slices, a bundle of sweet herbs, a tea- spoonful of Chyan, six anchovies, washed and picked clean, a quarter of a pound of beaten mace, a tea-spoonful of mushroom powder, and half a pint of essence of ham if you have it, lay over it a coarse paste, set it in the oven for three hours; when it comes out, take off the lid and scum off the fat, and brown it with a salamander. — This is the bottom dish.

Then blanch the fins, cut them off at the first joint, fry the first pinions a fine brown, and put them into a tossing pan with two quarts of strong brown gravy, a glass of red wine, and the blood of the turtle, a large spoonful of lemon pickle, the same of browning, two spoonfuls of mushroom catchup, Chyan and salt, an onion stuck with cloves, and a bunch of sweet herbs; a little before it is enough, put in an ounce of morels, the same of truffles, stew them gently over a flow fire for two hours; when they are tender, put them into another tossing pan, thicken your gravy with flour and butter and strain it upon them, give them a boil and serve them up. This is a corner dish.

Then take the thick or large part of the fins, blanch them in warm water, and put them in a tossing pan, with three quarts of strong veal gravy, a pint of Madeira wine, half a tea-spoonful of Chyan, a little salt, half a lemon, a little beaten mace, a tea spoonful of mushroom powder, and a bunch of sweet herbs; let them stew till quite tender, they will take two hours at least, then take them up into another tossing pan, strain your gravy, and make it pretty thick with flour and butter, then put in a few boiled forcemeat balls, which must be made of the veally part of your turtle, left out for that purpose; one pint of fresh mushrooms, if you cannot get them pickled ones will do, and eight artichoke bottoms boiled tender, and cut in quarters, shake them over the fire five or six minutes, then put in half a pint of thick cream, with the yolks of six eggs beaten exceeding well, shake it over the fire again till it looks thick and white, but do not let it boil; dish up your fins with the balls, mushrooms, and artichoke-bottoms over and round them. This is the top dish.

Then take the chicken part, and cut it like Scotch collops, fry them a light brown, then put in a quart of veal gravy, stew them gently a little more than half an hour, and put to it the yolks of four eggs boiled hard, a few morels, a score of oysters; thicken your gravy, it must be neither white nor brown, but a pretty gravy colour; fry some oyster patties and lay round it. This is a corner dish to answer the small fins. Then take the guts (which is reckoned the best part of the turtle) rip them open, scrape and wash them exceeding well, rub them well with salt, wash them through many waters, and cut them in pieces two inches long, then scald the maw or paunch, take off the skin, scrape it well, cut it into pieces about half an inch broad and two inches long, put some of the fishy part of your turtle in it, set it over a slow charcoal fire, with two quarts of veal gravy, a pint of Madeira wine, a little mushroom catchup, a few shallots, a little Chyan, half a lemon, and stew them gently four hours, till your gravy is almost consumed, then thicken it with flour, mixed with a little veal gravy, put in half an ounce of morels, a few force meat balls, made as for the fins; dish it up, and brown it with a salamander, or in the oven. This is the corner dish.

Then take the head, skin it, and cut it in two pieces, put it into a stew-pot with all the bones, hearts, and lights, to a gallon of water, or veal broth, three or four blades of mace, one shalot, a slice of beef beaten to pieces, and a bunch of sweet herbs, set them in a very hot oven, and let it stand an hour at least, when it comes out strain it into a tureen for the middle of the table.

Then take the hearts and lights, chop them very fine, put them in a stew-pan with a pint of good gravy, thicken it and serve it up; lay the head in the middle, fry the liver, lay it round the head upon the lights, garnish with whole slices of lemon. This is the fourth corner dish. N. B. The first course should be of turtle only, when it is dressed in this manner: but when it is with other victuals, it should be in three different dishes, but this way I have often dressed them, and have given great satisfaction. Observe to kill your turtle the night before you want it, or very early next morning, that you may have all your dishes going on at a time. Gravy for a turtle, a hundred weight, will take two legs of veal, also two shanks of beef.

To dress a TURTLE *about thirty pounds weight.*

WHEN you kill the turtle, which must be done the night before, cut off the head, and let it bleed two or three hours, then cut off the fins and the callipee from the callipash, take care you do not burst the gail, throw all the inwards into cold water, the guts and tripe keep by themselves, and slit them open with a penknife, and wash them very clean in scalding water, and scrape off all the inward skin; as you do them throw them into cold water, warn them out of that, and put them into fresh water, and let them lie all night, scalding the fins and edges of the callipash and callipee; cut the meat off the shoulders and hack the bones, and set them over the fire with the fins in about a quart of water, put in a little mace, nutmeg, Chyan, and salt, let it stew about three hours, then strain it and put the fins by for use, the next morning take some of the meat you cut off the shoulders, and chop it small as for sausages, with about a pound of beef or veal suet, sea soned with mace, nutmeg, sweet-marjoram, parsley, Chyan, and salt to your taste, and three or four glasses of Madeira wine, so stuff it under the two fleshy parts of the meat, cases if you have any left, lay it over to prevent the meat from burning, then cut the remainder of the meat and the fins in pieces the size of an egg, season it pretty high with Chyan, salt, and a little nutmeg, and put it into the callipash, take care that it be sewed or secured up at the end, to keep in the gravy, then boil up the gravy, and add more wine if required, and thicken it a little with butter and flour, put some of it to the turtle, and set it in the oven with a well buttered paper over it to keep it from burning, and when it is about half baked squeeze in the juice of one or two lemons and stir it up. Callipash or back will take half an hour more bakeing than the callipee, which two hours will do the guts must be cut in pieces two or three inches long, the tripe in less, and put into a mug of clear water, and set in the oven with the callipash, and when it is enough and drained from the water, it is to be mixed with the other parts and sent up very hot.

To dress a COD'S HEAD and SHOULDERS.

TAKE out the gills and the blood clean from the bone, warn the head very clean, rub over it a little salt, and a glass of allegar, then lay it on your fish plates when your water boils throw in a good handful of salt, with a glass of allegar, then put in your fish, and let it boil gently half an hour ; if it is a large one three quarters; take it up very carefully, and strip the skin nicely off, set it before a brisk fire, dredge it all over with flour, and baste it well with butter; when the froth begins to rise, throw over it some very fine white bread crumbs; you must keep basting it all the time to make it froth well ; when it is a fine white brown, dish it up, and garnish it with a lemon cut in slices, scraped horse-radish, bar berries, a few small fish fryed and laid round it, or fryed oysters; cut the roe and liver in slices, and lay over it a little of the lobster out of the sauce in lumps, and then serve it.

To make Sauce for the COD'S HEAD.

TAKE a lobster, if it be alive stick a skewer in the vent of the tail to keep the water out and throw an handful of salt in the water, when it boils put in the lobster, and boil it half an hour; if it has spawn on, pick them off, and pound them exceeding fine in a marble mortar, and put them into half a pound of good melted butter, then take the meat out of your lobster, pull it in bits, and put it in your butter, with a meat spoonful of lemon pickle, and the same of walnut catchup, a slice of an end of a lemon, one or two slices of horse radish, as much beaten mace as will lie on a six pence, salt and Chyan to your taste, boil them one minute, then take out the horse-radish and lemon, and serve it up in your sauce-boat. N. B. If you can get no lobster, you may make shrimp, cockle, or muscle sauce the same way; if there can be no kind of shell-fish got, you then may add two anchovies cut small, a spoonful of walnut liquor, a large onion stuck with cloves, strain it and put it in the sauce- boat.

Second way to dress a COD'S HEAD

TAKE out the gills and blood clean from the back-bone, wash it well, and put it on your plates when your water boils, put in two handfuls of salt, and half a pint of allegar, it will make your fish firmer, then put in the cod's head; if it is of a middle size, it will take an hour's boiling; then take it up, and strip off the skin gently, dredge it well with flour, and lay lumps of butter on it ; if it suits you better, you may send it to the oven, and if it is not brown all over, do it with a salamander: make your gravy sauce to it, and serve it up.

To dress young CODLINS like SALT FISH.

TAKE young codlins, gut and dry them well with a cloth, fill their eyes full of salt, throw a little on the back-bone, and let them lie all night, then hang them up by the tail a day or two: as you have occasion for them, boil them in spring water, and drain them well, dish them up, and pour egg sauce on them, and send them to the table.

To dress a SALT COD.

STEEP your salt fish in water all night, with a glass of vinegar, it will fetch out the salt, and make it eat like fresh fish; the next day boil it; when it is enough, pull it in flakes into your dish, then pour egg sauce over it, or parsnips boiled and beat fine with butter and cream; send it to the table on a water plate, for it will soon grow cold.

To make EGG SAUCE for a SALT COD.

BOIL your eggs hard, first half chop the whites, then put in the yolks, and chop them both together, but not very small, put them into half a pound of good melted butter, and let it boil up, then put it on the fish.

To dress COD SOUNDS.

STEEP your sounds as you do the salt cod, and boil them in a large quantity of milk and water, when they are very tender and white take them up, and drain the water out, then pour the egg sauce boiling hot over them, and serve them up.

To dress COD SOUNDS like little TURKEYS.

Boil your sounds as for eating, but not too much, take them up and let them stand till they are quite cold, then take a forcemeat of chopped oysters, crumbs of bread, a lump of butter, nutmeg, pepper, salt, and the yolks of two eggs, fill your sounds, with it, and skewer them up in the shape of a turkey, then lard them down each side, as you would do a turkey's breast, dust them well with flour, and put them in a tin oven to roast before the fire, and baste them well with butter: when they are enough pour on them oyster sauce; three are sufficient for a side dish; garnish with barberries; it is a pretty side dish for a large table, for a dinner in Lent.

To boil SALMON CRIMP.

SCALE your salmon, take out the blood, wash it well, and lay it on a fish-plate, put your water in a fish-pan with a little salt: when it boils put in your fish for half a minute, then take it out for a minute or two; when you have done it four times, boil it until it be enough; when you take it out of the fish-pan, set it over the water to drain; cover it well with a clean cloth dipped in hot water; fry some small fishes, or a few slices of salmon, and lay round it ; garnish with scraped horse-radish and fennel.

To make ROLLED SALMON.

TAKE a side of salmon when split and the bone taken out and scaled, strew over the inside pepper, salt, nutmeg, and mace, a few chopped oysters, parsley, and crumbs of bread, roll it up tight, put it into a deep pot, and bake it in a quick oven, make the common fish sauce and pour over it. Garnish with fennel, lemon, and horse-radish.

To make Sauce for a SALMON.

Boil a bunch of fennel and parsley, chop them small, and put it into some good melted butter, and send it to the table in a sauce-boat; another with gravy sauce. To make the gravy sauce, put a little brown gravy into a sauce-pan, with one anchovy, a tea spoonful of lemon pickle, a meat spoonful of liquor from your walnut pickle, one or two spoonfuls of the water that the fish was boiled in; it gives it a pleasant flavour; a stick of horse radish, a little browning and salt; boil them three or four minutes, thicken it with flour and a good lump of butter, and strain it through a hair sieve. N. B. This is a good sauce for most kinds of boiled fish.

To boil a TURBOT.

WASH your turbot clean (if you let it lie in the water it will make it soft) and rub it over with allegar, it will make it firmer, then lay it on your fish-plate, with the white side up, lay a cloth over it, and pin it tight under your plate, which will keep it from breaking, boil it gently in hard water, with a good deal of salt and vinegar, and scum it well, or it will discolour the skin, when it is enough, take it up and drain it, take the cloth carefully off, and slip it on your dish, lay over it fried oysters, or oyster patties; send in lobster or gravy sauce in sauce-boats. Garnish it with crisp parsley and pickles. N. B. Don't put in your fish till your water boils.

To boil a PIKE *with a pudding in the belly.*

TAKE out the gills and guts, wash it well, then make a good forcemeat of oysters chopped fine, the crumbs of half a penny loaf, a few sweet herbs, and a little lemon peel shred fine, nutmeg, pepper, and salt to your taste, a good lump of butter, the yolks of two eggs, mix them well together, and put them in the belly of your fish, sew it up, skewer it round, put hard water in your fish-pan, add to it a tea cupful of vinegar, and a little salt: when it boils put in the fish; if it be a middle size, it will take half an hour's boiling: garnish it with walnuts and pickled barberries, serve it up with oyster sauce in a boat, and pour a little sauce on the pike. You may dress a roasted pike the same way.

To stew CARP *white.*

WHEN the carp are scaled, gutted, and washed, put them into a stew-pan, with two quarts of water, half a pint of white wine, a little mace, whole pepper, and salt, two onions, a bunch of sweet herbs, a stick of horse-radish, cover the pan close, let it stand an hour and a half over a slow stove, then put a gill of white wine into a saucepan, with two anchovies chopped, an onion, a little lemon peel, a quarter of a pound of butter rolled in flour, a little thick cream, and a large tea cupful of the liquor the carp was stewed in; boil them a few minutes, drain your carp, add to the sauce, the yolks of two eggs, mixed with a little cream; when it boils up squeeze in the juice of half a lemon; dish up your carp, and pour your sauce hot upon it.

To dress CARP *the best way, and the sauce.*

KILL your carp, and save all the blood, scale and clean them very well, have ready some nice rich gravy made of beef and mutton, seasoned with pepper, salt, mace, and onion, strain it off before you stew your fish in it, boil your carp first before you stew it in the gravy, be careful you don't boil them too much before you put in the carp, then let it stew on a slow fire about a quarter of an hour, thicken the sauce with a good lump of butter rolled in flour: garnish your dish with fryed oysters, fryed toast cut three corner ways, pieces of lemon, scraped horse-radish, and the roe of the carp cut in pieces, some fryed and the other boiled, squeeze the juice of a lemon into the sauce just before you send it up; take care to dish it up handsomely and very hot.

Another CARP *Sauce.*

TAKE the liver of the carp clean from the guts, and three anchovies, with a little parsley, thyme, and one onion, chop all these small together, then take half a pint of Rhenish wine, four spoonfuls of elder vinegar, with the blood of the carp, put all these together to stew gently, and put it to the carp, which must first be boiled in water, a little salt, and a pint of wine; take care not to do it too much after the carp is put in the sauce: garnish with fryed oysters, fryed toast, scraped horse-radish, and pieces of lemon, with the roe cut in pieces and fryed: if you don't like elder vinegar, any other sort will do.

To make WHITE FISH *Sauce.*

WASH two anchovies, put them into a sauce pan, with one glass of white wine, and two of water, half a nutmeg grated, and a little lemon peel; when it has boiled five or six minutes, strain it through a sieve, add to it a spoonful of white wine vinegar, thicken it a little, then put in near a pound of butter rolled in flour, boil it well, and pour it hot upon your fish.

To make a very nice SAUCE *for most sorts of Fish.*

TAKE a little gravy made of either veal or mutton, put to it a little of the water that drains from your fish, when it is boiled enough, put it in a sauce-pan, and put in a whole onion, one anchovy, a spoonful of catchup, and a glass of white wine, thicken it with a good lump of butter rolled in flour, and a spoonful of cream; if you have oysters, cockles, or shrimps put them in after you take it off the fire, (but it is very good without) you may use red wine instead of white by leaving out the cream.

To make LOBSTER SAUCE.

BOIL half a pint of water with a little mace and whole pepper, long enough to take out the strong taste of the spice, then strain it off, melt three quarters of a pound of butter smooth in the water, cut your lobster in very small pieces flew it all together tenderly with anchovy, and send it up hot.

To make LOBSTER SAUCE *another way.*

BRUISE the body of a lobster into thick melted butter and cut the flesh into it in small pieces, stew all together and give it a boil, sea son with a little pepper, salt, and a very small quantity of mace.

To stew CARP *or* TENCH.

GUT and scale your fish, wash and dry them well with a clean cloth, dredge them well with flour, fry them in dripping, or sweet rendered suet, until they are a light brown, and then put them in a stew-pan, with a quart of water, and one quart of red wine, a meat spoonful of lemon pickle, another of browning, the same of walnut or mum catchup, a little mushroom powder, and Chyan to your taste, a large onion stuck with cloves, and a stick of horse-radish, cover your pan close to keep in the steam, let them stew gently over a stove fire, till your gravy is reduced to just enough to cover your fish in the dish then take the fish out, and put them on the dish you intend for table, set the gravy on the fire, and thicken it with flour and a large lump of butter, boil it a little, and strain it over your fish : garnish them with pickled mush rooms and scraped horse-radish, put a bunch of pickled barberries, or a sprig of myrtle in their mouths, and send them to the table. It is a top dish for a grand entertainment.

To dress a STURGEON.

TAKE what size of a piece of sturgeon you think proper, and wash it clean, lay it all night in salt and water, the next morning take it out, rub it well with allegar, and let it lie in it for two hours, then have ready a fish-kettle full of boiling water, with one ounce of bay salt, two large onions, and a few sprigs of sweet marjoram; boil your sturgeon till the bones will leave the fish, then take it up, take the skin off, and flour it well ; set it before the fire, baste it with fresh butter, and let it stand till it be a fine brown ; then dish it up, and pour into the dish, the same sauce as for the white carp; garnish with crisp parsley and red pickles. This is a proper dish for the top or middle.

To roast large EELS or LAMPREYS with a pudding in the belly.

SKIN your eels or lampreys, cut off the head, take the guts out, and scrape the blood clean from the bone, then make a good forcemeat of oysters or shrimps chopped small, the crumbs of half a penny loaf, a little nutmeg and lemon peel shred fine, pepper, salt, and the yolks of two eggs, put them in the belly of your fish, sew it up, turn it round on your dish, put over it flour and butter, pour a little water in your dish, and bake it in a moderate oven; when it comes out take the gravy from under it, and scum off the fat, then strain it through a hair sieve; add to it a tea spoonful of lemon pickle, two of browning, a meat spoonful of walnut catchup, a glass of white wine, one anchovy, and a slice of lemon, let it boil ten minutes, thicken it with butter and flour, send it up in a sauce-boat, dish your fish : garnish it with lemon and crisp parsley. This is a pretty dish for either corner or side for a dinner.

To Stew LAMPREYS.

SKIN and gut your lampreys, season them well with pepper, salt, cloves, nutmeg, and mace, not pounded too fine; and a little lemon peel shred fine; then cut some thin slices of butter into the bottom of your sauce-pan, put in the fish with half a pint of nice gravy, half the quantity of white wine and cyder, the same of claret, with a small bundle of thyme, winter savory, pot marjoram, and an onion sliced, stew them over a slow fire, and keep turning the lampreys till they are quite tender, when they are tender take them out and put in one anchovy, and thicken the sauce with the yolk of an egg, or a little butter, rolled in flour, and pour it over the fish and serve them up. — N. B. Roll them round a skewer before you put them into the pan.

To Stew FLOUNDERS, PLAICE, or SOLES.

HALF fry your fish in three ounces of butter a fine brown, then take up your fish, and put to your butter a quart of water, and boil it slowly a quarter of an hour with two anchovies, and an onion sliced, then put in your fish again, with a herring, and stew them gently twenty minutes, then take out your fish, and thicken the sauce with butter and flour, and give it a boil, then strain it through a hair sieve, over the fish, and send them up hot. — N. B. If you choose cockle or oyster-liquor, put it in just before you thicken the sauce, or you may send oysters, cockles, or shrimps in a sauce-boat to table.

A good way to STEW FISH.

MIX half a tumbler of wine with as much water as will cover the fish in the stew-pan and put in a little pepper and salt, three or four onions, a crust of bread toasted very brown, one anchovy, a good lump of butter, and set them over a gentle fire, make the stew-pan now and then that it may not burn; just before you serve it up, pour your gravy into a sauce-pan, and thicken it with a little butter rolled in flour, a little catchup and walnut pickle beat well together till smooth, then pour it on your fish, and set it over the fire to heat, and serve it up hot.

To boil MACKAREL.

GUT your mackarel and dry them carefully with a clean cloth, then rub them slightly over with a little vinegar, and lay them straight on your fish plate (for turning them round often breaks them) put a little salt in the water when it boils; put them into your fish-pan, and boil them gently fifteen minutes, then take them up and drain them well, and put the water that runs from them into a sauce-pan, with two tea spoonfuls of lemon pickle, one meat spoonful of walnut catchup, the same of browning, a blade or two of mace, one anchovy, a slice of lemon; boil them all together a quarter of an hour, then strain it through a hair sieve, and thicken it with flour and butter; send it in a sauce-boat, and parsley sauce in another; dish up your fish with the tails in the middle; garnish it with scraped horse radish and barberries.

To boil HERRINGS.

SCALE, gut, and wash your herrings, dry them clean, and rub them over with a little vinegar and salt, skewer them with their tails in their mouths, lay them on your fish plate, when your water boils put them in, they will take ten or twelve minutes boiling, when you take them up, drain them over the water, then turn the heads into the middle of your dish, lay round them scraped horse-radish, parsley and butter for sauce.

To fry HERRINGS.

SCALE Wash and dry your herrings well; lay them separately on a board, and set them to the fire two or three minutes before you want them, it will keep the fish from sticking to the pan, dust them with flour, when your dripping or butter is boiling hot put in your fish, a few at a time, fry them over a brisk fire, when you have fryed them all, set the tails up one against another in the middle of the dish, then fry a large handful of parsley crisp, take it out before it loses its colour, lay it round them, and parsley sauce in a boat) or if you like onions better fry them, lay some round your dish, and make onion sauce for them; or you may cut off the heads after they are fryed, chop them and put them into a sauce-pan, with ale, pepper, salt, and an anchovy, thicken it with flour and butter, strain it then put it in a sauce-boat.

To bake HERRINGS.

WHEN you have cleaned your herrings as above, lay them on a board, take a little black and Jamaica pepper, a few cloves, and a good deal of salt, mix them together, then rub it all over the fish, lay them straight in a pot, cover them with allegar, tie strong paper over the pot, and bake them in a moderate oven; if your allegar be good, they will keep two or three months; you may eat them either hot or cold.

To bake SPRATS.

RUB your sprats with salt and pepper, and to every two pints of vinegar put one pint of red wine, dissolve a penny-worth of cochineal, lay your sprats in a deep earthen dam, pour in as much red wine, vinegar, and cochineal as will cover them, tie a paper over them, set them in an oven all night.—They will eat well, and keep for some time.

To boil SCATE or RAY.

CLEAN your skate or ray very well, and cut it in long narrow pieces, then put it in boiling water with a little salt in it, when it has boiled a quarter of an hour take it out, slip the skin off, then put it into your pan again, with a little vinegar, and boil it till enough when you take it up, set it over the water to drain, and cover it close up, and when you dish it, be as quick as possible, for it soon grows cold, pour over it cockle, shrimp, or muscle sauce, lay over it oyster patties; garnish it with barberries and horse-radish.

To fry SOLES.

SKIN your soles as you do eels, but keep on their heads, rub them over with an egg, and strew over them bread crumbs, fry them over a brick fire in hogs-lard a light brown, serve them up with good melted butter, and garnish it with green pickles

To marinate SOLES.

BOIL them in salt and water, bone and drain them, lay them on a dish with the belly up, boil some spinage and pound it in a mortar, then boil four eggs hard, chop the whites and yolks separately, lay green, white, and yellow amongst the soles, serve them up with melted butter in a boat.

To broil HADDOCKS or WHITINGS.

GUT and wash your haddocks or whitings, dry them with a cloth, and rub a little vinegar over them, it will keep the skin on better, dust them well with flour, rub your gridiron with butter, and let it be very hot when you lay the fish on, or they will stick, turn them two or three times on the gridiron, when enough serve them up, and lay pickles round them, with plain melted butter, or cockle sauce, they are a pretty dish for supper.

A second Way

WHEN you have cleaned your haddocks or writings, as above, put them in a tin oven, and set them before a quick fire, when the skins be gin to rise, take them off, beat an egg, rub it over them with a feather, and strew over them a few bread crumbs, dredge them well with flour, when your gridiron is hot rub it well with butter or suet, it must be very hot before you lay the fish on, when you have turned them, rub a little cold butter over them, turn them as your fire requires until they are enough and a little brown; lay round them cockles, muscles, or red cabbage, you may either have shrimp sauce or melted butter.

To fry SMELTS or SPARLINGS.

DRAW the guts out at the gills, but leave in the melt or roe, dry them with a cloth, beat an egg and rub it over them with a feather, then strew bread crumbs over them, fry them with hogs-lard or rendered beef suet, when it is boiling hot put in your fish, shake them a little, and fry them a nice brown, drain them in a sieve, when you dish them put a basin in the middle of your dish with the bottom up, lay the tails of your fish on it, fry a handful of parsley in the fat your fish was fryed in, take it out of water as you fry it, and it will keep its colour and crisp sooner, put a little on the tails, and lay the rest in lumps round the edge of the dish, serve it up with good melted butter for sauce.

To fry PERCH or TROUT.

WHEN you have scaled, gutted, and washed your perch or trout, dry them well, then lay them separately on a board before the fire, two minutes before you fry them dust them well with flour, and fry them a fine brown in roast drippings or rendered suet, serve them up with melted butter and crisped parsley.

To dress PERCH in Water Sokey.

SCALE, gut, and wash your perch, put salt in your water, when it boils put in the fish, with an onion cut in slices, you must separate it into round rings, a handful of parsley picked and washed clean, put in as much milk as will turn the water white, when your fish is enough, put them in a soup dish, and pour a little of the water over them with the parsley and the onions, then serve it up with butter and parsley in a boat; onions may be omitted if you please. You may boil trout the same way.

To boil EELS.

SKIN, gut, and take the blood out of your eels cut off their heads, dry them, and turn them round on your fish plate, boil them in salt and water, and make parsley sauce for them.

To pitch-cock EELS.

SKIN, gut, and wash your eels, then dry them with a cloth, sprinkle them with pepper, salt, and a little dried sage, turn them backward and forward, and skewer them, rub your grid iron with beef suet, broil them a good brown, pot them on your dish with good melted butter, and lay round fried parsley.

To broil EELS,

WHEN you have skinned and cleansed your eels as before, rub them with the yolk of an egg, strew over them bread crumbs, chopped parsley, sage, pepper, and salt, baste them well with butter, and set them in a dripping-pan, roast or broil them on a gridiron, serve them up with parsley and butter for sauce.

To boil FLOUNDERS, *and all Kinds of Flat Fish.*

CUT off the fins, and nick the brown side under the head, then take out the guts, and dry them with a cloth, boil them in salt and water; make either gravy, shrimp, cockle, or muscle sauce, and garnish it with red cabbage.

To Stew OYSTERS, *and all Sorts of Shell Fish.*

WHEN you have opened your oysters, put their liquor into a tossing pan with a little beaten mace, thicken it with flour and butter, boil it three or four minutes, toast a slice of white bread, and cut it into three-cornered pieces, lay them round your dish, put in a spoonful of good cream, put in your oysters, and shake them round in your pan, you must not let them boil, for if they do it will make them hard and look small; serve them up in a little soup dish or plate. N. B. You may stew cockles, muscles, or any shell fish the same way.

To stew OYSTERS, COCKLES, *and* MUSCLES.

OPEN your fish clean from the shell, save the liquor, and let it stand to settle, then strain it through a hair sieve, and put to it as many crumbs of bread as will make it pretty thick, and boil them well together before you put in the fish, with a good lump of butter, pepper, and salt to your taste, give them a single boil, and serve them up. — N. B. You may make it a fish sauce by adding a glass of white wine just before you take it off the fire, and leaving out the crumbs of bread.

To scollop OYSTERS,

WHEN your oysters are opened, put them in a bason, and wash them out of their own liquor, put some in your scollop-shells, strew over them a few bread crumbs, and lay a slice of butter on them, then more oysters, bread crumbs, and a slice of butter on the top, put them into a Dutch oven to brown, and serve them up in the shells.

To Fry OYSTERS.

TAKE a quarter of an hundred of large oysters, beat the yolks of two eggs, add to it a little nutmeg, and a blade of mace pounded, a spoonful of flour, and a little salt, dip in your oysters, and fry them in hogs-lard a light brown ; if you choose, you may add a little parsley shred fine. N. B. They are a proper garnish for cods-head, calves-head, or most made dishes

To Make OYSTER LOAVES

TAKE small French rasps, or you may make little round loaves, make a round hole in the top, scrape out all the crumbs, then put your oysters into a tasting pan, with the liquor and crumbs that came out of your rasps or loaves, and a good lump of butter, stew them together five or six minutes, then put in a spoonful of good cream, fill your rasps or loaves, lay the bit of crust carefully on again, set them in the oven to crisp. Three are enough for a side dish.

To boil LOBSTERS.

TAKE your lobster, and put a skewer in the vent of the tail, to prevent the water from get ting into the body of the lobster, put it into a pan of boiling water, with a little salt in it, if it be a large one it will take half an hour's boiling; when you take it out, put a lump of butter in a cloth, and rub it over, it will strike the colour, and make it look bright.

To roast LOBSTERS.

HALF boil your lobster as before, rub it well with butter, and set it before the fire, baste it all over till the shell looks a dark brown, serve it up with good melted butter.

To flew LOBSTERS or SHRIMPS.

PICK your lobsters or shrimps in as large pieces as you can, and boil the shells in a pint of water, with a blade or two of mace, and a few whole pepper corns; when all the strength is come out of the shells and spice, strain it, and put in your lobsters or shrimps, and thicken it with flour and butter and give them a boil; put in a glass of white wine, or two spoonfuls of vinegar, and serve it up.

To make LOBSTER PATTIES to garnish Fish.

TAKE all the red seeds and the meat of a lobster, with a little pepper, salt, and crumbs of bread, mix them well with a little butter, make them up in small patties, and put them in either rich batter or thin paste, fry or bake them, and garnish your fish with them.

To pickle STURGEON.

Cut your sturgeon into what size pieces you please, wash it well, and tie it with mats ; to every three quarts of water put one quart of old strong beer, a handful of bay salt, and double the quantity of common salt, one ounce of ginger, two ounces of black pepper, one ounce of cloves, and one of Jamaica pepper, boil it till it will leave the bone, then take it up, the next day put in a quart of strong ale allegar, and a little salt, tie it down with strong paper, and keep it for use. — Don't put your sturgeon in till the water boils.

To pickle SALMON the Newcastle Way.

TAKE a salmon about twelve pounds, gut it, then cut off the head, and cut it across in what pieces you please, but don't split it; scrape the blood from the bone, and wash it well out, then tie it a-cross each way, as you do sturgeon, set on your fish-pan with two quarts of water, and three of strong beer, half a pound of bay salt, and one pound of common salt, when it boils scum it well, then put in as much fish as your liquor will cover, and when it is enough take it carefully out, lest you strip off the skin, and lay it on earthen dishes ; when you have done all your fish, let it stand till the next day, put it into pots, add to the liquor three quarts of strong beer allegar, half an ounce of mace, the same of cloves and black pepper, one ounce of long pepper, two ounces of white ginger, sliced, boil them well together half an hour, then pour it boiling hot upon your fish, when cold cover it well with strong brown paper. This will keep a whole year.

To pickle OYSTERS.

OPEN the largest and finest oysters you can. get, whole and clean from the shell, wash them in their own liquor, let it stand to settle, then pour it from the sediment into a sauce-pan, put to it a glass of Lisbon wine, as much white wine vinegar as you had oyster liquor, three or four blades of mace, a nutmeg sliced, a few white pepper corns, and a little salt, boil it five or six minutes, scum it, then put in your oysters, simmer them ten or twelve minutes, take them out, and put them in narrow-topped jars; when they are cold, pour over them rendered mutton suet, tie them down with a bladder, and keep them for use,

To pickle OYSTERS a second Way.

OPEN the oysters very carefully, and take off all the shells that stick to the fish, put them into a little water, and wash the oysters in it and strain the liquor, boil it with a little vinegar, whole pepper, salt, and mace, till it taste of the spices, then put in the oysters: if they are large they must boil eight minutes, if small, not so long; put them into pickling-pots, when the liquor is cold pour it upon the oysters. To half a hundred of oysters put six spoonfuls of water and four of very good vinegar, then tie bladders very close over them.

To collar MACKAREL.

GUT and slit your mackarel down the belly, cut off the head, take out the bones, take care you don't cut it in holes, then lay it flat upon its back, season it with mace, nutmeg, pepper, and salt, and a handful of parsley shred fine, strew it over them, roll them tight, and tie them well separately in cloths, boil them gently twenty minutes in vinegar, salt, and water, then take them out, put them into a pot, pour the liquor on them, or the cloth will stick to the fish, the next day take the cloth off your fish, put a little more vinegar to the pickle, keep them for use; when you send them to the table, garnish with fennel and parsley and put some of the liquor under them.

To pickle MACKAREL.

WASH and gut your mackarel, then skewer them round with their tails in their mouths, bind them with a fillet to keep them from breaking, boil them in salt and water about ten minutes, then take them carefully out, put to the water a pint of allegar, two or three blades of mace, a little whole pepper, and boil it all together; when cold pour it on the fish, and tie it down close.

To pot SALMON.

Let your salmon be quite fresh, scale and wash it well, and dry it with a cloth, split it up the back and take out the bone, season it well with white pepper and salt, a little nutmeg and mace, let it lie two or three hours, then put it in your pot, with half a pound of butter, tie it down, put it into the oven and bake it an hour, when it comes out, lay it on a flat dish that the oil may run from it, cut it to the size of your pots, lay it in layers till you fill the pot, with the skin upwards, put a board over it, lay on a weight to press it till cold, then pour over it clarified butter; when you cut it, the skin makes it look fibbed, you may send it to the table either cut in slices, or in the pot.

A second way.

WHEN you have any cold salmon left, take the skin off, and bone it, then put it in a marble mortar, with a good deal of clarified butter; season it pretty high with pepper, mace, and salt, shred a little fennel very small, beat them all together exceeding fine, then put it close down into a pot, and cover it with clarified butter.

To pot SMELTS *or* SPARLINGS.

DRAW out the guts with a skewer under the gills, the melt or roe must be left in, dry them well with a cloth, season them with salt, Mace, and pepper, lay them in a pot, with half a pound of melted butter over them, tie them down, and bake them in a slow oven three quarters of an hour; when they are almost cold, take them out of the liquor, put them into oval pots, cover them with clarified butter, and keep them for use.

To pickle SMELTS *or* SPARLINGS.

GUT them with a skewer under the gills, but leave the melt or roe in, dry them with a cloth, and skewer their tails in their mouths, put salt in your water, when it boils put in your fish for ten minutes, then take them up, put to the water a blade or two of mace, a few cloves, and a little allegar; boil them all together, and when it is cold put in your fish, and keep them for use.

To collar EELS.

CASE your eel, cut off the head, flit open the belly, take out the guts, cut off the fins, tail out the bones, lay it flat on the back, grate over it a small nutmeg, two or three blades of mace beat fine, a little pepper and salt,- strew over it a handful of parsley shred fine, with a few sage leaves, roll it up tight in a cloth, bind it well; if it be of a middle size, boil it in salt and water, three quarters of an hour, hang it up all night to drain, add to the pickle a pint of vinegar, a few pepper corns, and a sprig of sweet marjoram, boil it ten minutes, and let it stand till the next day, take off the cloth, and put your eels into the pickle, you may send them whole on a plate, or cut them in slices; garnish with green parsley. Lampreys are done the same way.

To pickle COCKLES.

WASH your cockles clean, put them in a sauce-pan, cover them close, set them over the fire, shake them till they open, then pick them out of the shells, let the liquor settle till it be clear, then put the same quantity of wine vinegar, and a little salt, a blade or two of mace, boil them together, and pour it on your cockles, and keep them in bottles for use. You must pickle muscles the same way.

To pot CHARS.

CUT off the fins, and- cheek-part of each side of the head of your chars, rip them open, take out the guts and the blood from the back bone, dry them well in a cloth, lay them on a board, and throw on them a good deal of salt, let them stand all night, then scrape it gently off them, and wipe them exceedingly well with a cloth, pound mace, cloves, and nutmeg, very fine, throw a little in the inside of them, and a good deal of salt and pepper on the outside, put them close down in a deep pot, with their bellies up, with plenty of clarified butter over them, set them in the oven, and let them stand for three hours when they come out, pour what butter you can off clear, lay a board over them, and turn them upside down, to let the gravy run from them, scrape the salt and pepper very carefully off, and season them exceeding well both inside and out with the above seasoning, lay them close into broad thin pots for that purpose, with the backs up, then cover them well with clarified butter; keep them in a cool dry place.

To pot EELS.

SKIN, gut, and clean your eels, cut them in pieces about four inches long, then season them with pepper, salt, beaten mace, and a little dryed sage rubbed very fine, rub them well with your seasoning, lay them in a brown pot, put over them as much butter as will cover them, tie them down with a strong papery set them in a quick oven for an hour and a half; take them out, when cold put them into small pots, and cover them with clarified butter. -N. B. You may pot lampreys the same way.

To pot LAMPREYS.

TAKE lampreys alive, and run a stick through their heads, and slit their tails, hang them up by their heads and they will bleed at the tail end; when they have done bleeding, cut them open, take out the guts, and wipe them until they are perfectly dry and clean, (you must not wash them with water) then rub them with pepper and salt, let them stand all night, and wipe them exceedingly dry again, then season them with pepper, salt, mace, and a little nutmeg, roll them up tight, put them in a pot with some butter, cover them up with strong paper, and bake them in a moderate oven; when they are enough and near cold, drain out the butter from them, put them in your potting pots, and cover them with clarified butter.

To pot LOBSTERS.

TAKE the meat out of the claws and belly of a boiled lobster, put it in a marble mortar, with two blades of mace, a little white pepper and salt, a lump of butter the size of half an egg, beat them all together till they come to a paste, put one half of it into your pot, take the meat out of the tail part, lay it in the middle of your pot, lay on it the other half of your taste, press it close down, pour over it clarified utter, a quarter of an inch thick. N. B. To clarify butter, put your boat into a clean saucepan, set it over a slow fire, when it is melted, scum it, and take it off the fire, let it stand a little, then pour it over your lobsters; take care you do not pour in the milk, which settles to the bottom of the saucepan.

A receipt to pot LOBSTERS, *which cost ten guineas.*

TAKE twenty good lobsters, and when cold pick all the meat out of the tails and claws (be careful to take out all the black gut in the tails, which must not be used) beat fine three quarters of an ounce of mace, a small nutmeg, and four or five cloves, with pepper and salt, season the meat with it; lay a layer of butter into a deep earthen pot, then put in the lobsters, and lay the rest of the butter over them (this quantity of lobsters will take at least four pounds of butter to bake them) tie a paper over the pot, set them in an oven, when they are baked tender, take them out, and lay them on a dish, to drain a little: then put them close down in your potting pots, but do not break them in small pieces, but lay them in as whole as you can, only splitting the tails. When you have filled your pots as full as you choose, take a spoonful or two of the red butter they were baked in, pour it on the top, and set it before the fire to let it melt in, then cool it, and melt a little white wax in the remainder of the butter, and cover them. N. B. Lay a good deal of the red hard part in the pot to bake, to colour the butter, but do not put it in the potting pots.

To pot SHRIMPS.

PICK the finest shrimps you can get, season them with a little beaten mace, pepper and salt to your taste, and with a little cold butter pound them all together in a mortar till it comes to a paste, put it down in small pots, and pour over them clarified butter.

To caveach SOLES.

FRY your soles in either oil or butter, boil some vinegar with a little water, two or three blades of mace, a very few cloves, some black pepper and a little salt, let it stand till cold, and when cold beat up some oil with it, lay your fish in a deep pot, and slice a good deal of shallots or onions between each fish, throw your liquor over it, and pour some oil on the top: it will keep three or four months, made rich and fryed in oil; it must be stopped well and kept in a dry place. Take out a little at a time when you use it.

To caveach FISH.

CUT your fish into pieces the thickness of your hand, season it with pepper and salt, let it lie an hour, dry it well with a cloth, flour it, and then fry it a fine brown in oil: boil a sufficient quantity of vinegar with a little garlick, mace, and whole pepper to cover the fish, add the same quantity of oil, and salt to your taste, mix well the oil and vinegar, and when the fish and liquor is quite cold, slice some onion to lay in the bottom of the pot, then a layer of fish, and onion, and so on till the whole fish is put up in the liquor must not be put in till it is quite cold.

A very good Way to preserve FISH.

TAKE any large fish, cut off the head, wash it clean, and cut it into thin slices, dry it well with a cloth, flour it and dip it in the yolks of eggs, fry it in plenty of oil till it is a fine brown, and well done, lay them to drain till cold, then lay them in your vessel, throw in betwixt the layers, mace, cloves, and sliced nutmeg, then make a pickle of the best white wine vinegar, shallots, garlick, white pepper, Jamaica pepper, long pepper, juniper berries and salt, boil it till the garlick is tender, and the pickle will be enough; when it is quite cold pour it on your film, with a little oil on the top; small fish are done whole; cover it close with a bladder.

To pickle SHRIMPS.

PICK the finest shrimps you can get, and put them into cold allegar and salt, put them into little bottles, cork them close, and keep them for use.

To pot red and black MOOR-GAME.

PLUCK and draw them, and season them with pepper, cloves, mace, ginger, and nutmeg, well beaten and sifted, with a quantity of salt not to overcome the spices, roll a lump of butter in the seasoning, and put it into the body of the fowls, rub the outside with seasoning, and then put them into pots with the breast downwards and cover them with butter, lay a paper, and then a paste over them, and bake them till they are tender, then take them out and lay them to drain, then put them into potting-pots with the breast upward, and take all the butter they were baked in clean from the gravy and pour upon them; fill up the pots with clarified butter, and keep them in a dry place.

58

CHAP III

Observations on Roasting and Boiling

WHEN you boil any kind of meat, particularly veal, it requires a great deal of care and neatness; be sure your copper is very clean and well tinned, fill it as full of soft water as is necessary, dust your veal well with fine flour, put it into your copper, set it over a large fire; some choose to put in milk to make it white, but I think it is better without; if your water happens to be the least hard it curdles the milk, and gives the veal a brown yellow cast, and often orange in lumps about the veal, so will oatmeal, but by dusting your veal, and putting it into the water when cold, it prevents the foulness of the water from hanging upon it; when the scum begins to rise take it clear off, put on your cover, let it boil in plenty of water as slow as possible, it will make your veal rise and plump: A cook cannot be guilty of a greater error than to let any sort of meat boil that it hardens the outside before the inside is warm, and discolours it, especially veal; for instance, a leg of veal twelve pounds weight, will require three hours and a half boiling, the slower it boils the whiter and plumper it will be; when you boil mutton or beef, observe to dredge them well with Flour before you put them into the kettle of cold water, keep it covered, and take off the scum; mutton or beef don't require so much boiling, nor is it so great a fault if they are a little short, but veal, pork, or lamb, is not so wholesome if they are not boiled enough; a leg of pork will require half an hour more boiling than a leg of veal of the same weight; when you boil beef or mutton, you may allow an hour for every four pound weight; it is the best way to put in your meat when the water is cold, it gets warm to the heart before the outside grows hard, a leg of lamb four pounds weight will require an hour and half boiling.

When you roast any kind of meat, it is a very good way to put a little salt and water in your dripping pan, baste your meat a little with it, let it dry, then dust it well with flour, baste it, with fresh butter, it will make your meat a better colour; observe always to have a brisk: clear fire, it will prevent your meat from dazing, and the froth from falling, keep it a good distance from the fire, if the meat is scorched, the outside is hard, and prevents the heat from penetrating into the meat, and will appear enough before it be little more than half done. Time, distance, basting often, and a clear fire, is the best method I can prescribe for roasting meat to perfection; when the steam draws near the fire, it is a sign of its being enough, but you will be the best judge of that from the time you put it down. Be careful when you roast any kind of wild fowl, to keep a clear brisk fire, roast them a light brown, but not too much; it is a great fault to roast them 'till the gravy runs out of them, it takes off the fine flavour,—Tame fowls require more roasting, they are a long time before they are hot through, and must be often basted to keep up a strong froth, it makes them rise better, and a finer colour.— Pigs and geese should be roasted before a good fire, and turned quick.—Hares and rabbits requires time and care, to see the ends are roasted enough; when they are half roasted, cut the neck skin, to let out the blood, or when they are cut up, they often appear bloody at the Neck.

To roast a PIG

STICK your pig just above the breastbone, run your knife to the heart, when it is dead put it in cold water for a few minutes, then run it over with a little resin beat exceeding fine, or its own blood, put your pig into a pail of scalding water half a minute, take it out, lay it on a clean table, pull off the hair as quick as possible, if it does not come clean off put it in again, when you have got it all clean off wash it in warm water, then in two or three cold waters, for fear the resin should taste; take off the four feet at the first joint, make a slit down the belly, take out all the entrails, put the liver, heart, and lights to the pettitoes, wash it well out of cold water, dry it exceedingly well with a cloth, hang it up, and when you roast it, put in a little shred sage, a tea spoonful of black pepper, two of salt, and a crust of brown bread, spit your pig, and felt up ; lay it down to a brisk clear fire, with a pig-plate hung in the middle of the fires when your pig is warm, put a lump of butter in a cloth, rub your pig often with it while it is roasting; a large one will take an hour and an half: when your pig is a fine brown, and the steam draws near the fire, take a clean cloth, rub your pig quite dry, then rub it well with a little cold butter, it will help to crisp it; then take a sharp knife, cut off the head, and take off the collar, then take off the ears and jaw-bone, split the jaw in two, when you have cut the pig down the back, which must be done before you draw the spit out, then lay your pig back to back on your dish, and the jaw on each side, the ears on each shoulder, and the collar at the shoulder, and pour in your sauce, and serve it up: garnish with a crust of brown bread grated.

To make Sauce for a PIG.

CHOP the brains a little, then put in a tea-cupful of white gravy with the gravy that runs out of the pig, a little bites anchovy, mix near half a pound of butter, with as much flour as will thicken the gravy, a slice of lemon, a spoonful of white wine, a little caper liquor and salt, shake it over the fire, and pour it into your dish; some like currants, boil a few and send them in a tea saucer with a glass of currant jelly in the middle of it.

A second way to make PIG Sauce.

CUT all the outside off a penny loaf, then cut it into very thin slices, put it into a saucepan of cold water, with an onion, a few pepper corns, and a little salt, boil it until it be a fine pulp, then beat it well, put in a quarter of a pound of butter, and two spoonfuls of thick cream, make it hot, and put it into a bason.

To dress a PIG'S PETTITOES.

TAKE up the heart, liver, and lights, when they have boiled ten minutes, and shred them pretty small, but let the feet boil till they are pretty tender, then take them out and split them; thicken your gravy with flour and butter, put in your mincemeat, a slice of lemon, a spoonful of white wine, a little salt, and boil it a little; beat the yolk of an egg, add to it two spoonfuls of good cream, and a little grated nutmeg, put in your pettitoes, shake it over the fire, but do not let it boil lay sippets round your dish, pour in your mincemeat, lay the feet over them the skin side up, and send them to the table.

To boil a GOOSE with ONION SAUCE.

TAKE your goose ready dressed, singe it and pour over it a quart of boiling milk, let it lie in it all night, then take it out and dry it exceeding well with a cloth, season it with pepper and salt, chop small a large onion, a handful of sage leaves, put them into your goose, sew it up at the neck and vent, hang it up by the legs till the next day, then put it into a pan of cold water, cover it close, and let it boil slowly one hour.

To Stew GOOSE GIBLETS.

CUT your pinions in two, the neck in four pieces, slice the gizzard, clean it well, stew them in two quarts of water, or mutton broth, with a bundle of sweet herbs, one anchovy, a few pepper corns, three or four cloves, a spoonful of catchup, and an onion; when the giblets are tender, put in a spoonful of good cream, thicken it with flour and butter, serve them up in a soup dish, and lay sippets round it.

To roast a GREEN GOOSE.

WHEN your goose is ready dressed, put in a good lump of butter, spit it, lay it down, finger it well, dust it with flour, baste it well with fresh butter, baste it three or four different times with cold butter, it will make the flesh rise better than if you was to baste it out of the dripping-pan; if it is a large one it will take three quarters of an hour to roast it; when you think it is enough, dredge it with flour, baste it till it is a fine froth, and your goose a nice brown, and dish it up with a little brown gravy under it: garnish with a crust of bread grated round the edge of your dish.

To make SAUCE for a GREEN GOOSE.

TAKE some melted butter, put in a spoonful of the juice of sorrel, a little sugar, a few codled gooseberries, pour it into your sauce-boats, and send it hot to the table.

To roast a STUBBLE GOOSE.

CHOP a few sage leaves, and two onions very fine, mix them with a good lump of butter, a teaspoonful of pepper, and two of salt, put it in your goose, then spit it and lay it down, singe it well, dust it with flour; when it is thoroughly hot baste it with fresh butter: if it be a large one it will require an hour and a half before a good clear fire; when it is enough, dredge and baste it, pull out the spit, and pour in a little boiling water.

To make SAUCE for a GOOSE.

PARE, core, and slice your apples, put them in a saucepan with as much water as will keep them from burning, set them over a very slow fire, keep them close covered till they are all of a pulp, then put in a lump of butter, and sugar to your taste, beat them well and send them to the table in a china basin.

To boil DUCKS with ONION SAUCE.

SCALD and draw your ducks, put them in warm water for a few minutes, then take them out, put them in an earthen pot, pour over them a pint of boiling milk, let them lie in it two or three hours when you take them out dredge them well with flour, put them in a copper of cold water, put on your cover, let them boil slowly twenty minutes, then take them out, and smother them with onion sauce.

To make ONION SAUCE.

BOIL eight or ten large onions, change the water two or three times while they are boiling, when enough chop them on a board to keep them from growing a bad colour, put them in, a saucepan with a quarter of a pound of butter, two spoonfuls of thick cream, boil it a little, and pour it over the ducks.

To roast DUCKS. .

WHEN you have killed and drawn your ducks, ibred one onion, and a few sage leaves, put them into your ducks with pepper and salt, spit, singe, and dust them with flour, baste them with butter; if your fire be very hot they will be roasted in twenty minutes, the quicker they are roasted the better they eat; just before you draw them, dust them with flour, and baste them with butter, put them on a dish, have ready your gravy made of the gizzards and pinions, a large blade of mace, a few pepper corns, a spoonful of catchup, the same of browning, a tea spoonful of lemon pickle, and one onion, strain it, pour it on your dim, and lend onion sauce in a boat.

To boil a TURKEY with OYSTER SAUCE.

LET your turkey have no meat the day before you kill it, when you are going to kill it give it a spoonful of allegar, it will make it white and eat tenders; when you have killed it hang it up by the legs for four or five days at least; when you have plucked it draw it at the rump, if you can take the breast-bone out nicely it will look much better, cut off the legs, put the end of the thighs into the body of the turkey, skewer them down, and tie them with a string, cut off the head and neck, then grate a penny loaf, chop a score or more of oysters fine, shred a little lemon peel, nutmeg, pepper, and salt to your palate, mix it up into a light force meat with a quarter of a pound of butter, a spoonful or two of cream, and three eggs, stuff the craw with it, and make the rest into balls and boil them; sew up the turkey, dredge it well with flour, put it into a kettle of cold water, cover it, and set it over the fire, when the scum begins to rise, take it off, put on your cover, let it boil very slowly for half an hour, then take off your kettle, and keep it close covered, if it be of a middle size let it stand half an hour in the hot water, the steam being kept in will stew it enough, make it rife, keep the skin whole; tender, and very white ; when you dish it up, pour over it a little of your oyster sauce, lay your balls round it, and serve it up with the rest of your sauce in a boat: garnish with lemon and barberries. — N. B. Observe to set on your turkey in time, that it may stew as above: it is the best way I ever found to boil one to perfection: when you are going to dish it up, set it over the fire to make it quite hot.

To make SAUCE *for a* TURKEY.

AS you open your oysters, put a pint into a bason, wash them out of their liquor, and put them in another baso : when the liquor is settled, pour it clean off into a saucepan, with a little white gravy, a tea spoonful of lemon pickle, thicken it with flour and a good lump of butter, boil it three or four minutes, put in a spoonful of good thick cream, put in your oysters, keep shaking them over the fire till they are quite hot, but do not let them boil, it will make them hard and look little.

A second way to make SAUCE *for a* TURKEY.

CUT a scrag end of a neck of veal in pieces, put them in a saucepan, with two or three blades of mace, one anchovy, a few sticks of celery, a little Chyan and salt, a glass of white wine, a spoonful of lemon pickle, a tea spoonful of mushroom powder or catchup, a quart of water, put on your cover, and let it boil until it be reduced to a pint, strain it, and thicken it with a quarter of a pound of butter rolled in flour, boil it a little, put in a spoonful of thick cream, and pout it over the turkey

To roast a TURKEY.

WHEN you have dressed your turkey as before, truss its head down to the legs, then make your forcemeat, take the crumbs of a penny loaf, a quarter of a pound of beef suet shred fine, a little sausage meat, or veal scraped and pounded exceeding fine, nutmeg, pepper, and salt to your palate, mix it up lightly with three eggs, stuff the craw with it, spit it, and lay it down a good distance from the fire, keep it clear and brisk, singe, dust, and baste it several times with cold butter, it makes the froth stronger than basting it with the hot out of the dripping-pan, and makes the turkey rise better: when it is enough, froth it up as before, dish it up, pour on your dim the same gravy as for the boiled turkey, only put in browning instead of cream: garnish with lemon and pickles, and serve it up; if it be a middle size it will require one hour and a quarter roasting.

To make SAUCE *for a* TURKEY.

CUT the crusts off a penny loaf, cut the rest in thin slices, put it in cold water, with a few pepper corns, a little salt and onion, boil it till the bread is quite soft, then beat it well, put in a quarter of a pound of butter, two spoonful of thick cream, and put it into a bason.

To boil FOWLS.

WHEN you have plucked your fowls, draw them at the rump, cut off the head, neck, and legs, take the breast-bone very carefully out, skewer them with the end of their legs in the body, tie them round with a string, singe, and dust them well with flour, put them in a kettle of cold water, cover it close, set it on the fire, when the scum begins to rise, take it off, put on your cover, and let them boil very slowly twenty minutes, take them off, cover them close, and the heat of the water will stew them enough in half an hour; it keeps the skin whole, and they will be both whiter and plumper than if they had boiled fast; when you take them up, drain them, pour over them white sauce, or melted butter.

To make WHITE SAUCE *for* FOWLS.

TAKE a scrag of veal, the necks of the fowls, or any bits of mutton or veal you have, put them in a sauce-pan, with a blade or two of mace, a few black pepper corns, one anchovy, a head of celery, a bunch of sweet herbs, a slice of the end of a lemon, put in a quart of water, cover it close, let it boil till it is reduced to half a pint, strain it, and thicken it with a quarter of a pound of butter, mixed with flour, boil it five or six minutes, put in two spoonfuls of pickled mushrooms, mix the yolks of two eggs with a teacupful of good cream and a little nutmeg, put in your sauce, keep shaking it over the fire, but do not let it boil.

To roast large FOWLS,

TAKE your fowls when they are ready dressed, put them down to a good fire, singe, dust, and baste them well with butter, they will be near an hour in roasting, make a gravy of the necks and gizzards, strain it, put in a spoonful of browning; when you dim them up, pour the gravy into the dish, serve them up with egg sauce in a boat.

To make EGG SAUCE.

BOIL two eggs hard, half chop the whites, then put in the yolks, chop them both together, but not very fine, put them into a quarter of a pound of good melted butter, and put it in a boat.

To boil young CHICKENS.

PUT your chickens in scalding water, as soon as the feathers will flip off take them out, or it will make the skin hard and break, when you have drawn them lay them in skimmed milk for two hours, then truss them with their heads on their wings, singe and dust them well with flour, put them in cold water, cover them close, set them over a very slow fire, take off the scum, let them boil slowly for five or six minutes, take them off the fire, keep them close covered in the water for half an hour, it will stew them enough, and make them both white and plump ; when you are going to dim them, set them over the fire to make them hot, drain them, pour over them white sauce made the same way as for the boiled fowls.

To roast young CHICKENS.

WHEN you roast young chickens, pluck them very carefully, draw them, only cut off the claws, truss them, and put them down to a good fire, singe, dust, and baste them with butter; they will take a quarter of an hour roasting, then froth them up, lay them on your dish, pour butter and parsley in the dish, and serve them up hot.

To roast PHEASANTS or PARTRIDGES.

WHEN you roast pheasants or partridges, keep them at a good distance from the fire, dust them, and baste them often with fresh butter; if your fire is good, half an hour will roast them; put a little gravy in the dish, made of a scrag of mutton, a spoonful of catchup, the same of browning, and a tea spoonful of lemon pickle, strain it, dish them up, with bread sauce, in a bason, made the same way as for the boiled turkey. N. B. When the pheasant is roasted, stick feathers on the tail before you send it to the table.

To roast RUFFS And REES.

THESE birds I never met with but in Lincolnshire; the best way is to feed them with white bread boiled in milk, they must have separate pots, for two will not eat out of one, they will be fat in eight or ten days; when you kill them, slip the skin off the head and neck with the feathers on, then pluck and draw them; when you roast them, put them a good distance from the fire, if the fire be good they will take about twelve minutes, when they are roasted slip the skin on again with the feathers on, send them up with gravy under them, made the same as for the pheasant, and bread sauce in a boat, and crisp crumbs of bread round the edge of the dish.

To roast WOODCOCKS or SNIPES.

PLUCK them, but do not draw them, put them on a small spit, dust and baste them well with butter, toast a few slices of a penny loaf, put them on a clean plate, and set it under the birds while they are roasting, if the fire be good they will take about ten minutes roasting; when you draw them lay them upon the toasts on the dish; pour melted butter round them, and serve them up.

To roast WILD DUCKS or TEAL.

WHEN your ducks are ready dressed, put in them a small onion, pepper, salt, and a spoonful of red wine, if the fire be good they will roast in twenty minutes, make gravy of the necks and gizzards, a spoonful of red wine, half an anchovy, a blade or two of mace, a slice of an end of a lemon, one onion, and a little Chyan pepper, boil it till it is wasted to half a pint, strain it through a hair sieve, put in a spoonful of browning, pour it on your ducks, serve them up with onion sauce in a boat : garnish your dish with raspings of bread.

To boil PIGEONS.

SCALD your pigeons, draw them, take the craw clean out, wash them in several waters, cut off the pinions, turn the legs under the wings, dredge them, and put them in soft cold Water, boil them very slowly a quarter of an hour, dish them up, pour over them good melted butter, lay round them a little brocoli in bunches, and send butter and parsley in a boat.

To roast PIGEONS.

WHEN you have dressed your pigeons, as before, roll a good lump of butter in chopped parsley, with pepper and salt, put in your pigeons, spit, dust, and baste them; if the fire be good they will be roasted in twenty minutes ; when they are enough lay round them bunches of asparagus, with parsley and butter for sauce.

To roast LARKS.

PUT a dozen of larks on a skewer, tie it to the spit at both ends, dredge and baste them, let them roast ten minutes, take the crumbs of a half-penny loaf, with a piece of butter the size of a walnut, put it in a tossing pan, and shake it over a gentle fire till they are a light brown, lay them betwixt your birds, and pour over them a little melted butter.

To boil RABBITS.

WHEN you have cased your rabbits, skewer them with their heads straight up, the fore-legs brought down, and the hind-legs straight, boil them three quarters of an hour at least, then smother them with onion sauce, made the same as for boiled ducks, pull out the jaw bones, stick them in their eyes, put a sprig of myrtle or bar berries in their mouths, and serve them up.

To roast RABBITS.

WHEN you have cased your rabbits, skewer their heads with their mouths upon their backs, stick their fore-legs into their ribs, skewer the hind-legs double, then make a pudding for them of the crumbs of half a penny loaf, a little parsley, sweet marjoram, thyme, and lemon peel, all shred fine, nutmeg, pepper and salt to your taste, mix them up into a light stuffing, with a quarter of a pound of butter, a little good cream, and two eggs, put it into the belly, and few them up, dredge, and baste them well with butter, roast them near an hour, serve them up with parsley and butter for sauce, chop the livers and lay them in lumps round the edge of your dish.

To roast a HARE.

SKEWER your hare with the head upon one shoulder, the fore legs stuck into the ribs, the hind-legs double, make your pudding of the crumb of a penny loaf, a quarter of a pound of beef marrow or suet, and a quarter of a pound of butter, shred the liver, a sprig or two of winter savory, a little lemon peel, one anchovy, a little Chyan pepper, half a nutmeg grated, mix them up in a light forcemeat, with a glass of red wine, and two eggs, put it in the belly of your hare, sew it up, put a quart of good milk in your dripping pan, baste your hare with it till it is reduced to half a gill, then dust and baste it well with butter, if it be a large one, it will require an hour and a half roasting.

To boil a TONGUE.

IF your tongue be a dry one, steep it in water all night, then boil it three hours, if you would have it eat hot, stick it with cloves, rub it over with the yolk of an egg, strew over it bread crumbs, baste it with butter, set it before the fire till it is a light brown; when you dish it up, pour a little brown gravy, or red wine sauce, mixed the same way as for venison, lay slices of currant jelly round it. N. B. If it be a pickled one, only wash it out of water.

To boil a HAM.

STEEP your ham all night in water, then boil it; if it be of a middle size, it will take three hours boiling, and a small one two hours and a half; when you take it up, pull off the skin, and rub it all over with an egg, strew on bread crumbs, baste it with butter, set it to the fire till it be a light brown if it be to eat hot, garnish with carrots and serve it up.

To roast a HAUNCH of VENISON.

WHEN you have spitted your venison, lay over it a large sheet of paper, then a thin common paste with another paper over it, tie it well to keep the paste from falling, if it be a large one it will take four hours roasting; when it is enough take off the paper and paste, dust it well with flour, and baste it with butter; when it is a light brown, dish it up with brown gravy in your dish, or currant jelly sauce, and send some in a boat.

To broil BEEF STEAKS.

CUT your steaks off a rump of beef about half an inch thick, let your fire be clear, rub your girdiron well with beef suet, when it is hot lay them on, let them broil until they begin to brown, turn them, and, when the other side is brown, lay them on a hot dish, with a slice of butter betwixt every steak; sprinkle a little pepper and salt over them, let them stand two or three minutes, then slice a shalot (as thin as possible) into a spoonful of water, lay on your steaks again, keep turning them till they are enough, put them on your dish, pour the shallot and water amongst them, and send them to the table.

A very good way to fry BEEF STEAKS.

CUT your steaks as for broiling, put them into a stew-pan with a stood lump of butter, set them over a very flow fire, keep turning them till the butter is become a thick white gravy, pour it into a bason, and pour more butter to them; when they are almost enough, pour all the gravy into your bason, and put more butter into your pan, fry them a light brown over a quick fire, take them out of the pan, put them in a hot pewter dish, slice a shalot among them, put a little in your gravy that was drawn from them, and pour it hot upon them: I think this is the best way of dressing beef steaks. Half a pound of butter will dress a large dish.

To dress BEEF STEAKS a common way.

FRY your steaks in butter a good brown, then put in half a pint of water, an onion sliced, a spoonful of walnut catchup, a little capes liquor, pepper and salt, cover them close with a dish, and let them stew gently; when they are enough, thicken the gravy with flour and butter and serve them up.

To broil MUTTON STEAKS.

CUT your steaks half an inch thick, when your gridiron is hot rub it with fresh suet, lay on your steaks, keep turning them as quick as possible, if you do not take great care the fat that drops from the steak will smoke them; when they are enough, put them into a hot dish, rub them well with butter, slice a shalot very thin into a spoonful of water, pour it on them with a spoonful of mushroom catchup and salt, serve them up hot.

To broil PORK STEAKS.

OBSERVE the same as for the mutton steaks, only pork requires more broiling; when they are enough put in a little good gravy; a little sage rubbed very fine strewed over them gives them a fine taste.

To hash BEEF.

CUT your beef in very thin slices, take a little of your gravy that runs from it, put it into a tossing pan with a teaspoonful of lemon pickle, a large one of walnut catchup, the same of browning, slice a shalot in, and put it over the fire; when it boils put in your beef; shake it over the fire till it is quite hot, the gravy is not to be thickened, slice in a small pickle cucumber; garnish with scraped horse-radish or pickled onions.

To hash VENISON.

CUT your venison in thin slices, put a large glass of red wine into a tossing pan, a spoonful of mushroom catchup, the same of browning, an onion stuck with cloves, and half an anchovy chopped small; when it boils, put in your venison, let it boil three or four minutes, pour it into a soup dish, and lay round it currant jelly, or red cabbage.

To hash MUTTON.

CUT your mutton in slices, put a pint of gravy or broth into a tossing pan, with one spoonful of mushroom catchup, and one of browning, slice in an onion, a little pepper and salt, put it over the fire, and thicken it with flour and butter; when it boils put in your mutton, keep shaking it till it is thoroughly hot, put it in a soup dish and serve it up.

To hash VEAL.

CUT your veal in thin round slices, the size of a half crown, put them into a sauce pan, with a little gravy and lemon peel cut exceeding fine, a tea spoonful of lemon pickle, put it over the fire, and thicken it with flour and butter; when it boils put in your veal, just before you dim it up put in a spoonful of cream, lay sippets round your dish and serve it up.

To warm up SCOTCH COLLOPS.

WHEN you have any Scotch collops left, put them into a stone jar till you want them, then put the jar into a pan of boiling water, let it stand till your collops are quite hot, then pour them into a dish, lay over them a few broiled bits of bacon, and they will eat as well as fresh ones.

To mince VEAL.

CUT your veal in slices, then cut it in little square bits, but do not chop it, put it into a saucepan with two or three spoonfuls of gravy, a slice of lemon, a little pepper and salt, a good lump of butter rolled in flour, a teaspoonful of lemon pickle, and a large spoonful of cream; keep shaking it over the fire till it boils, but do not let it boil above a minute, if you do it will make your veal eat hard: put sippets round your dish and serve it up.

To hash a TURKEY.

TAKE off the legs, cut the thighs in two pieces, cut off the pinions and break in pretty large pieces, take off the skin or it will give the gravy a greasy taste, put it into a stew-pan, with a pint of gravy, a tea spoonful of lemon pickle, a slice of the end of a lemon, and a little beaten mace; boil your turkey six or seven minutes (if you boil it any longer it will make it hard) then put it on your dish, thicken your gravy with flour and butter, mix the yolks of two eggs with a spoonful of thick cream, put it in your gravy, shake it over your fire till it is quite hot, but do not let it boil, strain it, and pour it over your turkey: lay sippets round, serve it up, and garnish with lemon or parsley.

To hash FOWLS.

CUT up your fowl as for eating, put it in a tossing pan, with half a pint of gravy, a tea spoonful of lemon pickle, a little mushroom catchup, a slice of lemon, thicken it with flour and butter; just before you dish it up put in a spoonful of good cream; lay sippets round your dish and serve it up.

A nice way to dress a COLD FOWL.

PEEL off all the skin, and pull the flesh off the bones in as large pieces as you can, then dredge it with a little flour, and fry it a nice brown in butter, toss it up in rich gravy, well seasoned, and thicken it with a piece of butter rolled in flour; just before you send it up squeeze in the juice of a lemon.

To hash a WOODCOCK, or PARTRIDGE.

CUT your woodcock up as for a eating, work the entrails very fine with the back of a spoon, mix it with a spoonful of red wine, the same of water, half a spoonful of allegar, cut an onion in slices and pull it into rings, roll a little butter in flour, put them all in your tossing pan, and shake it over the fire till it boils, then put in your woodcock, and when it is thoroughly hot, lay it in your dish with sippets round it, strain the sauce over the woodcock, and lay on the onion in rings; it is a pretty corner dish for dinner or supper.

To hash a WILD DUCK.

CUT up your duck as for eating, put it in a tossing pan, with a spoonful of good gravy, the same of red wine, a little of your onion sauce, or an onion sliced exceeding thin; when it has boiled two or three minutes, lay the duck in your dish, pour the gravy over it, it must not be thickened, you may add a teaspoonful of caper liquor, or a little browning.

To hash a HARE.

Cut your hare in small pieces, if you have any of the pudding left, rub it small, put to it a large glass of red wine, the same quantity of water, half an anchovy chopped small, an onion stuck with four cloves, a quarter of a pound of butter rolled in flour, shake them all together over a flow fire, till your hare is thoroughly hot, it is a bad custom to let any kind of hash boil longer (it makes the meat eat hard) send your hare to the table in a deep dish, lay sippets round it, but take out the onion, and serve it up.

To boil CABBAGE.

CUT off the outside leaves, and cut it in quarters, pick it well, and wash it clean, boil it in a large quantity of water, with plenty of salt in it; when it is tender, and a fine light green, lay it on a sieve to drain, but don't squeeze it, if you do, it will take off the flavour; have ready some very rich melted butter, or chop it with cold butter. — Greens must be boiled the same way.

To boil a COLLYFLOWER.

WASH and clean your collyflower, boil it in plenty of milk and water (but no salt) till it be tender; when you dish it up, lay greens under it; pour over it good melted butter, and send it up hot.

To boil BROCOLI in Imitation of ASPARAGUS.

TAKE the side shoots of brocoli, strip off the leaves, and with a pen-knife take off all the out-rind up to the heads, tie them in bunches, and put them in salt and water, have ready a pan of boiling water, with a handful of salt in it, boil them ten minutes; then lay them in bunches, and pour over them good melted butter.

To Stew SPINAGE.

WASH your spinage well in several waters, put it in a cullendar, have ready a large pan of boiling water, with a handful of salt, put it in, let it boil two minutes, it will take off the strong earthy taste, then put it into a sieve, squeeze it well, put a quarter of a pound of butter into a tossing pan, put in your spinage, keep turning and chopping it with a knife until it be quite dry and green, lay it upon a plate, press it with another, cut it in the shape of sippets or diamonds, pour round it very rich melted butter, it will eat exceeding mild, and quite a different taste from the common way.

To boil ARTICHOKES.

IF they are young ones, leave about an inch of the stalks, put them in a strong salt and water for an hour or two, then put them in a pan of cold water, set them over the fire, but do not cover them, it will takeoff their colour; when you dish them up, put rich melted butter, in small cups or pots, like rabbits, put them in the dish with your artichokes, and send them up.

To boil ASPARAGUS.

SCRAPE your asparagus, tie them in small bunches, boil them in a large pan of water with salt in it; before you dish them up toast some slices of white bread, and dip them in the boiling water, lay the asparagus on your toasts, pour on them very rich melted butter, and serve them up hot.

To boil FRENCH BEANS.

CUT the end's of your beans off, then cut them slantways, put them in a strong salt and water, as you do them, let them stand an hour, boil them in a large quantity of water with a handful of salt in it, they will be a fine greens when you dish them up, pour on them melted butter, and send them up.

To boil WINDSOR BEANS.

BOIL them in a good quantity of salt and water, boil and chop some parsley, put it in good melted butter; serve them up with bacon in the middle if you choose it.

To boil GREEN PEASE.

SHELL your pease just before you want them, put them into boiling water, with a little salt and a lump of loaf sugar, when they begin to dent in the middle they are enough, strain them in a sieve, put a good lump of butter into a mug, give your pease a make, put them on a dish, and send them to the table. — Boil a sprig of mint in another water, chop it fine, and lay it in lumps round the edge of your dish.

To boil PARSNIPS.

WASH your parsnips very well, boil them till they are soft, then take off the skin, beat them in a bowl with a little salt, put to them a little cream and a lump of butter, put them in a tossing pan, and let them boil till they are like alight custard pudding, put them on a plate, and send them to the table.

CHAP IV

Observations on MADE DISHES

BE careful the tossing pan is well tinned, quite clean, and not gritty and put every ingredient into your white sauce, and have it of a proper thickness, and well boiled, before you put in eggs and cream, for they will not suit much to the thickness, nor stir them with a spoon after they are in, nor set your pan on the fire for it will gather at the bottom and be in lumps, but hold your pan a good height from the fire, and keep shaking the pan round one way, it will keep the sauce from curdling, and be sure you don't let it boil; it is the best way to take up your meat, collops, or hash, or any other kind of dish you are making, with a fish slice, and strain your sauce upon it, for it is almost impossible to prevent little bits of meat from mixing with the sauce, and by this method the sauce will cook clear.

In the brown made dishes take special care no fat is on the top of the gravy, but skim it clean off, and that it be of a fine brown, and taste of no one thing in particular; if you use any wine put it in some time before your dish is ready, to take off the rawness, for nothing can give a made dish a more disagreeable taste than raw wine, or fresh anchovy: When you use fried forcemeat balls, put them on a sieve to drain the fat from them, and never let them boil in your sauce, it will give it a greasy look, soften the balls -, the best way is to put them in after your meat is dished up. You may use pickled mushrooms, artichoke bottoms, morels, truffles, and forcemeat balls in almost every made dish, and in several, you may use a roll of forcemeat instead of balls, as in the porcupine breast of veal, and where you can use it, it is much handsomer than balls, especially in a mock turtle, collared or raggooed breast of veal, or any large made dish

To make LEMON PICKLE.

TAKE two dozen of lemons, grate off the out-rinds very thin, cut them in four quarters, but leave the bottoms whole, rub on them equally half a pound of bay salt, and spread them on a large pewter dish, put them in a cool oven, or let them dry gradually by the fire till all the juice is dried into the peels, then put them into a pitcher well glazed ; with one ounce of mace, half an ounce of cloves beat fine, one ounce of nutmeg cut in thin slices, four ounces of garlick peeled, half a pint of mustard seed bruised a little, and tied in a muslin bag, pour two quarts of boiling white wine vinegar upon them, close the pitcher well up; and let it stand five or six days by the fire; shake it well up every. days, then tie it up and let it stand for three months to take off the bitter; when you bottle it ; put the pickle and lemon in a hair sieve, press them well to get out the liquor, and let it stand till another day, then pour off the fine and bottle it ; let the other stand three or four days and it will refine itself, pour it off and bottle it, let it stand again and bottle it, till the whole is refined: it may be put in any white sauce, and will not hurt the colour; it is very good for fish sauce and made dishes, a tea spoonful is enough for white, and two for brown sauce for a fowl; it is a most useful pickle and gives a pleasant flavour: be sure you put it in before you thicken the sauce, or put any cream in, lest the sharpness make it curdle.

Browning for MADE DISHES.

BEAT small four ounces of treble refined sugar, put it in a clean iron frying pan, with one ounce of butter, set it over a clear fire, mix it very well together all the time; when it begins to be frothy, the sugar is dissolving, hold it higher over the fire, have ready a pint of red wine; when the sugar and butter is of a deep brown, pour in a little of the wine, stir it well together, then add more wine, and keep stirring it all the time; put in half an ounce of Jamaica pepper, six cloves, four shalots peeled, two or three blades of mace, three spoonfuls of mushroom catchup, a little salt, the out-rinds of one lemon, boil them slowly for ten minutes, pour it into a bason, when cold take off the scum very clean, and bottle it for use.

To dress a MOCK TURTLE.

TAKE the largest calf's head you can get, with the skin on, put it in scalding water tilt you find the hair will come off, clean it well, and wash it in warm water, and boil it three quarters of an hour, then take it out of the water and slit it down the face, cut off all the- meat along with the skin as clean from the bone as you can, and be careful you do not break the ears off, lay it on a flat dish, and stuff the ears with forcemeat, and tie them round with cloths, take the eyes out, and pick all the rest of the meat clean from the bones, put it in a tossing pan, with the nicest and softest part of another calf's head, without the skin on, boiled as long as the above, and three quarts of veal gravy, lay the skin in the pan on the meat with the flesh side up, cover the pan close, and let it stew over a moderate fire one hour, then put in three sweetbreads fryed a light brown, one ounce of morels, the same of truffles, five artichoke bottoms boiled,, one anchovy, boned and chopped small, a tea spoonful of Chyan pepper, a little salt, half a lemon, three pints of Madeira wine, two meat spoonful of mushroom catchup, one of lemon pickle, half a pint of mushrooms, and let them stew slowly half an hour longer, and thicken it with flour and butter; have ready the yolks of four eggs boiled hard, and the brains of both heads boiled, cut the brains the size of nutmegs, and make a rich forcemeat, and spread it on the caul of a leg of veal, roll it up and boil it in a cloth one hour; when boiled, cut it in three parts, the middle largest, then take up the meat into the dish, and lay the head over it with the skin side up, and put the largest piece of forcemeat between the ears, and make the top of the ears to meet round it; (this is called the crown of the turtle) lay the other slices of the forcemeat opposite to each other at the narrow end, and lay a few of the truffles, morels, brains, mushrooms, eggs, and artichoke bottoms upon the face and round it, strain the gravy boiling hot upon it, be as quick in dishing it up as possible, for it soon goes cold.

MOCK TURTLE *a second way.*

DRESS the hair of a calf's head as before, boil it half an hour, when boiled cut it in pieces half an inch thick, and one inch and a half long, put it into a stew pan, with two quarts of veal gravy, and salt to your taste; let it stew one hour, then put in a pint of Madeira wine, half a tea spoonful of Chyan pepper, truffles and morels one ounce each, three or four artichoke bottoms boiled and cut in quarters; when the meat begins to look clear, and the gravy strong, put in half a lemon, and thicken it with flour and butter, fry a few forcemeat balls, beat four yolks of hard boiled eggs in a mortar very fine, with a lump of butter, and make them into balls the size of pigeons eggs; put the forcemeat balls and eggs in after you have dished it up. N. B. A lump of butter put in the water makes the artichoke bottoms boil white and sooner.

To make an ARTIFICIAL TURTLE.

SCALD a calf's head, cut it in pieces one inch thick, two broad, and four long, parboil a salmon's liver, cut it in ten or twelve pieces, season the whole with beaten mace, salt, and Chyan, put them into a well-lined copper dish, with a pint and half of gravy made of veal, six anchovies, a blade of mace, and a sprig of sweet marjoram (your gravy must be very good) a pint of Madeira wine, the juice of four or five lemons strained from the feeds, the yolks of ten or twelve eggs boiled hard, and about three dozen of forcemeat balls, made as the receipt directs; let it stew gently about an hour, always keep it close covered, and stir in a lump of butter the size of an orange, with a tea spoonful of fine flour rolled in it, and let it stew full two hours longer: if you perceive it wants addition of seasoning, etc, add to it a few minutes before you serve it up, which must be in a soup dish or tureen, with the yolks and slices of lemon on the top; take care to skim off the fat before you dish it up.

To make FORCEMEAT *for an* ARTIFICIAL TURTLE

TAKE a pound of the fat of a loin of veal, the same of lean, with six boned anchovies, beat them fine in a marble mortar, season with mace, Chyan, salt, a little shred parsley, sweet marjoram, some juice of lemon, and three or four spoonfuls of Madeira wine, mix these well together, and make it into little balls, dust them with a little fine flour, and put them into your dish to stew about half an hour before you serve it up; the green skin of a salmon's head is a very great addition to your turtle; boil it a little, then stew it among the rest of the other things.

To make a CALF'S HEAD *Hash*

CLEAN your calf's head exceeding well, and boil it a quarter of an hour; when it is cold cut the meat into thin broad slices, and put it into a tossing pan, with two quarts of gravy; and when it has stewed three quarters of an hour, add to it one anchovy, a little beaten mace, and Chyan to your taste, two tea spoonfuls of lemon pickle, two meat spoonfuls of walnut catchup, half an ounce of truffles and morels, a slice or two of lemon, a bundle of sweet herbs, and a glass of white wine, mix a quarter of a pound of butter with flour, and put it in a few minutes before the head is enough ; take your brains and put them into hot water, it will make them skin sooner, and beat them fine in a bason, then add to them two eggs, one spoonful of flour, a bit of lemon peel shred fine, chop small a little parsley, thyme, and sage, beat them very well together, strew in a little pepper and salt, then drop them in little cakes into a panful of boiling hog's lard, and fry them a light brown, then lay them on a sieve to drain; take your hash out of the pan with a fish slice, and lay it on your dish, and strain your gravy over it, lay upon it a few mushrooms, forcemeat balls, the yolks of four eggs boiled hard, and the brain-cakes; garnish with lemon and pickles. It is proper for a top or side dish.

To dress a CALF'S HEAD the best -way..

TAKE a calf's head with the skin on, and scald off all the hair and clean it very well, cut it in two, take out the brains, boil the head very white and tender, take one part quite off the bone, and cut it into nice pieces with the tongue, dredge it with a little flour, and let it stew on a slow fire for about half an hour in rich white gravy made of veal, mutton, and a piece of bacon, seasoned with pepper, salt, onion, and a very little mace; it must be strained off before the hash is put in it, thicken it with a little butter rolled in flour: the other part of the head must be taken off in one whole piece, stuff it with nice forcemeat, and roll it like a collar, and stew it tender in gravy, then put it in the middle of the dish, and the hash all round, garnish it with forcemeat balls, fried oysters, and the brains made into little cakes dipped in rich butter and fried. You may add wine, morels, truffles, or what you please to make it good and rich.

To dress a CALF'S HEAD SURPRISE.

DRESS off the hair of a large calf's head as directed in the mock turtle, then take a sharp pointed knife and raise off the skin, with as much of the meat from the bones as you possibly can get, that it may appear like a whole head when it is stuffed, and be careful you do not cut the skin in holes, then scrape a pound of fat bacon, the crumb of two penny loaves, grate a small nutmeg with salt, Chyan pepper, and shred lemon peel to your taste, the yolks of six eggs well beat, mix all up into a rich forcemeat, put a little into the ears and stuff the head with the remainder, have ready a deep narrow pot that it will just go in, with two quarts of water, half a pint of white wine, two spoonfuls of lemon pickle, the same of walnut and mush room catchup, one anchovy, a blade or two of mace, a bundle of sweet herbs, a little salt and Chyan pepper, lay a coarse paste over it to keep in the steam; and set it in a very quick oven two hours and a half, when you take it out lay your head in a soup dish, skim the fat clean off the gravy, and strain it through a hair sieve into a tossing pan, thicken it with a lump of butter rolled in flour; when it has boiled a few minutes, put in the yolk of six eggs well beat, and mixed with half a pint of cream, but do not let it boil, it will curdle the eggs; you must have ready boiled a few forcemeat balls, half an ounce of truffles and morels, it would make the gravy too dark a colour to stew them in it; Pour your gravy over your head, and garnish with the truffles, morels, forcemeat balls, mushrooms, and barberries, and serve it up. This is a handsome top dish at a small expence.

To grill a CALF'S HEAD.

WASH your calf's head clean and boil it almost enough, then take it up and hash one half, the other half rub over with the yolk of an egg, a little pepper and salt, strew over it bread crumbs, parsley chopped small, and a little grated lemon peel, set it before the fire and keep basting it all the time to make the froth rise; when it is a fine light brown, dish up your hash, and lay the grilled side upon it. Blanch your tongue, slit it down the middle, and lay it on a soup plate: skin the brains, boil them with a little sage and parsley; chop them fine, and mix them with some melted butter, and a spoonful of cream, make them hot, and pour them over the tongue, serve them up, and they are sauce for the head.

To collar a CALF'S HEAD.

TAKE a calf's head with the skin on and scald it, clean it well, then bone it, season it with pepper, salt, cloves, mace, and a little ginger, all ground very fine, take some cochineal, dissolve it in some water, rub it on the inside of the head with a little bay salt and a large handful of chopped parsley, roll it up light in a cloth, and boil it till you think it is enough in a pickle made of all sorts of sweet herbs, spices, and some red wine, then unroll the cloth and roll it tight again, and put weights upon it as it lies in the pickle to press it close till it is cold, then boil some bran and water with some bay and common salt, strain it off, and when they are both cold put it in the head, and let it lie three or four days before you use it.

To make a PORCUPINE *of a* BREAST OF VEAL,

BONE the finest and largest breast of veal you can get, rub it over with the yolks of two eggs, spread it on a table, lay over it a little bacon cut as thin as possible, a handful of parsley shred fine, the yolks of five hard boiled eggs, chopped small, a little lemon peel cut fine, nutmeg, pepper, and salt to your taste, and the crumb of a penny loaf steeped in cream, roll the breast close, and skewer it up, then cut fat bacon and the lean of ham that has been a little boiled, or it will turn the veal red, and pickled cucumbers about two inches long to answer the other lardings, and lard it in rows, first ham, then bacon, then cucumbers, till you have larded it all over the veal; put it in a deep earthen pot, with a pint of water, and cover it and set it in a flow oven two hours; when it comes from the oven slum the fat off, and strain the gravy through a sieve into a stew-pan, put in a glass of white wine, a little lemon pickle and caper liquor, a spoonful of mushroom catchup, thicken it with a little butter, rolled in flour, lay your porcupine on the dish, and pour it hot upon it, cut a roll of forcemeat in four slices, lay one at each end and the other at the sides ; have ready your sweetbread cut in slices, and fried, lay them round it with a few mushrooms. It is a grand bottom dish when game is not to be had. N. B. Make the forcemeat of a few chopped oysters, the crumbs of a penny loaf, half a pound of beef suet shred fine, and the yolks of four eggs, mix them well together with nutmeg, Chyan pepper, and salt to your palate, spread it on a veal caul, and roll it up close like a collared eel, bind it in a cloth and boil it one hour.

To ragoo a BREAST OF VEAL.

HALF roast a breast of veal, then bone it and put it in a tossing pan, with a quart of veal gravy, one ounce of morels, the same of truffles, stew it till tender, and just before you thicken the gravy, put in a few oysters, pickled mushrooms, and pickled cucumbers, cut in small square pieces, the yolks of four eggs boiled hard, cut your sweetbread in slices, and fry it a light brown, dish up your veal and pour the gravy hot over it, lay your sweetbread round, morels, truffles, and eggs upon it: garnish with pickled barberries; this is proper for either top or side for dinner, or bottom for supper.

To collar a BREAST OF VEAL.

TAKE the finest breast of veal, bone it, and rub it over with the yolks of two eggs, and strew over it some crumbs of bread, a little grated lemon, a little pepper and salt, a handful of chopped parsley, roll it up tight and bind it hard with twine, wrap it in a cloth, and boil it one hour and a half, then take it up to cool, when a little cold take off the cloth, and clip off the twine carefully, lest you open the veal, cut it in five slices, lay them on a dish with the sweetbread boiled and cut in thin slices and laid round them, with ten or twelve forcemeat balls; pour over your white sauce, and garnish with barberries or green pickles. The white sauce must be made thus: Take a pint of good veal gravy, put to it a spoonful of lemon pickle, half an anchovy, a teaspoonful of mushroom powder, or a few pickled mushrooms, give it a gentle boil; then put in half a pint of cream, the yolks of two eggs beat fine, shake it over the fire after the eggs and cream is in, but do not let it boil, it will curdle the cream. It is proper for a top dish at night, or a side dish for dinner.

A boiled BREAST OF VEAL.

SKEWER your breast of veal, that it will lie flat in the dish, boil it one hour (if a large one an hour and a quarter) make a white sauce as before-mentioned for the collared one, pour it over, and garnish it with pickles.

Neck of VEAL CUTLETS.

CUT a neck of veal into cutlets, fry them a fine brown, then put them into a tossing pan, and stew them till tender in a quart of good gravy, then add one spoonful of browning, the game of catchup, some fried forcemeat balls, a few truffles, morels, and pickled mushrooms, a little salt, and Chyan pepper, thicken your gravy with flour and butter, let it boil a few minutes, lay your cutlets in the dish, with the top of the ribs in the middle, pour your sauce over them, lay your balls, morels, truffles, and mushrooms over the cutlets, and send them up.

A Neck of VEAL a-la-royal.

CUT off the scrag-end and part of the chine, bone to make it lie flat in the dish, then chop a few mushrooms, shalots, a little parsley and thyme, all very fine, with pepper and salt, cut middle-sized lards of bacon, and roll them in the herbs, &c. and lard the lean part of the neck, put it in a slew-pan with some lean bacon or shank of ham, and the chine-bone and scrag cut in pieces, with three or four carrots, onions, a head of celery, and a little beaten mace, pour in as much water as will cover the pan very close, and let it stew slowly for two or three hours, till tender, then strain half a pint of the liquor out of the pan through a fine sieve, set it over a stove, and let it boil, keep stirring it till it is dry at the bottom, and of a good brown; be sure you do not let it burn, then add more of the liquor strained free from fat, and keep stirring it till it becomes a fine thick brown glaze, then take the veal out of the stew-pan, and wipe it clean, and put the larded side down upon the glaze, set it over a gentle fire five or six minutes to take the glaze, then lay it in the dish with the glazed side up, and put into the same stew-pan as much flour as will lie on a six-pence, stir it about well, and add some of the braise liquor, if any left; let it boil till it is of a proper thickness, strain it and pour it in the bottom of the dim, squeeze in a little juice of lemon and serve it up.

Bombarded VEAL.

CUT the bone nicely out of a fillet, make a forcemeat of the crumbs of a penny loaf, half a pound of fat bacon scraped, a little lemon peel or lemon thyme, parsley, two or three sprigs of sweet marjoram, one anchovy, chop them all very well, grate a little nutmeg, Chyan pepper and salt to your palate, mix all up together with egg and a little cream, and fill up the place where the bone came out with the forcemeat, then cut the fillet across, in cuts about one inch from another all round the fillet, fill one nick, with forcemeat, a second with boiling spinage, that is boiled and well squeezed, a third with bread crumbs, chopped oysters, and beef marrow, then forcemeat, and fill them up as above all round the fillet, wrap the caul close round it, and put it in a deep pot with a pint of water, make a coarse paste to lay over it, to keep the oven from giving it a fiery taste; when it comes out of the oven, skim off the fat and put the gravy in a stew-pan, with a spoonful of lemon pickle, and another of mushroom catchup, two of browning, half an ounce of morels, and truffles, five boiled artichoke bottoms cut in quarters, thicken the sauce with flour and butter, give it a gentle boil, and pour it upon the veal into your dish.

To make a FRYCANDO of VEAL.

CUT steaks half an inch thick, and six inches long, out of the thick part of a leg of veal, lard them with small cardoons, and dust them with flour, put them before the fire to broil a fine brown, then put them into a large tossing pan with a quart of good gravy and let it stew half an hour, then put in two tea-spoonfuls of lemon pickle, a meat spoonful of walnut catch up, the same of browning, a slice of lemon, a little anchovy and Chyan, a few morels and truffles; when your fricandos are tender, take them up, and thicken your gravy with flour and butter, strain it, place your fricandos in the dish, pour your gravy on them: garnish with lemons and barberries. You may lay round them forcemeat balls fried, or forcemeat rolled in a veal caul, and yolks of eggs boiled hard.

To make VEAL OLIVES.

CUT the thick part of a leg of veal in thin slices, flatten them with the broad side of a cleaver, rub them over with the yolk of an egg strew over every piece a very thin slice of bacon, strew over them a few bread crumbs, a little lemon peel, and parsley chopped small, pepper, salt, and nutmeg, roll them up close and skewer them tight, then rub them with the yolk of eggs, and roll them in bread crumbs and parsley chopped small, put them into a tin dripping-pan to bake or fry them; then take a pint of good gravy, add to it a spoonful of lemon pickle, the same of walnut catchup, and one of browning, a little anchovy and Chyan pepper, thicken it with flour and butter, serve them up with forcemeat balls, and strain the gravy hot upon them: garnish with pickles, and strew over them a few pickled mushrooms. — You may dress veal cutlets the same way, but not roll them.

To make VEAL OLIVES a second Way.

CUT large collops of a fillet of veal, and hack them very well with the back of a knife, spread forcemeat very thin over every one, roll them up and roast them, or bake them in an oven, make a ragoo of oysters and sweet-breads diced, a few morels and mushrooms, and lay them in the dish with the rolls of veal; if you have oysters enough, chop and mix some with the forcemeat, it makes it much better; force meat balls look very pretty round them; there must be nice brown gravy in the dish, and they must be sent up hot.

To dress SCOTCH COLLOPS *white*.

CUT them off the thick part of a leg of veal, the size and thickness of a crown piece, put a lump of butter into a tossing pan, and set it over a slow fire or it will discolour your collops; before the pan is hot lay the collops in, and keep turning them over till you feel the butter is turned to thick white gravy; put your collops and gravy in a pot, and set them upon the hearth, to keep warm, put cold butter again into your pan every time you fill it, and fry them as above, and so continue till you have finished; when you have fried them pour your gravy from them into your pan, with a tea spoonful of lemon pickle, mushroom catchup, caper liquor, beaten mace, Chyan pepper, and salt, thicken with flour and butter, when it has boiled five minutes, put in the yolks of two eggs well beat and mixed, with a tea-cupful of rich cream; keep shaking your pan over the fire till your gravy looks of a fine thickness, then put in your collops and shake them, when they are quite hot, put them on your dish with forcemeat balls, strew over them pickled mushrooms : garnish with barberries and kidney-beans.

To dress SCOTCH COLLOPS *brown*.

CUT your collops the same way as the white ones, but brown your butter before you lay ht your collops, fry them over a quick fire, shake and turn them, and keep them on a fine froth : when they are a light brown, put them into a pot, and fry them as the white ones; when you have fried them all brown, pour all the gravy from them into a clean tossing-pan, with half a pint of gravy made of the bones and bits you cut the collops off, two teaspoonfuls of lemon pickle, a large one of catchup, the same of browning, half an ounce of morels, half a lemon, a little anchovy, Chyan, and salt to your taste, thicken it with flour and butter, let it boil five or six minutes, then put in your collops, and shake them over the fire; if they boil it will make them hard ; when they have simmered a little, take them out with an egg spoon, and lay them on your dish, strain your gravy and pour it hot on them, lay over them force meat balls, and little slices of bacon curled round a skewer and boiled, throw a few mushrooms over: garnish with lemon and barberries, and serve them up.

To dress SCOTCH COLLOPS *the French Way.*

TAKE a leg of veal, and cut your collops pretty thick, five or six inches long, and three inches broad, rub them over with the yolk of an egg, put pepper and salt, and grate a little nutmeg on them, and a little shred parsley; lay them on an earthen dish, and set them before the fire, baste them with butter,. and let them be a fine brown, then turn them on the other side, and rub them as above, baste and brown them the same way; when they are thoroughly enough, make a good brown gravy with truffles and - morels, dish up your collops, lay truffles and morels, and the yolks of hard boiled eggs over them: garnish with crisp parsley and lemon.

SWEET-BREADS *a-la-daub.*

TAKE three of the largest and finest sweet breads you can get, put them in a sauce pan of boiling water for five minutes, then take them out, and when they are cold lard them with a row down the middle, with very little pieces of bacon, then a row on each side with lemon peel cut the size of wheat straw; then a row on each side of pickled cucumbers, cut very fine, put them in a tossing pan, with good veal gravy, a little juice of lemon, a spoonful of browning, stew them gently a quarter of an hour; a little before they are ready thicken them with flour and butter, dish them up and pour the gravy over, lay round them bunches of boiled celery, or oyster patties: garnish with stewed spinage, green coloured parsley, stick a bunch of barberries in the middle of each sweet-bread. It is a pretty corner dish for either dinner or supper.

Forced SWEETBREADS.

PUT three sweet-breads in boiling water five minutes, beat the yolk of an egg a little, and rub it over them with a feather, strew on bread crumbs, lemon peel, and parsley shred very fine, nutmeg, salt, and pepper to your palate, set them before the fire to brown, and add to them a little veal gravy, put a little mushroom powder, caper liquor, or juice of lemon and browning, thicken it with flour and butter, boil it a little, and pour it in your dish, lay in your sweet- breads, and lay over them lemon peel in rings, cut like straws: garnish with pickles.

To fricassee SWEET-BREADS *brown.*

SCALD three sweet-breads, when cold cut them in slices the thickness of a crown piece, dip them in batter, and fry them in fresh butter a nice brown, make a gravy for them as the last, stew your sweet-breads slowly in the gravy eight or ten minutes, lay them on your dish, and pour the gravy over them: garnish with lemon or barberries.

To Fricassee SWEET-BREADS *white.*

SCALD and slice the sweet- breads as before, put them in a tossing pan, with a pint of veal gravy, a spoonful of white wine, the same of mushroom catchup, a little beaten mace, stew them a quarter of an hour, thicken your gravy with flour and butter a little before they are enough; when you are going to dish them up, mix the yolk of an egg with a tea-cupful of thick cream, and a little grated nutmeg, put it into your tossing pan, and shake it well over the fire, but do not let it boil, lay your sweet- breads on your dish, and pour your sauce over them: garnish with pickled red beet-root and kidney- beans.

To ragoo SWEET-BREADS.

RUB them over with the yolk of an egg, strew over them bread crumbs and parsley, thyme and sweet marjoram shred small, and pepper and salt, make a roll of forcemeat like a sweet bread, and put it in a veal caul, and roast them in a Dutch oven, take some brown gravy, and put to it a little lemon pickle, mushroom catchup, and the end of a lemon, boil the gravy, and when the sweet-breads are enough, lay them in a dish, with a forcemeat in the middle, take the rind of the lemon out, and pour the gravy into the dish and serve them up.

To Stew a FILLET of VEAL.

TAKE a fillet of a cow calf, stuff it well under the elder, at the bone and quite through to the shank, put it in the oven with a pint of water under it, till it is a fine brown, then put it in a stew-pan with three pints of gravy, stew it tender, put in a few morels, truffles, a tea spoonful of lemon pickle, a large one of browning, and one of catchup, and a little Chyan pepper, thicken with a lump of butter rolled in flour, dish up your veal, strain your gravy over, lay round forcemeat balls: garnish with pickles and lemon.

To ragoo a FILLET of VEAL.

LARD your fillet and half roast it, then put it in a tossing pan, with two quarts of good gravy, cover it close, and let it stew till tender, then add one spoonful of white wine, one of browning, one of catchup, a tea spoonful of lemon pickle, a little caper liquor, half an ounce of morels, thicken with flour and butter, lay round it a few yolks of eggs.

A good Way to dress a MIDCALF.

TAKE a calf's heart, stuff it with good forcemeat, and send it to the oven in an earthen dish with a little water under it, lay butter over it, and dredge it with flour, boil half the liver and all the lights together half an hour, then chop them small, and put them in a tossing pan with a pint of gravy, one spoonful of lemon pickle and one of catchup, squeeze in half a lemon, pepper and salt, thicken with a good piece of butter rolled in flour; when you dish it up, pour the minced meat in the bottom, and have ready fried a fine brown the other half of the liver cut in thin slices, and little bits of bacon, set the heart in the middle, and lay the liver and bacon over the minced meat, and serve it up.

To disguise a LEG *of* VEAL.

LARD the top side of a leg of veal in rows with bacon, and stuff it well with forcemeat made of oysters, then put it into a large sauce pan with as much water as will cover it, put on a close lid to keep in the steam, stew it gently till quite tender, then take it up and boil down the gravy in the pan to a quart, skim off the fat and add half a lemon, a spoonful of mushroom catchup, a little lemon pickle, the crumbs of half a penny loaf grated exceeding fine, boil it in your gravy till it looks thick, then add half a pint of oysters, if not thick enough, roll a lump of butter in flour and put it in, with half a pint of good cream, and the yolks of three eggs, shake your sauce over the fire, but do not let it boil after the eggs are in lest it curdle; put your veal in a deep dish, and pour the sauce over it: garnish with crisped parsley and fried oysters. It is an excellent dish for the top of a. large table,

HARICO *of a* NECK *of* MUTTON.

CUT the best end of a neck of mutton into chops, in single ribs, flatten them, and fry them a light brown, then put them into a large sauce pan with two quarts of water, a large carrot cut in, slices, cut at the edge like wheels; when they have stewed a quarter of an hour, put in two turnips cut in square slices, the white part of a head of celery, a few heads of asparagus, two cabbage lettuces fried, and Chyan to your taste, boil them all together till they are tender, the gravy is not to be thickened; put it into a tureen, or soup dish. It is proper for a top dish,

To dress a NECK *of* MUTTON *to eat like* VENISON.

CUT a large neck before the shoulder is taken off, broader than usual, and the flap of the shoulder with it, to make it look handsomer; stick your neck all over in little holes with a sharp penknife, and pour a bottle of red wine upon it, and let it lie in the wine four or five days, turn and rub it three or four times a day, them take it out and hang it up for three days in the open air out of the sun, and dry it often with a cloth to keep it from musting; when you roast it baste it with the wine it was steeped in if any left, if not, fresh wine, put white paper three or four folds to keep in the fat, roast it thoroughly, and then take off the skin, and froth it nicely, and serve it up.

To make FRENCH STEAKS *of a* NECK *of* MUTTON.

LET your mutton be very good and large, and cut off most part of the fat of the neck, and then cut the steaks two inches thick, make a large hole through the middle of the fleshy part of every steak with a penknife, and stuff it with forcemeat made of bread crumbs, beef suet, a little nutmeg, pepper and salt, mixed up with the yolk of an egg; when they are stuffed, wrap them in writing paper, and put them in a Dutch oven, set them before the fire to broil, they will take near an hour, put a little brown gravy in your dish, and serve them up in the papers.

A SHOULDER *of* MUTTON *surprised.*

HALF boil a shoulder, then put it in a tossing-pan with two quarts of veal gravy, four ounces of rice, a tea spoonful of mushroom powder, a little beaten mace, and stew it one our, or till the rice is enough, then take up your mutton and keep it hot, put to the rice half a pint of good cream, and a lump of butter rolled in flour, shake it well and boil it a few minutes; lay your mutton on the dish and pour it over: garnish with barberries or pickles, and send it up.

To dress a SHOULDER *of* MUTTON, *called* HEN *and* CHICKENS.

HALF roast a shoulder, then take it up, and cut off the blade at the first joint, and both the flaps to make the blade round, score the blade, round in diamonds; throw a little pepper and salt over it, and setting a tin oven to broil, cut the flaps and the meat off the shank in thin slices into the gravy that runs out of the mutton, and put a little good gravy to it, with two spoonfuls of walnut catchup, one of browning, a little Chyan pepper, and one or two shalots; when your meat is tender, thicken it with flour and butter, put your meat in the dish with the gravy, and lay the blade on the top, broiled a dark brown: garnish with green pickles, and serve it up.

To boil a SHOULDER *of* MUTTON *with* ONION SAUCE.

PUT your shoulder in when the water is cold, when enough smother it with onion sauce, made the same as for boiled ducks. — You may dress a shoulder of veal the same way.

A SHOULDER *of* MUTTON *and* CELERY SAUCE.

BOIL it as before till it is quite enough, pour over it celery sauce, and lend it to the table. —

N. B. The sauce — Wash and clean ten heads of celery, cut off the green tops, and take off the outside stalks, cut them into thin bits, and boil it in gravy till it is tender, thicken it with flour and butter, and pour it over your mutton. — A shoulder of veal roasted with this sauce is very good.

MUTTON *kebobed*.

CUT a loin of mutton in four pieces, take off the skin, and rub them with the yolk of an egg, strew over them a few breadcrumbs, and a little shred parsley, turn them round and spit them, roast them and keep basting all the while with fresh butter, to make the froth rise; when they are enough, put a little brown gravy under, and serve them up: garnish with pickles.

To grill a BREAST *of* MUTTON.

SCORE a breast of mutton in diamonds, and rub it over with the yolk of an egg, then strew on a few bred crumbs and shred parsley, put it in a Dutch oven to broil, baste it with fresh butter, pour in the dim good caper sauce, and serve it up.

Split LEG *of* MUTTON *and* ONION SAUCE.

SPLIT the leg from the shank to the end, stick a skewer in to keep the nick open, baste it with red wine till it is half roasted, then take the wine out of the dripping-pan, and put to it one anchovy, set it over the fire till the anchovy is dissolved, rub the yolk of a hard egg in a little cold butter, mix it with the wine, and put it in your sauce-boat, put good onion sauce over the leg when it is roasted, and serve it up.

To force a LEG *of* MUTTON.

RAISE the skin and take out the lean part of the mutton, chop it exceeding fine, with one anchovy, shred a bundle of sweet herbs, grate a penny loaf, half a lemon, nutmeg, pepper, and salt to your taste, make them into a force meat, with three eggs and a large glass of red wine, fill up the skin with the forcemeat, but leave the bone and shank in their place, and it will appear like a whole leg, lay it on an earthen dish with a pint of red wine under it, and send it to the oven; it will take two hours and a half ; when it comes out take off all the fat, strain the gravy over the mutton, lay round it hard yolks of eggs and pickled mushrooms: garnish with pickles, and serve it up.

To dress SHEEP'S RUMPS and KIDNEYS.

BOIL six sheeps' rumps in veal gravy, then lard your kidneys with bacon, and let them be fore the fire in a tin oven ; when the rumps are tender, rub them over with the yolk of an egg, a little Chyan and grated nutmeg, skim the fat off the gravy, put it in a clean tossing pan, with three ounces of boiled rice, a spoonful of good cream, a little mushroom powder or catchup, thicken it with flour and butter, and give it a gentle boil, fry your rumps a light brown ; when you dish them up, lay them round on your rice, so that the small ends meet in the middle, and lay a kidney between every rump, garnish with red cabbage or barberries, and serve it up. It is a pretty side or corner dish.

To dress a LEG of MUTTON to eat like VENISON.

GET the largest and fattest leg of mutton you. can get, cut out like a haunch of venison; as soon- as it is killed, whilst it is warm, it will eat the tenderer, take out the bloody vein, stick it in, several places in the underside with a sharp- pointed knife, pour over it a bottle of red wine, turn it in the wine four or five times a day for five days, then dry it exceeding well with a clean cloth, hang it up in the air with the thick end uppermost for five days, dry it night and morning to keep it from being damp, or growing musty; when you roast it, cover it with paper, and paste as you do venison ; serve it up with venison sauce.—— It will take four hours roasting.

A BASQUE of MUTTON.

TAKE the caul of a leg of veal; lay it in a copper dish the size of a small punch bowl, take the lean of a leg of mutton, that has been kept a week, chop it exceeding small, take half its weight in beef marrow, the crumbs of a penny loaf, the yolks of four eggs, two anchovies, half a pint of red wine, the rind of half a lemon grated, mix it like sauceage-meat, and lay it in your caul in the inside of your dish, close up the caul, and bake it in a quick oven; when it comes out lay your dish upside-down, and turn the whole out, pour over it brown gravy, and send it up with venison sauce in a boat : garnish with pickle.

OXFORD JOHN.

TAKE a stale leg of mutton, cut it in at thin collops as you possibly can, take out all the fat sinews, season them with mace, pepper, and salt, strew among them a little shred parsley, thyme, and two or three slots, put a good lump of butter into a stew-pan; when it is hot put in all your collops, keep stirring them with a wooden spoon till they are three parts done, then add half a pint of gravy, a little juice of lemon, thicken it a little with flour and butter, let them simmer four or five minutes, and they will be quite enough, if you let them boil, or have them ready before you want them, they will grow hard: serve them up hot, with fried bread cut in dices, over and round them.

To boil a LEG of LAMB and LOIN fried.

CUT your leg from the loin, boil the leg three quarters of an hour, cut the loin in handsome steaks, beat them with a cleaver, and fry them a good brown, then stew them a little in strong gravy, put your leg on the dish, and lay your steaks round it, pour on your gravy, lay round lumps of stewed spinage, and crisped parsley on every steak, send it to the table with gooseberry sauce in a boat.

To force a QUARTER of LAMB.

TAKE a hind quarter and cut off the shank, raise the thick part of the flesh from the bone, with a knife, stuff the place with white force meat, and stuff it under the kidney, half roast it, then put it in a tossing-pan, with a quart of mutton gravy, cover it close up, and let it stew gently: when it is enough take it up and lay it on your dish, skim the fat off the gravy, and strain it, then put in a glass of Madeira wine, one spoonful of walnut catchup, two of browning, half a lemon, a little Chyan, half a pint of oysters, thicken it with a little butter rolled in flour, pour your gravy hot on your lamb and serve it up.

To dress a LAMB'S HEAD and PURTENANCE.

SKIN the head and split it, take the black part out of the eyes, then wash and clean it exceeding well, lay it in warm water till it looks white, wash and clean the purtenance, take off the gall, and lay them in water, boil it half an hour, then mince your heart, liver, and lights, very small, put the mincemeat in a tossing-pan with a quart of mutton gravy, a little catchup, pepper and salt, half a lemon, thicken it with flour and butter, a spoonful of good cream, and just boil it up; when your head is boiled, rub it over with the yolk of an egg, strew over it bread crumbs, a little shred parsley, pepper and salt, baste it well with butter, and brown it before the fire, or with a salamander, put the purtenance on your dish, and lay the head over it: garnish with lemon or pickle, and serve it up.

To fricassee LAMB STONES.

SKIN six lamb stones, or what quantity you please, dip them in batter, and fry them in hog's-lard a nice brown, have ready a little veal gravy, thicken it with flour and butter, put in a tea spoonful of lemon pickle, a little mushroom catchup, a slice of lemon, a little grated nutmeg, beat the yolk of an egg, and mix it with two spoonfuls of thick cream, put in your gravy, keep shaking it over the fire till it looks white and thick, then put in the lamb stones, and give them a shake; when they are hot, dish them up, and lay round them boiled forcemeat balls.

To roast a PIG in Imitation of LAMB.

LET your pig be a month or five weeks old, divide it down the middle, take off the shoulder, and leave the rest to the hind part, then take the skin off, draw sprigs of parsley all over the outside, which must be done by running a skewer or larding pin, and sticking the stalk of the parsley in it to spit it and roast it before a quick fire, dredge it and baste it well with fresh butter, roast it a fine brown, and send it up with a froth on it: garnish with green parsley, it will eat and look like fat lamb.— It is eat with salad.

To barbecue a PIG.

DRESS a pig of ten weeks old as if it were to be roasted, make a forcemeat of two anchovies, six sage leaves, and the liver of the pig, all chopped very small; then put them into a marble mortar, with the crumbs of half a penny loaf, four ounces of butter, half a tea spoonful of Chyan pepper, and half a pint of red wine, beat them all together to a paste, put it in your pig's belly and sew it up, lay your pig down at a good distance before a large brisk fire, singe it well, put in your dripping-pan three bottles of red wine, baste it with the wine all the time it is roasting, when it is half roasted, put under your pig two penny loaves, if you have not wine enough, put in more, when your pig is near enough, take the loaves and sauce out of your dripping-pan, put to the sauce one anchovy chopped small, a bundle of sweet herbs, and half a lemon, boil it a few minutes, then draw your pig, put a small lemon or apple in the pig's mouth, and a loaf on each side, strain your sauce and pour it on them boiling hot, lay bar berries, and slices of lemon round it, and send it up whole to the table. — It is a grand bottom dish. It will take four hours roasting.

To barbecue a LEG of PORK.

LAY down your leg to a good fire, put into the dripping-pan two bottles of red wine, baste your pork with it all the time it is roasting, when it is enough, take up what is left in the pan, put to it two anchovies, the yolks of three eggs boiled hard and pounded fine, with a quarter of a pound of butter, and half a lemon, a bunch of sweet herbs, a teaspoonful of lemon pickle, a spoonful of catchup, and one of tarragon vinegar, or a little tarragon shred small, boil them a few minutes, then draw your pork, and cut the skin down from the bottom of the shank in rows an inch broad, raise every other row and roll it to the shank, strain your sauce and pour it on boiling hot, lay oyster patties all round the pork, and sprigs of green parsley.

To stuff a CHINE of PORK.

TAKE a chine that has been hung about a month, boil it half an hour, then take it up and make holes in it all over the lean part, one inch from another, stuff them betwixt the joints with shred parsley, rub it all over with the yolk of eggs, strew over it bread crumbs, baste it and set it in a Dutch oven, when it is enough lay round it boiled brocoli, or stewed spinage: garnish with parsley.

To roast a HAM or a GAMMON of BACON.

HALF boil your ham or gammon, then take off the skin, dredge it with oatmeal sifted very fine, baste it with fresh butter, it will make a stronger froth than either flour or bread crumbs, then roast it; when it is enough dish it up and pour brown gravy on your dish: garnish with green parsley and send it to the table.

To force the Inside of a SURLOIN of BEEF.

SPIT your sirloin, then cut off from the in side all the skin and fat together, and then take off all the flesh to the bones, chop the meat very fine with a little beaten mace, two or three slots, one anchovy, half a pint of red wine, a little pepper and salt, and put it on the bones again, lay your fat and skin on again, and skewer it close and paper it well, when roasted take off the fat, and dish up the sirloin, pour over it a sauce made of a little red wine, a shalot, one anchovy, two or three slices of horse-radish, and serve it up.

To dress the inside of a cold SURLOIN of BEEF.

CUT out all the inside (free from fat) of the sirloin in pieces as thick as your finger and about two inches long, dredge it with a little flour, and fry it in nice butter of a light brown, then drain it, and toss it up in rich gravy that has been well seasoned with pepper, salt, shallot, and an anchovy; just before you send it up, add two spoonfuls of vinegar taken from pickled capers: garnish with fried oysters, or what you please.

BOUILLIE BEEF.

TAKE the thick end of a brisket of beef, put it into a kettle of water quite covered over, let it boil fast for two hours, then keep stewing it close by the fire for six hours more, and as the water wastes fill up the kettle, put in with the beef some turnips cut in little balls, carrots, and some clary cut in pieces: an hour before it is done take out as much broth as will fill your soup dish, and boil in it for that hour turnips and carrots cut out in balls or in little square pieces, with some celery, salt and pepper to- your taste, serve it up in two dishes, the beef by itself, and the soup by itself; you may put pieces of fried bread, if you like it, in your soup, boil in a few knots of greens, and if you think your soup will not be rich enough, you may add a pound or two of fried mutton chops to your broth when you take it from the beef, and let it stew for that hour in the broth, but be sure to take out the mutton when you send it to the table: the soup must be very clear.

To Stew a RUMP of BEEF.

HALF roast your beef, then put it in a large saucepan or caldron, with two quarts of water, and one of red wine, two or three blades of mace, a shalot, one spoonful of lemon pickle, two of walnut catchup, the same of browning, Chyan pepper and salt to your taste, let it stew over a gentle fire, close covered for two hours, then take up your beef, and lay it on a deep dish, skim off the fat, and strain the gravy, and put in one ounce of morels, and half a pint of mushrooms, thicken your gravy and pour it over your beef, lay round it forcemeat balls: garnish with horse-radish, and serve it up.

To stew a RUMP of BEEF a second Way.

STUFF your beef with three cloves of garlick in different parts, make a hole with a skewer, and get in the garlick as far as about one half your finger can reach, stuff it likewise in several places with forcemeat, in the making of which, put some fat bacon cut in very small slices, then put your beef into the pot the right side under, cut about a pound of suet over it, five or six ounces of bacon sliced, and as much water as will cover it, then set the pot over the fire, let it boil for three quarters of an hour, then cover the pot quite close, and let it stew for four hours over a moderate fire, after which take it up, and pour every drop of liquor from it, and put a quart of claret over it, and set it on a very slow fire while you are preparing the sauce, which is to be either of turnips, or carrots, or pallets, cut as for a ragoo; put in as much broth as you think sufficient, with some of the clear gravy free from fat that you poured off the beef, in a stew-pan; boil them a little with morels, truffles, and a glass of claret, and a little butter rolled in flour, which must be tossed up together, and dish it up very hot.

A FRICANDO of BEEF.

CUT a few slices of beef five or six inches long, and half an inch thick, lard it with bacon, dredge it well with flour, and set it before a brisk fire to brown, then put it in a tossing pan, with a quart of gravy, a few morels and truffle, half a lemon, and stew them half an hour, then add one spoonful of catchup, the same of browning, and a little Chyan, thicken your sauce and pour it over your fricando, lay round them force meat balls, and the yolks of hard eggs.

To a-la-mode BEEF.

TAKE the bone out of a rump of beef, lard the top with bacon, then make a forcemeat of four ounces of marrow, two heads of garlick, the crumbs of a penny loaf, a few sweet herbs chopped small, nutmeg, pepper and salt to your taste, and the yolks of four eggs well beat, mix it up, and stuff your beef where the bone came out, and in several places in the lean part, skewer it round and bind it about with a fillet, put it in a pot with a pint of red wine, and tie it down with strong paper, bake it in the oven for three hours; when it comes out, if you want to eat it hot, skim the fat off the gravy, and add half an ounce of morels, a spoonful of pickled mush rooms, thicken it with flour and butter, dish up your beef and pour on the gravy, lay round it forcemeat balls, and send it up.

To make a PORCUPINE of the FLAT RIBS of BEEF.

BONE the flat ribs, and beat it half an hour with a paste pin, then rub it over with the yolks of eggs, strew over it bread crumbs, parsley, leeks, sweet marjoram, lemon peel shred fine, nutmeg, pepper, and salt, roll it up very close, and bind it hard, lard it across with bacon, then a row of cold boiled tongue, a third row of pickled cucumbers, a fourth row of lemon peel, do it all over in rows as above till it is larded all round, it will look like red, green, white, and yellow dices, then split it or put it in a deep pot with a pint of water, lay over the caul of veal to keep it from scorching, tie it down with strong paper, and send it to the oven, when it comes out skim off the fat, and strain your gravy into a saucepan, add to it two spoonfuls of red wine, the same of browning, one of mushroom catch up, half a lemon, thicken it with a lump of butter rolled in flour, dish up the meat, and pour the gravy on the dish, lay round forcemeat balls: garnish with horse-radish, and serve it up.

To make BRISKET *of BEEF a-la-royal.*

BONE a brisket of beef, and make holes in it with a knife, about an inch one from another, fill one hole with fat bacon, a second with chopped parsley, and a third with chopped oysters, seasoned with nutmeg, pepper, and salt, till you have done the brisket over, then pour a pint of red wine boiling hot upon the beef, dredge it well with flour, send it to the oven, and bake it three hours or better; when it comes out of the oven take off the fat, and strain the gravy over your beef: garnish with pickles, and serve it up.

BEEF OLIVES.

CUT slices off a rump of beef about six inches long and half an inch thick, beat them with a paste pin, and rub them over with the yolk of an egg, a little pepper, salt, and beaten mace, the crumbs of half a penny loaf, two ounces of marrow sliced fine, a handful of parsley chopped small, and the out-rind of half a lemon grated, strew them all over your steaks, and roll them up, skewer them quite close, and set them before the fire to brown, then put them into a tossing pan with a pint of gravy, a spoonful of Catchup, the same of browning, a tea spoonful of lemon pickle, thicken it with a little butter rolled in flour: lay round forcemeat balls, mushrooms; or the yolks of hard eggs.

To make MOCK HARE of a BEAST'S HEART.

WASH a large beast's heart clean, and cut off the deaf ears, and stuff it with some force meat, as you do a hare, lay a caul of veal, or paper over the top, to keep in the stuffing, roast it either in a cradle spit or hanging one, it will take an hour and a half before a good fire, baste it with red wine; when roasted take the wine out of the dripping-pan, and skim off the fat, and add a glass more of wine, when it is hot put in some lumps of red currant jelly, and pour it in the dish, serve it up, and send in red currant jelly cut in slices on a saucer.

BEEF HEART *larded*.

TAKE a good beast's heart, stuff it as before, and lard it all over with little bits of bacon, dust it with flour, and cover it with paper, to keep it from being too dry, and send it to the oven; when baked put the heart on your dish, take off the fat and strain the gravy through a hair sieve, put it in a saucepan with one spoonful of red wine, the same of browning, and one of lemon pickle, half an ounce of morals, one anchovy cut small, a little beaten mace, thicken it with flour and butter, pour it hot on your heart, and serve it up: garnish with barberries.

To Stew OX PALATES.

WASH four ox palates in several waters, and then lay them in warm water for half an hour, then wash them out and put them in a pot, and tie them down with strong paper, and send them to the oven with as much water as will cover them, or boil them till tender, then skin them, and cut them in pieces, half an inch broad and three inches long, and put them in a tossing pan with a pint of veal gravy, one spoonful of Madeira wine, the same of catchup and browning, one onion stuck with cloves, and a slice of lemon, stew them half an hour, then take out the onion and lemon, thicken your sauce, and put them in a dish; have ready boiled artichoke bottoms, cut them in quarters, and lay them over your palates, with forcemeat balls and molds: garnish with lemon, and serve them up.

To fricando OX PALATES.

WHEN you have warned and cleaned your palates as before, cut them in square pieces, lard them with little bits of bacon, fry them in hog's lard, a pretty brown, and put them in a sieve to drain the fat from them, then take better than half a pint of beef gravy, one spoonful of red wine, half as much of browning, a little lemon pickle, one anchovy, a shallot, and a bit of horse radish; give them a boil, and strain your gravy, then put in your palates, and stew them half an hour, make your sauce pretty thick, dish them up, and lay round them stewed spinage pressed and cut like sippets, and serve them up.

To fricassee OX PALATES.

CLEAN your palates very well as before, put them in a stew-pot, and cover them with water, set them in the oven for three or four hours; when they come from the oven strip off the skins, and cut them in square pieces, season them with mace, nutmeg, Chyan, and salt, mix a spoonful of flour with the yolks of two eggs, dip in your palates, and fry them a light brown, then put them in a sieve to drain; have ready half a pint of veal gravy, with a little caper liquor, a spoonful of browning, and a few mushrooms, thicken it well with flour and butter, pour it hot on your dish, and lay in your palates: garnish with fried parsley and barberries.

Ta Stew a TURKEY with CELERY SAUCE.

TAKE a large turkey, and make a good white forcemeat of veal, and stuff the craw of the turkey, skewer it as for boiling, then boil it in soft water till it is almost enough, and then take up your turkey, and put it in a pot with some of the water it was boiled in, to keep it hot, put seven or eight heads of celery, that are washed and cleaned very well, into the water that the turkey was boiled in, till they are tender, then take them up, and put in your turkey with the breast down, and stew it a quarter of an hour, then take it up, and thicken your sauce with half a pound of butter and flour to make it pretty thick, and a quarter of a pint of rich cream, then put in your celery; pour the sauce and celery hot upon the turkey's breast, and serve it up. It is a proper dish for dinner or supper.

To Stew a TURKEY brown.

WHEN you have drawn the craw out of your turkey, cut it up the back, and take out the entrails, that the turkey may appear whole, and take all the bones out of the body very carefully, the rump, legs, and wings are to be left whole, then take the crumb of a penny loaf, and chop half a hundred of oysters very small, with half a pound of beef marrow, a little lemon peel cut fine, and pepper and salt, mix them well up together with the yolks of four eggs, and stuff your turkey with it, sew it up and lard it down each side with bacon, half roast it, then put it into a tossing pan with two quarts of veal gravy, and cover it close up; when it has stewed one hour, add a spoonful of mushroom catchup, half an anchovy, a slice or two of lemon, a little Chyan pepper, and a bunch of sweet herbs; cover them close up again, and stew it half an hour longer, then take it up and skim the fat off the gravy, and strain it, thicken it with flour and butter, let it boil a few minutes, and pour it hot upon your turkey: lay round it oyster patties, and serve it up.

A TURKEY A LA DAUB, to be sent up hot.

CUT the turkey down the back just enough to bone it, without spoiling the look of it, then stuff it with a nice forcemeat made of oysters, chopped fine, crumbs of bread, pepper, salt, shalots, a very little thyme, parsley and butter, fill it as full as you like, and sew it up with a thread, tie it up in a clean cloth and boil it very white, but not too much. You may serve it up with oyster sauce made good, or take the bones with a piece of veal, mutton, and bacon and make a rich gravy seasoned with pepper, salt, shallots, and a little bit of mace; strain it off through a sieve, and stew your turkey in it (after it is half boiled) just half an hour, dish it up in the gravy after it is well skimmed, strained, and thickened with a few mushrooms stewed white, or stewed pallets, forcemeat balls, fried oysters, or sweet-breads, and pieces of lemon. Dish it up with the breast upwards; if you send it up garnished with pallets, take care to have them stewed tender first ; before you add them to the turkey, you may put a few morels and truffles in your sauce if you like it, but take care to wash them clean.

TURKEY A-LA-DAUB, *to be sent up cold.*

BONE the turkey and season it with pepper and salt, then spread over it some slices of ham, upon that some forcemeat, upon that a fowl, boned and seasoned as above, then more ham and forcemeat, then sew it up with thread; cover the bottom of the stew-pan with veal and ham, then lay in the turkey the breast down, chop all the bones to pieces, and put them on the turkey, cover the pan and set it on the fire five minutes, then put in as much clear broth as will cover it, let it boil two hours, when it is more than half done, put in one ounce of isinglass and a bundle of herbs. When it is done enough take out the turkey, and strain the jelly through a hair sieve, skim off all the fat, and when it is cold lay the turkey upon it the breast down, and cover it with the rest of the jelly. Let it (land in some cold place ; when you serve it up, turn it on the dish it is to be served in : if you please you may spread butter over the turkey's breast, and put some green parsley or flowers, or what you please, and in what form you like.

FOWLS *a la braize*.

SKEWER your fowl as for boiling, with the legs in the body, then lay over it a layer of fat bacon, cut in pretty thin slices, then wrap it round in beet leaves, then in a caul of veal, and put it into a large saucepan with three pints of water, a glass of Madeira wine, a bunch of sweet herbs, two or three blades of mace, and half a lemon, stew it till quite tender, take it up and skim off the fat, make your gravy pretty thick with flour and butter, and strain it through a hair sieve, and put to it a pint of oysters, a tea-cup full of thick cream, keep making your to fling pan over the fire, and when it has simmered a little, serve up your fowl with the bacon, beet leaves, and caul on, and pour your sauce hot upon it : garnish with barberries, or red beetroot.

To force a FOWL.

TAKE a large fowl, pick it clean and cut it down the back, take out the entrails and take the skin off whole, cut the flesh from the bones and chop it with half a pint of oysters, one ounce of beef marrow, a little pepper and salt, mix it up with cream, then lay the meat on the bones and draw the skin over it and sew up the back, then cut large thin slices of bacon, and lay them over the breast of your fowl-, tie the bacon on with a packthread in diamonds, it will take one hour roasting by a moderate fire, make a good brown gravy sauce, pour it upon your dish, take the bacon off and lay in your fowl, and serve it up: garnish with pickles, mush rooms, or oysters. — It is proper for a side dish for dinner, or top for supper.

To Stew PALLETS *and* CHICKENS.

TO every pallet or chicken take an anchovy, a little parsley and shallot, with the liver of the chickens, shred all these together very fine, and salt to your taste, and stuff the birds with it, turn them up short as for boiling, tie them in cloths, boil the pallets an hour at least, the chickens not above fifteen or twenty minutes in milk and water with a little salt in it; make the sauce with a little white gravy and white wine, and with it stew a good many oysters and shallots, beat it up thick with a lump of butter, (you may, if you please, leave out the wine, and mix a little cream in the sauce instead of it) your gravy must be made of veal ; when the chickens are boiled, and the pallets are stewed tender, toss them up together in the gravy and oysters, send them hot to the table, the chickens in the middle, and the pallets round them, with a few white balls made of veal; you may add sweet-breads. This is a very good way to stew a turkey. The water the pallets were boiled in will be extremely good to make gravy, adding to it a good piece of veal, mutton, and bacon.

To fricassee CHICKENS.

SKIN them and cut them in small pieces, wash them in Warm water, and then dry them very clean with a cloth, season them with pepper and salt, and then put them into a stew-pan with a little fair water, and a good piece of butter, a little lemon pickle, or half a lemon, a glass of white wine, one anchovy, a little mace and nutmeg, an on/on stuck with cloves, a bunch of lemon thyme and sweet marjoram, let them stew together till your chickens are tender, and then lay them on your dish, thicken the gravy with flour and butter, strain it, then beat the yolks of three eggs a little, and mix them with a large tea-cup full of rich cream, and put it in your gravy, and shake it over the fire, but do not let it boil, and pour it over your chickens.

To force CHICKENS.

ROAST your chickens better than half, take off the skin, then the meat, and chop it small with shred parsley and crumbs of bread, pepper and salt, and a little good cream, then put in the meat and close the skin, brown it with a salamander, and serve it up with white sauce.

To make artificial CHICKENS *or* PIGEONS.

MAKE a rich forcemeat with veal, lamb, or chickens, seasoned with pepper, salt, parsley, a shallot, a piece of fat bacon, a little buttery, and the yolk of an egg; work it up in the shape of pigeons or chickens, putting the foot of the bird you intend it for in the middle, so as just to appear at the bottom, roll the forcemeat very well in the yolk of an egg, then in the crumbs of bread, send them to the oven, and bake it a light brown, do not let them touch each other, put them on tin plates well buttered, as you send them to the oven: you may send them to the table dry, or gravy in the dish, just as you like.

To marinate a GOOSE

CUT your goose up the back bone, then take out all the bones, and stuff it with forcemeat, and sew up the back again, fry the goose a good brown, then put it into a deep stew-pan with; two quarts of good gravy and cover it close, and stew it two hours, then take it out and skim off the fat, add a large spoonful of lemon pickle, one of browning, and one of red wine, one anchovy shred fine, beaten mace, pepper and salt to your palate, thicken it with flour and butter, boil it a little, dish up your goose, and strain your gravy over it. — N. B. Make your stuffing thus, take ten or twelve sage leaves, two large onions, two or three large sharp apples, shred them very fine, mix them with the crumbs of a penny loaf, four ounces of beef marrow, one glass of red wine, half a nutmeg grated, pepper, salt, and a little lemon peel shred small, make a light stuffing with the yolks of four eggs, observe to make it one hour before you want it.

To Stew DUCKS.

TAKE three young ducks, lard them down each side the breast, dust them with flour and set them before the fire to brown, then put them in a stew-pan with a quart of water, a pint of red wine, one spoonful of walnut catchup, the same of browning, one anchovy, half a lemon, a clove of garlick, a bundle of sweet herbs, Chyan pepper to your taste, let them stew slowly for half an hour or till they are tender, lay them on a dish and keep them hot, skim off the fat, strain your gravy through a hair sieve, add to it a few morels and truffles, boil it quick till reduced to little more than half a pint, pour it over your ducks and serve it up. It is proper for a side dish for dinner, or bottom for supper.

To Stew DUCKS with GREEN PEAS.

HALF roast your ducks, then put them into a stew-pan with a pint of good gravy, a little mint, and three or four sage leaves chopped small, cover them close, and stew them half an hour, boil a pint of green peas as for eating, and put them in after you have thickened the gravy; dish up your ducks and pour the gravy and peas over them.

DUCKS a-la-braize

DRESS and singe your ducks, lard them quite through with bacon rolled in shred parsley, thyme, onions, beaten mace, cloves, pepper and salt, put in the bottom of a stew-pan a few slices of fat bacon, the same of ham or gammon of bacon, two or three slices of veal or beef, lay your ducks in with the breast down, and cover the ducks with slices the same as put under them, cut in a carrot or two, a turnip, one onion, a head of celery, a blade of three, four or five cloves, a little whole pepper, cover them close down, and let them simmer a little over a gentle stove till the breast is a light brown, then put in some broth or water, cover them as close down again as you can, stew them gently betwixt two and three hours till enough, then take parsley, onion, or shalot, two anchovies, a few gherkins or capers, chop them all very fine, put them in a stew-pan with part of the liquor from the ducks, a little browning, and the juice of half a lemon, boil it up, and cut the ends of the bacon even with the breast of your ducks, lay them on your dish, pour the sauce hot upon them, and serve them up; some put garlick instead of onions.

DUCKS *a-la-mode*

SLIT two ducks down the back, and bone them carefully, make a forcemeat of the crumbs of a penny loaf, four ounces of fat bacon scraped, a little parsley, thyme, lemon peel, two shallots, or onions shred very fine, with pepper, salt, and nutmeg to your taste, and two eggs, stuff your ducks with it and sew them up, lord them down each side of the breast with bacon, dredge them well with flour, and put them in a Dutch oven to brown, then put them into a stew-pan with three pints of gravy, a glass of red wine, a tea spoonful of lemon pickle, a large one of walnut and mushroom catchup, one of browning, and one anchovy, with Chyan pepper to your taste, stew them gently over a slow fire for an hour, when enough, thicken your gravy, and put in a few truffles and morels, strain your gravy and pour it upon them. You may a-la-mode a goose the same way.

PIGEONS *compote.*

TAKE six young pigeons and skewer them as you do for boiling, put forcemeat into the craws, lard them down the breast, and fry them brown, then put them into a strong brown gravy, and let them stew three quarters of an hour, thicken it with a lump of butter rolled in flour, when you dish them up, lay forcemeat balls round them, and strain the gravy over them.— The forcemeat must be made thus : grate the crumbs of half a penny loaf, and scrape a quarter of a pound of fat bacon, instead of suet, chop a little parsley, thyme, two shalots or an onion, grate a little nutmeg, lemon peel, some pepper and salt, mix them all up with eggs. It is proper for a top dim for a second course, or a side dish for the first.

PIGEONS in a bole

PICK, draw, and wash four young pigeons, stick their legs in their belly as you do boiled pigeons season them with pepper, salt, and beaten mace, put into the belly of every pigeon a lump of butter the size of a walnut, lay your pigeons in a pye dish, pour over them a batter made of three eggs, two spoonfuls of flour, and half a pint of good milk, bake it in a moderate oven, and serve them to table in the same dish.

PIGEONS transmogrified.

PICK and clean six small young pigeons, but do not cut off their heads, cut off their pinions, and boil them ten minutes in water, then cut off the ends of six large cucumbers and scrape out the seeds, put in your pigeons, but let the heads be cut at the ends of the cucumbers, and flick a bunch of barberries in their bills, and then put them in a tossing pan with a pint of veal gravy, a little anchovy, a glass of red wine, a spoonful of browning, a little slice of lemon, Chyan and salt to you taste, stew them seven minutes, take them out, thicken your gravy with a little butter rolled in flour, boil it up and strain it over your pigeons, and serve them up.

To broil PIGEONS.

TAKE young pigeons, pick and draw them, split them down the back, and season them with pepper and salt, lay them on the gridiron with the breast upward, then turn them, but be careful you do not burn the skin, rub them over with butter, and keep turning them till they are enough, dish them up, and lay round them crisped parsley, and pour over them melted butter, or gravy which you please, and send them up.

To boil PIGEONS in RICE.

WHEN you have picked and drawn your pigeons, turn the legs under the wings, and cut off the pinions, then lay over every pigeon thin slices of bacon, and a large beet leaf, wrap them in clean cloths separately, and boil them till enough, have ready four ounces of rice boiled soft, and put into a sieve to drain, put the rice into a little good veal gravy thickened with flour and butter, boil your rice a little in the gravy, and add two spoonfuls of good cream, take your pigeons out of the cloths and leave on the bacon and beet leaves, pour the rice over them and serve them up.

To *fricando* PIGEONS.

PICK, draw, and wash your pigeons very clean, stuff the craws, and lard them down the sides of the breast, fry them in butter a fine brown, and then put them into a tossing-pan with a quart of gravy, stew them till they are tender, then take off the fat, and put in a tea-spoonful of lemon pickle, a large spoonful of browning, the same of walnut catchup, a little Chyan and salt, thicken your gravy and add half an ounce of morels, and four yolks of hard eggs; lay the pigeons in your dish, and put the morels and eggs round them, and strain your sauce over them: garnish with barberries and lemon peel, and serve it up.

Jugged PIGEONS

TAKE six pigeons, pluck and draw them, wash them clean and dry them with a cloth, season them with beaten mace, white pepper, and salt, put them in a jug, and put half a pound of butter upon them, stop up your jug close with a cloth that no steam can get out, set it in a kettle of boiling water, and let it boil one hour and a half, then take out your pigeons, and put the gravy that is come from the-pigeons into a pan, and put to it one spoonful of wine, one of catchup, a slice of lemon, half an anchovy chopped small, and a bundle of sweet herbs, boil it a little, thicken it with a little butter rolled in flour, lay your pigeons on the dish, and strain the gravy on them: garnish with parsley and red cabbage, and serve them up, you may lay mushrooms or forcemeat balls. — It is a pretty side or corner dish.

Boiled PIGEONS and BACON

TAKE six young pigeons, wash them clean as before, turn their legs under their wings, boil them in milk and water by themselves twenty minutes, have ready boiled a square piece of bacon, takeoff the skin and brown it, put the bacon in the middle of your dish, and lay the pigeons round it, and lumps of stewed, spinage, pour plain melted butter over them, and send parsley and butter in a boat.

PIGEONS *fricassee*.

CUT your pigeons as you would do chickens for fricassee, fry them a light brown, then put them into some good mutton gravy, and stew them near half an hour, and then put in half an ounce of morels, a spoonful of browning, and a slice of lemon, take up your pigeons, and thicken your gravy, strain it over your pigeons, and lay round them forcemeat balls, and garnish with pickles.

PARTRIDGE *in panes*

HALF roast two partridges, and take the flesh from them, and mix it with the crumbs of a penny loaf steeped in rich gravy, six ounces of beef marrow, or half a pound of fat bacon scraped, ten morels boiled soft and cut small, two artichoke bottoms boiled and shred small, the yolks of three eggs, pepper, salt, nutmeg, and shred lemon peel to your palate, work them together, and bake them in moulds the shape of an egg, and serve them up cold of in jelly: garnish with curled parsley.

To stew PARTRIDGES.

TRUSS your partridges as for roasting, stuff the craws, and lard them down each side of the breast, then roll a lump of butter in pepper, salt, and beaten mace, and put it into the bellies, sew up the vents, dredge them well and fry them a light brown, then put them into a stew-pan with a quart of good gravy, a spoonful of Madeira wine, the same of mushroom catchup, a tea- spoonful of lemon pickle, and half the quantity of mushroom powder, one anchovy, half a lemon, a sprig of sweet marjoram, cover the pan close, and stew them half an hour, then take them out and thicken the gravy, boil it a little and pour it over the partridges, and lay round them artichoke bottoms boiled and cut in quarters, and the yolks of four hard eggs, if agreeable.

To stew PARTRIDGES *a second Way.*

TAKE three partridges when dressed, singe them, blanch and beat three ounces of almonds, and grate the same quantity of fine white bread, chop three anchovies, mix them with six ounces of butter, stuff the partridges, and sew them up at both ends, truss them, and wrap slices of fat bacon round them, half roast them, then take one and pull the meat off the breast, and beat it in a marble mortar, with the forcemeat it was stuffed with, have ready a strong gravy made of ham and veal, strain it into a stew-pan, then take the bacon off the other two, wipe them clean and put them into the gravy with a good deal of shalots, let them stew till tender, then take them out, and boil the gravy till it is almost as thick as bread sauce, then add to it a glass of sweet oil, the same of Champagne, and the juice of a China orange, put your partridges in, and make them hot : garnish with slices of bacon and lemon.

To stew a HARE

WHEN you have paunched and cased your hare, cut her as for eating, put her into a large sauce-pan with three pints of beef gravy, a pint of red wine, a large onion stuck with cloves, a bundle of winter savory, a slice of horse radish, two blades of beaten mace, one anchovy, a spoonful of walnut or mum catchup, one of browning, half a lemon,

Chyan and salt to your taste, put on a close cover, and set it over a gentle fire, and stew it for two hours, then take it up into a soup dish, and thicken your gravy with a lump of butter rolled in flour, boil it a little, and strain it over your hare : garnish with lemon peel cut like straws, and serve it up.

To jug a HARE

CUT the hare as for eating, season it with pepper, salt, and beaten mace, put it into a jug or pitcher, with a close top, put to it a bundle of sweet herbs, and set it in a kettle of boiling water, let it stand till it is tender, then take it up and pour the gravy into a tossing-pan, with a glass of red wine, one anchovy, a large onion stuck with cloves, a little beaten mace, and Chyan pepper to your taste, boil it a little and thicken it: dish up your hare and strain the gravy over it, then send it up.

To Florendine a HARE

TAKE a grown hare, and let her hang up four or five days, then case her, and leave on the cars, and take out all the bones except the head which must be left on whole, lay your hare flat on the table, and lay over the in side a forcemeat, and then roll it up to the head, skewer it with the head and ears leaning back, tie it with pack thread as you would a collar of veal, wrap it in a cloth, and boil it an hour and a half in a sauce pan, with a cover on it, with two quarts of water ; when your liquor is reduced to one quart put in a pint of red wine, a spoonful of lemon pickle, and one of catchup, the same of browning, and stew it till it is reduced to a pint, thicken it with butter rolled in flour, lay round your hare a few morels, and four slices of forcemeat, boiled in a caul of a leg of veal : when you dish it up, draw the jaw-bones, and stick them in the eyes for horns, let the ears lie back on the rolls and stick a sprig of myrtle in the mouth, strain over your sauce, and serve it up: garnish with barberries and parley. Forcemeat for the hare: — take the crumb of a penny loaf, the liver stirred fine, half a pound of fat bacon scraped, a glass of red wine, one anchovy, two eggs, a little winter savory, sweet marjoram, lemon thyme, pepper, salt, and nutmeg to your taste.

To hodge-podge a HARE

CUT the hare in pieces as you do far stewing, and put it into the pitcher, with two or. three onions, some salt and a little pepper, a bunch of sweet herbs and a piece of butter: stop the pitcher very close, that no steam may get out, set it in a kettle full of boiling water, keep the kettle filled up as the water wastes, let it stew four or five hours at least. You may when you first put in the hare into the kettle put in lettuce, cucumbers, celery, and turnips if you like it better.

To Florendine RABBITS

TAKE three young rabbits, skin them, but leave on the ears, wash and dry them with a cloth, take out the bones carefully, leaving the head whole, then lay them flat, make a force meat of a quarter of a pound of bacon scraped, it answers better than suet, it makes the rabbits eat tenderer and whiter ; add to the bacon the crumbs of a penny loaf, a little lemon thyme, or lemon peel shred fine, parsley chopped small, nutmeg, Chyan, and salt to your palate; mix them up together with an egg, and spread it over the rabbits, roll them up to the head, skewer them straight, and close the ends to prevent the force meat from coming out, skewer the ears back, and tie them in separate cloths, and boil them half an hour; when you dish them up take out the jaw-bones, and stick them in the eyes for ears, put round them forcemeat balls and mushrooms, have ready a white sauce made of veal gravy, a little anchovy, the juice of half a lemon, or a tea spoonful of lemon pickle, strain it, take a quarter of a pound of butter rolled in flour, so as to make the sauce pretty thick, keep stirring it whilst the flour is dissolving, beat the yolk of an egg, put to it some thick cream, nutmeg, and salt, mix it with the gravy, and let it simmer a little over the fire, but not boil, for it will curdle the cream, pour it over the rabbits, and serve it up.

RABBITS *surprised.*

TAKE young rabbits, skewer them, and put the same pudding as for the roasted rabbits, when they are roasted, draw out the jaw-bones and stick them in the eyes to appear like horns, then take off all the meat from the back clean from the bones, but leave them whole, chop the meat exceeding fine with a little shred parsley, lemon peel, one ounce of beef marrow, a spoonful of good cream, and a little salt, beat the yolks of two hard eggs, and a piece of butter the size of a walnut, in a marble mortar, very fine, then mix all together, and put it in a tossing-pan, when it has stewed five minutes, lay it on the rabbit when you take the meat off, and put it close down with your hand, to appear like a whole rabbit, then heat a salamander, and brown it all over, pour a good brown gravy made as thick as cream in the dish, stick a bunch of myrtle in their mouths, and serve them up with their livers broiled and frothed. To fricassee

RABBITS *brown.*

CUT your rabbits as for eating, fry them in butter a light brown, put them into a mine pan, with a pint of water, a tea spoonful of lemon pickle, a large spoonful of mushroom catchup, the same of browning, one anchovy, a slice of lemon, Chyan pepper and salt to your taste, stew them over a flow fire till they are enough, thicken your gravy, and strain it, dish up your rabbits, and pour the gravy over.

To fricassee RABBITS *white.*

CUT your rabbits as before, and put them into a tossing-pan, with a pint of veal gravy, a teaspoonful of lemon pickle, one anchovy, a slice of lemon, a little beaten mace, Chyan pepper and salt, stew them over a flow fire, when they are enough, thicken your gravy with flour and butter, strain it, then add the yolks of two eggs mixed with a large tea-cupful of thick cream, and a little nutmeg grated in it, do not let it boil, and serve it up.

To make a nice WHET before DINNER.

CUT some slices of bread half an inch thick, fry them in butter, but not too hard, then split some anchovies, take out the bones, and lay half an anchovy on each piece of bread, have ready some Cheshire cheese, grated, and some chopped parsley mixed together, lay it pretty thick over the bread and anchovy, baste it with butter, and brown it with a salamander: it must be done on the dish in which you send it to table.

A fine Haricot by way of SOUP.

GET a large neck of mutton, cut it in two parts, put the scrag part into a stew-pan with four large turnips and four carrots in a gallon of water, let it boil gently over a slow fire till all the goodness is out of the meat, but not boiled to pieces, then braise the turnips and two of the carrots fine into the soup, by way of thickening it, cut and fry six onions in nice butter, and put them in, then cut the other part of the mutton in very good chops not too large, try them in butter, and put them to the soup, and let it stew very slow till the chops are very tender, cut the other two carrots that were boiled into any shape, and put them in just before you take it off the fire, and season it to your taste with pepper and salt, and serve it up very hot in a soup dish.

A Haricot of MUTTON or LAMB,

CUT a neck or loin of mutton or lamb in nice steaks and fry them a light brown, have ready some good gravy made of the scrag of the mutton, and some veal with a piece of lean bacon and a few capers, season to your taste with pepper, salt, thyme, and onions, which must be strained off and added to the steaks, just one hour before you send them to the table; take care to do it on a slow fire, dish them up handsomely with turnips and carrots cut in dice, with a good deal of gravy thickened with a piece of butter rolled in a very little flour; if they are not tender they will not be good. Send them up very hot.

To Harico a NECK of MUTTON a second Way.

TAKE a neck of mutton and cut it into chops, flour them, and put them into a stew-pan, set them over the fire, and keep them turning till brown, then take them out and put a little more into the same pan, and keep it stirring till brown over the fire, with a bunch of sweet herbs, a bay leaf, an onion, and what other spice you please boil them well together, and then strain the broth through a sieve into an earthen pan by itself, and skim the fat off, which done, is a good gravy, then add turnips and carrots, with two small onions, a little celery, then place your mutton in a stew-pan with the celery and other roots, then put the gravy to them, and as much water as will cover them : keep it over a gentle fire till ready to serve up.

A hodge-podge of MUTTON.

CUT a neck or loin of mutton into steaks, take off all the fat, then put the steaks into a pitcher, with lettuce, turnips, carrots, two cucumbers cut in quarters, four or five onions, and pepper and salt; you must not put any water to it, and stop the pitcher very close, then set it in a pan of boiling water, let it boil four hours, keep the pan supplied with fresh boiling water as it wastes.

To dress CUCUMBERS with EGGS.

TAKE six large young cucumbers, pare, quarter, and cut them into squares, about the size of a dice, put them into boiling water, let them boil up, and take them out of the water, and put them into a stew pan, with an onion stuck with cloves, a good slice of ham, a quarter of butter, and a little salt, set it over the fire a quarter of an hour, keep it close covered, scum it well, and shake it often, as it is apt to burn; then dredge in a little flour over them, and put in as much veal gravy as will just cover the cucumbers, and stir it well together and keep a gentle fire under it till no scum will rise; then take out the ham and onion, and put in the yolks of two eggs beat up with a tea-cupful of good cream, stir it well for a minute, then take it off the fire, and just before you put it in the dish squeeze in a little lemon juice: have ready five or six poached eggs to lay on the top.

To stew PEAS.

TAKE a quart of young peas, wash them and put them into a stew-pan with a quarter of a pound of butter, three cabbage lettuces cut small, five or six young onions, with a little thyme, parsley, pepper and salt, and let them stew all together for a quarter of an hour, then put to them a pint of gravy, with two or three slices of bacon or ham, and let them stew all together till the peas are enough, then thicken them up with a quarter of a pound of butter, rolled in flour.

To Fricassee MUSHROOMS.

PEEL and scrape the inside of the mushrooms, throw them into salt and water, if buttons, rub them with flannel, take them out and boil them with fresh salt and water, when they are tender put in a little shred parsley, an onion stuck with cloves, toss them up with a good lump of butter rolled in a little flour; you may put in three spoonfuls of thick cream, and a little nutmeg cut in pieces, but take care to take out the nutmeg and onion before you serve it to table: you may leave out the parsley, and stew in a glass of wine if you like it.

CHAP V.

Observations on PIES

RAISED Pies should have a quick oven, and well closed up, or your pie will fall in the sides; it should have no water put in, till the minute it goes to the oven, it makes the crust sad, and is a great hazard of the pie running.— light paste requires a moderate oven, but not too slow, it will make them sad, and a quick oven will catch and burn it, and not give it time to rise; tarts that are iced, require a slow oven, or the icing will be brown, and the paste not be near baked. These sorts of tarts ought to be made of sugar paste, and rolled very thin.

To make crisp PASTE for TARTS.

TAKE one pound of fine flour mixed with one ounce of loaf sugar beat and sifted, make it into a stiff paste with a gill of boiling cream, and three ounces of butter in it, work it well, roll it very thin, when you have made your tarts, beat the white of an egg a little, rub it over them with a feather, sift a little double refined sugar over them, and bake them in a moderate oven.

ICING a second Way.

BEAT the white of an egg to a strong froth, put in by degrees four ounces of double refined sugar, with as much gum as will lie on a six pence, beat and sifted fine, beat them half an hour, then lay it over your tarts the thickness of a straw.

To make a light PASTE for TARTS.

TAKE one pound of fine flour, beat the white of an egg to a strong froth, mix it with as much water as will make three quarters of a pound of flour into a pretty stiff paste, roll it out very thin, lay the third part of half a pound of butter in thin pieces, dredge it with part of the quarter of your flour left out for that purpose, roll it up tight, then with your paste-pin roll it out again, do so until all your half pound of butter and flour is done, cut it in square pieces, and make your tarts; it requires a quicker oven than crisp paste.

To make an APPLE TART.

SCALD eight or ten large codlins, when cold skin them, take the pulp and beat it as fine as you can with a silver spoon, then mix the yolks of six eggs and the whites of four, beat all together as fine as possible, put in grated nut meg and sugar to your taste, melt some fine fresh butter, and beat it till it is like a fine thick cream, then make a fine puff paste, and cover a tin petty-pan with it, and pour in the ingredients, but do not cover it with the paste; bake it a quarter of an hour, then slip it out of the petty-pan on a dish, and strew fine sugar finely beat and lifted all over it.

To make PASTE for a GOOSE PYE.

TAKE eighteen pounds of fine flour, put six pounds of fresh butter, and one pound of rendered beef suet in a kettle of water, boil it two or three minutes, then pour it boiling hot upon your flour, work it well into a pretty stiff paste, pull it in lumps to cool, and raise your pye, bake it in a hot oven; you may make any raised pie the same way, only take a smaller quantity in proportion.

To make a cold PASTE for DISH PIES.

TAKE a pound of fine flour, rub it into half a pound of butter, beat the yolks of two eggs, put them into as much water as will make it a stiff paste, roll it out, then put your butter on in thin pieces, dust it with flour, roll it up tight, when you have done it so for three times, roll it out pretty thin, and bake it in a quick oven.

To make PASTE for CUSTARDS

PUT half a pound of butter in a pan of water, take two pounds of flour, when your butter boils, pour it on your flour, with as much water as will make it into a good paste, work it well, and when it has cooled a little raise your custards, put a paper round the inside of them, when they are half baked fill them. — When you make any kind of dripping paste, boil it four or five minutes in a good quantity of water to take the strength off it; when you make a cold crust with suet, shred it fine, pour part of it into the flour, then make it into a paste, and roll it out as before (only strew in it suet instead of butter).

To make a FRENCH PYE.

TO two- pounds of flour put three quarters of a pound of butter, make it into a paste, and raise the walls of the pye, then roll out some paste thin as for a lid, cut it into vine leaves, or the figures of any moulds you have, if you have no moulds, you may make use of a crocran, and pick out pretty shapes, beat the yolks of two eggs, and rub the outside of the walls of the pye with it, and lay the wine leaves or shapes round the walls, and rub them over with the eggs, fill the pye with the bones of the meat, to keep the steam in, that the crust may be well soaked; it is to go to table without a lid. Take a calf's head, wash and clean it well, boil it half an hour, when it is cold cut it in thin slices, and put it in a tossing-pan with three pints of veal gravy, and three sweet-breads cut thin, and let it stew one hour, with half an ounce of morels, and half an ounce of trusties, then have ready two calves feet boiled and boned, cut them in small pieces, and put them into your tossing-pan, with a spoonful of lemon pickle and one of browning, Chyan pepper, and a little salt, when the meat is tender thicken the gravy a little with flour and butter, strain it, and put in a few pickled mushrooms, but fresh ones if you can get them ; put the meat into the pye you took the bones out, and lay the nicest part at the top, have ready a quarter of an hundred of asparagus heads, strew them over the top of the pye and serve it up.

A *Yorkshire* GOOSE PYE.

TAKE a large fat goose, split it down the back, and take all the bones out, bone a turkey and two ducks the same way, season them very well with pepper and salt, with six woodcocks, lay the goose down on a clean dish, with the skin-side down, and lay the turkey into the goose with the skin down, have ready a large hare cleaned well, cut in pieces, and stewed in the oven, with a pound of butter, a quarter of an ounce of mace beat fine, the same of white pepper, and salt to your taste, till the meat will leave the bones, and scum the butter off the gravy, pick the meat clean off, and beat it in a marble mortar very fine, with the butter you took off, and lay it in the turkey; take twenty-four pounds of the finest flour, six pounds of butter, half a pound of fresh rendered suet, make the paste pretty thick, and raise the pye oval, roll out a lump of paste, and cut it in vine leaves, or what form you please, rub the pye with the yolks of eggs, and put your ornaments on the walls, then turn the hare, turkey, and goose upside- down, and lay them in your pye, with the ducks at each end, and the woodcocks on the sides, make your lid pretty thick and put it on; you may lay flowers, or the shape of the fowls in paste, on the lid, and make a hole in the middle of your lid; the walls of the pye are to be one inch and a half higher than the lid, then rub it all over with the yolks of eggs, and bind it round with three fold paper, and lay the same over the top; it will take four hours baking in a brown bread oven, when it comes out, melt two pounds of butter in the gravy that comes from the hare, and pour it hot in the pye through a tun-dish, close it well up, and let it be eight or ten days before you cut it; if you send it any distance, make up the hole in the middle with cold butter to prevent the air from getting in.

A HARE PYE.

CUT a large hare in pieces, season it well with mace, nutmeg, pepper, and salt, put it in a jug with half a pound of butter, cover it close up with a paste or cloth, set it in a copper of boiling water, and let it stew one hour and a half, then take it out to cool, and make a rich forcemeat of a quarter of a pound of scraped bacon, two onions, a glass of red wine. the crumb of a penny loaf, a little winter savory, the liver cut small, a little nutmeg, season it high with pepper and salt, mix it well up with the yolks of three eggs, raise the pye and lay the forcemeat in the bottom, lay in the hare, with the gravy that came out of the hare, lay the lid on, and put flowers or leaves on it; it will take an hour and a half to bake it. — It is a handsome side dish for a large table.

A SALMON PYE.

BOIL your salmon as for eating, take off the skin, and all the bones out and pound the meat in a mortar very fine, with mace, nutmeg, pepper, and salt to your taste, raise the pye, and put flowers or leaves on the walls, put the salmon in and lid it, bake it an hour and a half, when it comes out of the oven take off the lid, and put in four ounces of rich melted butter, cut a lemon in slices, and lay over it, stick in two or three leaves of fennel, and send it to table without a lid.

A BEEF STEAK PYE.

BEAT five or six rump steaks very well with a paste pin, and season them well with pepper and salt, lay a good puff paste round the dish, and put a little water in the bottom, then lay the steaks in, with a lump of butter upon every steak, and put on the lid, cut a little paste in what form you please, and lay it on.

A THATCHED HOUSE PYE.

TAKE an earthen dish that is pretty deep, rub the inside with two ounces of butter, then spread over it two ounces of vermicelli, make a good puff paste, and roll it pretty thick, and lay it on the dish; take three or four pigeons, season them very well with pepper and salt, and put a good lump of butter in them, and lay them in the dish with the breast down, and put a thick lid over them, and bake it in a moderate oven; when enough take the dish you intend for it, and turn the pye on to it, and the vermicelli will appear like thatch, which gives it the name of thatched house pye. It is a pretty side or corner dish for a large dinner, or a bottom for supper.

EGG and BACON PYE to eat cold:

STEEP a few thin slices of bacon all night in water to take out the salt, lay your bacon in the dish, beat eight eggs, with a pint of thick cream, put in a little pepper and salt, and pour upon the bacon, lay over it a good cold paste, bake a day before you want it in a moderate oven.

A CALF'S HEAD PYE.

PARBOIL a calf's head, when cold cut it in pieces, season it well with pepper and salt, put it in a raised crust, with half a pint of strong gravy, bake it an hour and a half, when it comes out of the oven, cut off the lid, and chop the yolks of three hard eggs small, strew them over the top of the pye, and lay three or four slices of lemon, and pour on some good melted butter, and send it to the table without a lid.

A savoury CHICKEN PYE.

LET your chickens be small, season them with mace, pepper, and salt, put a lump of butter into every one of them, lay them in the dish with the breasts up, and lay a thin slice of bacon over them, it will give them a pleasant flavour, then put in a pint of strong gravy, and make a good puff paste, lid it and bake it in a moderate oven: French cooks generally put morels and yolks of eggs chopped small.

A MINCE PYE.

BOIL a neat's tongue two hours, then skin it, and chop it as small as possible, chop very small three pounds of fresh beef suet, three pounds of good baking apples, four pounds of currants clean washed, picked, and well dried before the fire, one pound of jar raisins stoned, and chopped small, and one pound of powder sugar, mix them all together with half an ounce of mace, the same of nutmeg grated, cloves and cinnamon a quarter of an ounce of each, and one pint of French Brandy, and make a rich puff paste; as you fill the pye up, put in a little candied citron and orange cut in little pieces, what you have to spare; put close down in a pot and cover it up, put no citron or orange in till you use it.

To make a MINCE PYE without MEAT.

CHOP fine three pounds of suet, and three pounds of apples, when pared and cored, wash and dry three pounds of currants, stone and chop one pound of jar raisins, beat and sift one pound and a half of loaf sugar, cut small twelve ounces of candied orange peel, and six ounces of citron, mix all well together with a quarter of an ounce of nutmeg, half a quarter of an ounce of cinnamon, six or eight cloves, and half a pint of French brandy, pot it close up, and keep it for use.

A CODLING PYE.

GATHER small codlings, put them in a clean brass pan with spring water, lay vine leaves on them, and cover them with a cloth wrapped round the cover of a pan to keep in the steam, when they grow softish peel off the skin, and put them in the same water with the vine leaves, hang them a great height over the fire to green, when you see them a fine green, take them out of the water and put them in a deep dish, with as much powder or loaf sugar as will sweeten them, make the lid of rich puff paste, and bake it; when it comes from the oven take off the lid, and cut it in little pieces like sippets, and stick them round the inside of the pye with the points upward, pour over your codlings a good custard made thus. Boil a pint of cream, with a stick of cinnamon, and sugar enough to make it a little sweet, let it stand till cold, then put in the yolks of four eggs well beaten, set it on the fire and keep stirring it till it grows thick, but do not let it boil, lest it curdle, then pour it into your pye, pare a little lemon thin, cut the peel like straws, and lay it on your codlings over the top.

An HERB PYE for LENT.

TAKE lettuce, leeks, spinage, beets, and parsley, of each a handful, give them a boil, then chop them small, and have ready boiled in a cloth one quart of groats, with two or three onions in them, put them in a frying-pan with the herbs and a good deal of salt, a pound of butter, and a few apples cut thin, stew them a few minutes over the fire, fill your dish or raised crust with its one hour will bake it ; then serve it up.

A VENISON PASTY,

BONE a breast or shoulder of venison, season it well with mace, pepper, and salt, lay it in a deep pot with the best part of a neck of mutton, cut in slices, and laid over the venison, pour in a large glass of red wine, put a coarse paste over it and bake it two hours in an oven, then lay the venison in a dish, and pour the gravy over it, and put one pound of butter over it; make a good puff paste, and lay it near half an inch thick, round the edge of the dish, roll out the lid, which must be a little thicker than the paste on the edge of the dish, and lay it on, then roll out another lid pretty thin, and cut in flowers, leaves, or whatever form you please, and lay it on the lid; if you do not want it, it will keep in the pot that it was baked in eight or ten days, but keep the crust on to prevent the air from getting into it. — A breast and shoulder of venison is the most proper for a pasty.

An HOTTENTOT PYE

BOIL and bone two calf's feet, clean very well a calf's chitterling, boil it and chop it small, take two chickens and cut them up as for eating, put them in a stew-pan, with two sweet breads, a quart of veal or mutton gravy, half an ounce of morels, Chyan pepper and salt to your palate, stew them all together an hour over a gentle fire, then put in six forcemeat balls that have been boiled, and the yolks of four hard eggs, and put them in a good raised crust that has been baked for it, strew over the top of your pye a few green peas boiled as for eating; or peel and cut some young green brocoli stalks about the size of peas, give them a gentle boil, and strew them over the top of your pye, and send it up hot without a lid, the same way as the French pye.

A BRIDE'S PYE.

BOIL two calf's feet, pick the meat from the bones, and chop it very fine, shred small one pound of beef suet, and a pound of apples, wash and pick one pound of currants very small, dry them before the fire, stone and chop a quarter of a pound of jar raisins, a quarter of an ounce of cinnamon, the same of mace and nutmeg, two ounces of candied citron, two ounces of candied lemon cut thin, a glass of brandy and one of champagne, put them in a China dish with a rich puff paste over it, roll another lid and cut it in leaves, flowers, figures, and put a glass ring in it.

An EEL PYE.

SKIN and warn your eels very clean, cut them in pieces one inch and a half long, season them with pepper, salt, and a little dried sage rubbed small, raise your pies about the size of the inside of a plate, fill your pies with eels, lay a lid over them, and bake them in a quick oven: they require to be well baked.

To make a LOBSTER PYE.

TAKE two or three good fresh lobsters, take out all the meat and cut it in large pieces, put a fine puff paste round the edge of your dish, then put in a layer of lobsters, and a layer of oysters, with bread crumbs and slices of butter, a little pepper and salt, then a layer of lobsters, &c. till your dish is full, then take the red part of the lobster, pound it fine with chopped oysters, crumbs of bread, and a little butter; make them into small balls and fry them, then lay them upon the top of your pye; boil the shells of your oysters to make a little gravy, put to it a little pepper and salt and the oyster liquor, strain it through a sieve, and fill your pye with it, then lay on your crust, and stick a few small claws in the middle of your pye, and send it to the oven. — It is a genteel corner dish for dinner.

A Yorkshire GIBLET PYE.

WHILST the blood of your goose is warm, put in a teacupful of groats to swell, grate the crumbs of a penny loaf, and pour a gill of boiling milk on them, shred half a pound of beef suet very fine, chop two leaks, and four or five leaves of sage small, three yolks of eggs, pepper, salt, and nutmeg to your palate, mix them all up together, have ready the giblets seasoned very well with pepper and salt, and lay them round a deep dish, then put a pound of fat beef over the pudding in the middle of the dish, pour in half a pint of gravy, lay on a good paste, and bake it in a moderate oven.

A ROOK PYE.

SKIN and draw six young rooks, and cut out the back bones, season them well with pepper and salt, put them in a deep dish with a quarter of a pint of water, lay over them half a pound of butter, make a good puff paste, and cover the dish, lay a paper over, for it requires a good deal of baking.

A *sweet* VEAL PYE.

LAY marrow or beef suet shred very fine in the bottom of your dish, cut into steaks the best end of a neck of veal, and lay them in, strew over them some marrow or suet, it makes them eat tenderer, stone a quarter of a pound of jar raisins, chop them a little, wash half a pound of currants and put them over the steaks, cut three ounces of candied citron, and two ounces of candied orange, and lay them on the top, boil half a pint of sweet mountain or sack, with a stick of cinnamon, and pour it in, lay a light paste round the dish, and then lid it, an hour will bake it; when it comes out of the oven, put in a glass of French brandy or shrub, and serve it up.

An OLIVE PYE.

CUT a fillet of veal in thin slices, rub them over with yolks of eggs, strew over them a few crumbs of bread, shred a little lemon peel very fine, and put it on them with a little grated nutmeg, pepper, and salt, roll them up very tight, und lay them in a pewter dish, pour over them half a pint of good gravy made of bones, put half a pound of butter over it, make a light paste, and lay it round the dish, roll the lid half an inch thick, and lay it on. Make a beef olive pye the same way.

A *savoury* VEAL PYE.

CUT a loin of veal into steaks, season it with beaten mace, nutmeg, pepper, and salt, lay the meat in your dish with sweet-breads seasoned with the meat, and the yolks of six hard eggs, a pint of oysters, and half a pint of good gravy, lay round your dish a good puff paste, half an inch thick, and cover it with a lid the same thickness, bake it in a quick oven an hour and a quarter; when you take it out of the oven, cut off the lid, then cut the lid in eight or ten pieces, and stick it round the inside of the rim, cover the meat with slices of lemon, and serve it up.

To make savoury PATTIES.

TAKE one pound of the inside of a cold loin of veal, or the same quantity of cold fowl, that have been either boiled or roasted, a quarter of a pound of beef suet, chop them as small as possible, with six or eight sprigs of parsley, season them well with half a nutmeg grated fine, pepper and salt, put them in a tossing pan, with half a pint of veal gravy, thicken the gravy with a little flour and butter, and two spoonfuls of cream, and make them over the fire two minutes, and fill your patties. You must make your patties thus : Raise them of an oval form, and bake them as for custards, cut some long narrow bits of paste, and bake them on a dusting box, but not to go round, they are for handles; fill your patties when quite hot with the meat, then set your handles across the patties; they will look like baskets if you have nicely pinched the walls of the patties, when you raised them; five will be a dish, you may make them with sugar and currants instead of parsley.

Fried PATTIES.

CUT half a pound of a leg of veal very small, with six oysters, put the liquor of the oysters to the crumb of a penny loaf, mix them together with a little salt, put it in a tossing-pan, with a quarter of a pound of butter, and keep stirring it for three or four minutes over the fire, then make a good puff paste, roll it out, and cut it in little bits about the size of a crown piece, some round, square, and three-cornered, put a little of the meat upon them, and lay a lid on them, turn up the edges as you would a pasty, to keep the gravy in, fry them in a pan full of hog's lard; they are a pretty corner dish for dinner or supper: if you want them for garnish to a cod's head, put in only oysters ; they are very pretty for a calf's head hash.

Sweet PATTIES.

TAKE the meat of a boiled calf's foot, two large apples, and one ounce of candied orange, chop them very small, grate half a nutmeg, mix them with the yolk of an egg, a spoonful of French brandy, and a quarter of a pound of currants clean washed and dried, make a good puff paste, roll it in different shapes, as the fried ones, and fill them the same way; you may either bake or fry them. They are a pretty side dish for supper.

Common PATTIES

TAKE the kidney part of a very fat loin of veal, chop the kidney, veal, and sat very small all together, season it with mace, pepper, and salt, to your taste, raise little patties the size of a tea-cup, fill them with your meat, put thin lids on them, bake them very crisp, five is enough for a side dish.

To make fine PATTIES.

SLICE either turkey, house lamb, or chicken, with an equal quantity of the fat of lamb, loin of veal, or the inside of a sirloin of beef, a little parsley, thyme, and lemon-peel shred, put it all in a marble mortar, and pound it very fine, season it with white pepper and salt, then make a fine puff paste, roll it out in thin square sheets, put the forcemeat in the middle, cover it over, close them all round, and cut the paste even. Just before they go into the oven wash them over with the yolk of an egg, and bake them twenty minutes in a quick oven; have ready a little white gravy seasoned with pepper, salt, and a little shalot, thickened up with a little cream or butter; as soon as the patties come out of the oven, make a hole in the top and pour in some gravy, you must take care not to put too much gravy in, for fear of its running out at the sides, and spoiling the patties.

To make common FRITTERS.

TAKE half a pint of ale and two eggs, beat in as much flour as will make it rather thicker than a common pudding, with nutmeg and sugar to your taste, let it stand three or four minutes to rise, then drop them with a spoon into a pan of boiling lard, fry them a light brown, drain them on a sieve, serve them up with sugar grated over them, and wine sauce in a boat.

To make APPLE FRITTERS.

PARE the largest baking apples you can get, take out the core with an apple scraper, cut them in round slices, and dip them in batter, made as for common fritters, fry them crisp, serve them up with sugar grated over them, and wine sauce in a boat. — They are proper for a side dish for supper.

To make CLARY FRITTERS.

BEAT two eggs exceeding well with one spoonful of cream, one of ratifia water, one ounces of loaf sugar, and two spoonfuls of flour, grate in half a nutmeg, have ready washed and dried clary leaves, dip them in the batter and fry them a nice brown; serve them up with quarters of Seville oranges, laid round them, and good melted butter in a boat.

To make RASBERRY FRITTERS.

GRATE two Naples biscuits, pour over them half a gill of boiling cream, when it is almost cold, beat the yolks of four eggs to a strong froth, beat the biscuits a little, then beat both together exceeding well, put to it two ounces of sugar, and as much juice of raspberry as will make it a pretty pink colour, and give it a proper sharpness, drop them into a pan of boiling lard, the size of a walnut; when you dish them up, stick bits of citron in some, and blanched almonds cut lengthways in others; lay round them green and yellow sweetmeats and serve them up. They are a pretty corner dish for either dinner or supper.

To make a TANSEY FRITTER.

TAKE the crumb of a penny loaf, pour on it half a pint of boiling milk, let it stand an hour, then put in as much juice of tansey as will give it a flavour, but not to make it bitter, then make it a pretty green with the juice of spinage, put to it a spoonful of ratafia water, or brandy, sweeten it to your taste, grate the rind of half a lemon, beat the yolks of four eggs, mix them all together, put them in a tossing-pan with four ounces of butter, stir it over a flow fire till it is quite thick, take it off, and let it stand two or three hours, then drop them into a pan full of boiling lard, a spoonful is enough for a fritter, serve them up with slices of orange round them, grate sugar over them, and wine sauce in a boat.

To make PLUMB FRITTERS with RICE.

GRATE the crumbs of a penny loaf, pour over it a pint of boiling cream, or good milk, let it stand four or five hours, then beat it exceeding fine, put to it the yolks of five eggs, four ounces of sugar, and a nutmeg grated; beat them well together, and fry them in hog's lard; drain them on a sieve, and serve them up with white wine sauce under them. N. B. You may put currants in if you please.

To make WATER FRITTERS.

TAKE a quart of water, five or six spoonfuls of flour (the batter must be very thick) and a little salt; mix all these together, and beat the yolks and whites of eight eggs with a little brandy, then strain them through a hair sieve, and put them to the other things; the longer they stand before you fry them the better. Just before you fry them, melt about half a pound of butter very thick, and beat it well in; you must not turn them, and take care not to burn them: the best thing to fry them in is fine lard.

To make FRENCH BANCEES.

TAKE half a pint of water, a bit of lemon peel, a bit of butter the bigness of a walnut, a little orange-flower water; let these boil three or four minutes; then take out the lemon peel, and add to it a pint of flour, keep the water boiling and stirring all the while till it is stiff, then take it off the fire and put in six eggs, leaving out the whites of three ; beat these well for about half an hour, till they come to a stiff paste, drop them into a pan of boiling lard with a tea-spoon; if they are of a right lightness they will be very nice ; keep shaking the pan all the time till they are of a light brown. A large dam will take six or seven minutes boiling; when done enough, put them into a dish that will drain them, set them by the fire, and strew some sugar over them.

To make GERMAN PUFFS.

PUT half a pint of good milk into a tossing- pan, and dredge it in flour till it is thick as hasty- pudding, keep stirring it over a slow fire till it is all of a lump, then put it in a marble mortar; when it is cold put to it the yolks of eight eggs, four ounces of sugar, a spoonful of rose water, grate a little nutmeg, and the rind of half a lemon, beat them together an hour or more, when it looks light and bright, drop them into a pan of boiling lard with a tea-spoon, the size of a large nutmeg, they will rise and look like a large yellow plumb if they are well beat: as you fry them, lay them on a sieve to drain; grate sugar round your dish, and serve them up with sack for sauce. — It is a proper corner dish for dinner, or supper.

To make GOFERS.

BEAT three eggs well, with three spoonfuls of flour and a little salt, then mix them with a pint of milk, an ounce of sugar, and half a nutmeg grated, beat them well together, then make your gofer tongs hot, rub them with fresh butter, fill the bottom part of your tongs, and clap the top up, then turn them, and when a fine brown on both sides, put them in a dish, and pour white wine sauce over them, five is enough for a dish, do not lay them one upon another, it will make them soft. — You may put in currants if you please.

To make WAFER PANCAKES,

BEAT four eggs well with two spoonfuls of fine flour, and two of cream, one ounce of loaf sugar, beat and sifted, half a nutmeg grated, put a little cold butter in a clean cloth, and rub your pan well with it, pour in your batter and make it as thin as a wafer, fry it only on one side, put them on a dish, and grate sugar betwixt every pancake, and send them hot to the table.

To make CREAM PANCAKES.

TAKE the yolks of two eggs, mix them with half a pint of good cream, two ounces of sugar, rub your pan with lard, and fry them as thick as possible, grate sugar over them, and serve them up hot.

To make CLARY PANCAKES

BEAT three eggs with three spoonfuls of fine flour, and a little salt, exceeding well, mix them with a pint of milk, and put lard into your pan; when it is hot, pour in your batter as thin as possible, then lay in your clary leaves, and pour a little more batter thin over them, fry them a fine brown, and serve them up.

To make BATTER PANCAKES.

BEAT three eggs with a pound of flour, very well, put to it a pint of milk, and a little fat, fry them in lard or butter, grate sugar over them, cut them in quarters and serve them up.

To make fine PANCAKES.

TAKE a pint of cream, eight eggs, (leave out two of the whites) three spoonfuls of sack or orange-flower water, a little sugar if it be agreeable, a grated nutmeg; the butter and cream must be melted over the fire; mix all together with three spoonfuls of flour; butter the frying-pan for the first, let them run as thin as you can in the pan, fry them quick, and send them up hot.

To make TANSEY PANCAKES.

BEAT four eggs, and put to them half a pint of cream, four spoonfuls of flour, and two of fine sugar, beat them a quarter of an hour, then put in one spoonful of the juice of tansey, and two of the juice of spinage with a little grated nutmeg, beat all well together, and fry them in fresh butter: garnish them with quarters of Seville oranges, grate double refined sugar over them, and send them up hot.

To make a pink-coloured PANCAKE.

BOIL a large beet root tender, and beat it fine in a marble mortar, then add the yolks of four eggs, two spoonfuls of flour, and three spoonfuls of good cream, sweeten it to your taste, and grate in half a nutmeg, and put in a glass of brandy; beat them all together half an hour, fry them in butter, and garnish them with green sweetmeats, preserved apricots, or green sprigs of myrtle. — It is a pretty corner dish for either dinner or supper.

CHAP VI.

Observations on PUDDINGS

BREAD and custard puddings require time, and a moderate oven, that will raise, and not burn them; batter and rice puddings a quick oven, and always butter the pan or dish before you pour the pudding in; when you boil a pudding, take great care your cloth is very clean, dip it in boiling water, and flour it well, and give your cloth a shake; if you boil it in a bason, butter it, and boil it in plenty of water, and turn it often, and don't cover the pan; when enough take it up into a bason, let it stand a few minutes to cool, then untie the string, wrap the cloth round the bason, lay your dish over it, and turn the pudding out, and take the bason and cloth off very carefully, for very often a light pudding is broken in turning out.

A Hunting PUDDING.

BEAT eight eggs, and mix them with a pint of good cream, and a pound of flour, beat them well together, and put to them a pound of beef suet chopped very fine, a pound of currants well cleaned, half a pound of jar raisins stoned and chopped small, a quarter of a pound of powdered sugar, two ounces of candied citron, the same of candied orange cut small, grate a large nutmeg, and mix all well together, with half a gill of brandy, put it in a cloth, and tie it up close, it will take four hours boiling.

To make a baked ALMOND PUDDING.

BOIL the skins of two lemons very tender, and beat them very fine, beat half a pound of almonds in rose water, and a pound of sugar, very fine, melt half a pound of butter and let it stand till quite cold; beat the yolks of eight eggs and the whites of four, mix them, and beat them all together with a little orange-flower water, and bake it in the oven.

To make a baked APPLE PUDDING.

HALF a pound of apples well boiled and pounded, half a pound of butter beaten to a cream, and mixed with the apples before they are cold, and six eggs with the whites well beaten and strained, half a pound. of sugar, pounded and sifted, the rinds of two lemons, well boiled and beaten; sift the peel into clean water twice in the boiling, put a thin crust in the bottom and rims of your dish. Half an hour will bake it.

A boiled CUSTARD PUDDING.

BOIL a stick or two of cinnamon in a quart of thin cream, with a quarter of a pound of sugar ; when it is cold put in the yolks of six eggs well beat, and mix them together ; set it over a slow fire, and stir it round one way, till it grows pretty thick, but do not let it boil, take it off and let it stand till it be quite cold, butter a cloth very well, and dredge it with flour, put in your custard, and tie it up very close, it will take three quarters of an hour boiling; when you take it up, put it in a round basin to cool a little, then untie the cloth, and lay the dish on the bowl and turn it upside down ; be careful how you take off the cloth, for a very little will break the pudding, grate over it a little sugar; for sauce, white wine thickened with flour and butter, put in the dish.

A LEMON PUDDING.

BLANCH and beat eight ounces of Jordan almonds, with orange flower- water, add to them half a pound of cold butter, the yolks of ten eggs, the juice of a large lemon, half the rind grated fine, work them in a marble mortar, or wooden bason till they look white and light, lay a good puff paste pretty thin in the bottom of a China dish, and pour in your pudding; it will take half an hour baking.

To make a LEMON PUDDING *a second Way.*

GRATE the rinds of four lemons, and the juice of two or three, as they are in size, then take two biscuits grated, three quarters of a pound of boiled butter, with half a pound of sugar dissolved in the yolks of twelve eggs, and four whites well beat, with a little salt and a quarter of a nutmeg grated; mix all together very well and put it into a dish; put a nice paste round the edge before it goes into the oven. Half an hour will bake it.

To make a LEMON PUDDING *a third way.*

TAKE a pound of flour well dried and sifted, a pound of fine sugar beat and sifted, the rind of a lemon grated, twelve eggs, the yolks beat a little by themselves, and the whites beat till they are all froth, then gently mix all together, put it in a pan, and bake it just half an hour.

A ground RICE PUDDING.

BOIL four ounces of ground rice in water, till it be soft, then beat the yolks of four eggs, and put to them a pint of cream, four ounces of sugar, and a quarter of a pound of butter, mix them all well together; you may either boil or bake it.

An ORANGE PUDDING.

BOIL the rind of a Seville orange very soft, beat it in a marble mortar, with the juice, put to it two Naples biscuits grated very fine, half a pound of butter, a quarter of a pound of sugar, and the yolks of six eggs, mix them well together, lay a good puff paste round the edge of your China dish, bake it in a gentle oven, half an hour; you may make a lemon pudding the same way, by putting in a lemon instead of the orange.

To make an ORANGE PUDDING *a second way*

TAKE the rinds of six oranges, boil them till they are tender, changing the water as often as you find it bitter, cut them very fine, then pound and sift three quarters of a pound of loaf sugar, wash very well three quarters of a pound of butter, then take twelve eggs, leaving four of the whites out; mix all well together, butter the bottom of the dish well, and make a rich crust, which must be put at the bottom. Bake it nicely; it must not be too brown.

CALF'S FOOT PUDDING.

BOIL a gang of calf's feet, take the meat from the bones and chop it exceeding fine, put to it the crumb of a penny loaf, a pound of beef suet shred very small, half a pint of cream, eight eggs, a pound of currants well cleansed, four ounces of citron cut small, two ounces of candied orange cut like straws, a large nutmeg grated, and a large glass of brandy, mix them all very well together, butter your cloth, and dust it with flour, tie it close up, boil it three hours; when you take the pudding up, it is best to put it in a bowl that will just hold it, and let it stand a quarter of an hour, before you turn it out, lay your dish upon the top of the bason and turn it upside down.

A boiled RICE PUDDING.

BOIL a quarter of a pound of rice in water, till it be soft, and put it in a hair sieve to drain, beat it in a marble mortar, with the yolks of five eggs, a quarter of a pound of butter, the same of sugar, grate a small nutmeg, and the rind of half a lemon, work them well together for half an hour, then put in half a pound of currants well washed and cleaned, mix them well together, butter your cloth and tie it up ; boil it an hour, and serve it up with white wine sauce.

BREAD PUDDING.

TAKE the crumb of a penny loaf, and pour on it a pint of good milk boiling hot, when it is cold, beat it very fine, with two ounces of butter and sugar to your palate, grate half a nutmeg in it, beat it up with four eggs, and put them in and beat all together near half an hour, tie it in a cloth and boil it an hour, you may put in half a pound of currants for change, and pour over it white wine sauce.

To make a boiled BREAD PUDDING *a second Way.*

TAKE the inside of a penny loaf, grate it fine, add to it two ounces of butter, take a pint and a half of milk, with a stick of cinnamon; boil it and pour it over the bread, and cover it close till it is cold, then take six eggs beat up very well with rose water, mix them all well together, sweeten to your taste, and boil it one hour.

To make a Nice PUDDING.

BOIL half a pint of milk with a bit of cinnamon, four eggs with the whites well beaten, the rind of a lemon grated, half a pound of suet chopped fine, as much bread as will do; pour your milk on the bread and suet, keep mixing it till cold, then put in the lemon peel, eggs, a little sugar, and some nutmeg grated fine. Either bake or, boil it, as you think proper.

To make a PLAIN PUDDING.

BEAT the yolks and whites of three eggs, with two large spoonfuls of flour, a little salt, and half a pint of good milk or cream, make it the thickness of a pancake batter, and beat all very well together. Half an hour will boil it.

To make a SIPPET PUDDING.

CUT a penny loaf as thin as possible, put a layer of bread in the bottom of a pewter dish, then strew over it a layer of marrow, or beef suet, a handful of currants, then lay a layer of bread, and so on till you fill your dish; as the first lay, let the marrow or suet, and currants be at the top, beat four eggs and mix them with a quart of cream, a quarter of a pound of sugar, and a large nutmeg grated, pour it on your dish, and bake it in a moderate oven, when it comes out of the oven, pour over it wine sauce.

An APRICOT PUDDING.

TAKE twelve large apricots, pare them, and give them a scald in water, till they are soft; then take out the stones, grate the crumb of a penny loaf, and pour on it a pint of cream boiling hot, let it stand till half cold, then add a quarter of a pound of sugar, and the yolks of four eggs, mix all together with a glass of Madeira wine, pour it in a dish, with thin puff paste round; bake it half an hour in a moderate oven.

A TRANSPARENT PUDDING.

BEAT eight eggs very well, and put them in a pan, with half a pound of butter, and the same weight of loaf sugar beat fine, a little grated nutmeg, set it on the fire and keep stirring it till it thickens like buttered eggs, then put it in a baton to cool, roll a rich puff paste very thin, lay it round the edge of a China dish, then pour in the pudding, and bake it in a moderate oven half an hour, it will cut light and clear. — It is a pretty pudding for a corner for dinner and a middle for supper.

VERMICELLI PUDDING.

BOIL four ounces of vermicelli in a pint of new milk till it is soft, with a stick or two of cinnamon, then put in half a pint of thick cream, a quarter of a pound of butter, a quarter of a pound of sugar, and the yolks of four beaten eggs. Bake it in an earthen dish without a paste.

A red SAGO PUDDING.

TAKE two ounces of sago, boil it in water, with a stick of cinnamon till it be quite soft and thick, let it stand till quite cold, in the mean time grate the crumb of a halfpenny loaf, and pour over it a large glass of red wine, chop four ounces of marrow, and half a pound of sugar, and the yolks of four beaten eggs, beat them all together for a quarter of an hour, lay a puff paste round your dish, and send it to the oven; when it comes back stick it over with blanched almonds cut the long way, and bits of citron cut the same ; send it to table.

A boiled TANSEY PUDDING.

GRATE four Naples biscuits, put as much cream boiling hot as will wet them, beat the yolks of four eggs, have ready a few chopped tansey leaves, with as much spinage as will make it a pretty green, be careful you do not put too much tansey in, it will make it bitter, mix all together when the cream is cold with a little sugar, and set it over a slow fire till it grows thick, then take it off, and when cold put it in a cloth, well buttered and floured, tie it up close and let it boil three quarters of an hour, take it up in a bason, and let it stand one quarter, then turn it carefully out, and put white wine sauce round it.

A TANSEY PUDDING with ALMONDS.

BLANCH four ounces of almonds, and beat them very fine with rose water, slice a French roll very thin, put on a pint of cream boiling hot, beat four eggs very well, and mix with the eggs when beaten a little sugar and grated nut meg, a glass of brandy, a little juice of tansey, and the juice of spinage to make it green, put all the ingredients into a stew-pan, with a quarter of a pound of butter, and give it a gentle boil; you may either boil it or bake it in a dish, either with a crust or writing paper.

A TANSEY PUDDING of ground RICE.

BOIL six ounces of ground rice in a quart of good milk, till it is soft; then put in half a pound of butter, with six eggs very well beat, and sugar and rose water to make it palatable; beat some spinage in a mortar, with a few leaves of tansey, squeeze out the juice through a cloth, and put it in; mix all well together, cover your dish with writing paper well buttered, and pour it in; three quarters of an hour will bake it ; when you dish it up stick it all over with a Seville or sweet orange in half quarters.

A SAGO PUDDING *another Way.*

BOIL two ounces of sago till it is quite thick in milk, beat six eggs, leaving out three of the whites, put to it half a pint of cream, two spoonfuls of sack, nutmeg and sugar to your taste; put a paste round your dish.

Little CITRON PUDDINGS.

TAKE half a pint of cream, one spoonful of fine flour, two ounces of sugar, a little nutmeg, mix them all well together, with the yolks of three eggs, put it in tea-cups, and stick in it two ounces of citron cut very thin, bake them in a pretty quick oven, and turn them out upon, a China dish. — Five is enough for a side dish.

A *baked* TANSEY PUDDING.

GRATE the crumb of a penny loaf, pour on it a pint of boiling milk, with a quarter of a pound of butter in it, let it stand till almost cold, then beat five eggs, and put them in with a quarter of a pound of sugar, a large nutmeg grated, and a glass of brandy, stir them about and put them in a tossing pan, with as much juice of spinage as will green it, and a little tansey chopped small, stir it about over a slow fire till it grows thick, butter a sheet of writing paper and lay it in the bottom of a pewter dish, pin the corners of the paper to make it stand one inch above the dish, to keep the pudding from spreading, and let it stand three quarters of an hour in the oven; when baked, put the dish over it you send it up in, and turn it out upon it, take off the paper, stick it round with a Seville orange cut in half quarters, stick one quarter in the middle, and serve it up with wine sauce. It will look as green as if it had not been baked, when turned out.

A *green* CODLING PUDDING.

GREEN a quart of codlings, as for a pye, rub them through a hair sieve with the back of a wooden spoon, and as much of the juice of beets as will green your pudding, put in the crumbs of half a penny loaf, half a pound of butter, and three eggs well beaten; beat them all together with half a pound of sugar, and two spoonfuls of cyder; lay a good paste round the rim of the dish, and pour it in. — Half an hour will bake it.

To make a common RICE PUDDING.

WASH half a pound of rice, put to it three pints of good milk, mix it well with a quarter of a pound of butter, a stick or two of cinnamon beaten fine, half a nutmeg grated, - one egg well beat, a little salt and sugar to your taste. One hour and a half will bake it in a quick oven; when it comes out take off the top, and put the pudding in breakfast cups, turn them into a hot dish like little puddings, and serve it up.

A MARROW PUDDING.

POUR on the crumb of a penny loaf a pint of cream boiling hot, cut a pound of beef marrow very thin, beat four eggs very well, then add a glass of brandy, with sugar and nutmeg to your taste, and mix them all well up together; you may either boil or bake it, three quarters of an hour will do it, cut two ounces of citron very thin, and stick them all over it when you dish it up.

MARROW PUDDING *a second Way.*

HALF boil four ounces of rice, shred half a pound of marrow very fine, stone a quarter of a pound of raisins, chop them very small, with two ounces of currants well cleansed, beat four eggs a quarter of an hour, mix it all together with a pint of good cream, a spoonful of brandy, sugar and nutmeg to your taste; you may either bake it or put it in hogs skins.

MARROW PUDDING *a third Way*.

BLANCH half a pound of almonds, put them in cold water all night, and next day beat them in a marble mortar very fine, with orange- flower, or rose water, take the crumb of a penny loaf, and pour on them a pint of boiling cream; whilst the cream is cooling, beat the yolks of four eggs and two whites a quarter of an hour, add a little sugar, and grate nutmeg to your palate, have ready shred the marrow of two bones, and mix them all well together with a little candied orange cut small, this is usually made to fill in skins, but it is a good baked pudding: if you put it in skins, do not fill them too full, for it will swell, but boil them gently.

WHITE PUDDINGS *in* SKINS.

WASH half a pound of rice in warm water, boil it in milk till it is soft, put it in a sieve to drain, blanch and beat half a pound of Jordan almonds very fine, with rose water, wash and dry a pound of currants, then cut in small bits a pound of hog's lard, take six eggs and beat them well, half a pound of sugar, a large nutmeg grated, a stick of cinnamon, a little mace, and a little salt, mix them very well together, fill your skins and boil them.

To make a QUAKING PUDDING.

BOIL a quart of cream and let it stand till almost cold, then beat four eggs a full quarter of an hour, with a spoonful and a half of flour, then mix them with your cream, add sugar and nut meg to your palate, tie it close up in a cloth well buttered, and let it boil an hour and turn it care fully out.

To make a QUAKING PUDDING *a second Way* .

TAKE a pint of good cream, the yolks of ten eggs and a whites, beat them very well, and run them through a fine sieve; then take two heaped spoonfuls of flour, and a spoonful or two of cream, beat it with the flour till it be smooth, then mix all together, and tie it close up in a dish or bason well rubbed with butter, and dredged with flour, the water must boil when you put in the pudding. One hour will boil it; serve it up with wine sauce in a boat.

To make a YORKSHIRE PUDDING *to bake under* MEAT.

BEAT four eggs with four large spoonfuls of fine flour, and a little salt, for a quarter of an hour, put to them one quart and a half of milk, mix them well together, then butter a dripping- pan and set it under beef, mutton, or a loin of veal when roasting, and when it is brown cut it in square pieces and turn it over; when well browned on the underside, send it to table on a dish. — You may mix a boiled pudding the same way.

A boiled MILK PUDDING.

POUR a pint of new milk boiling hot on three spoonfuls of fine flour, beat the flour and milk for half an hour, then put in three eggs and beat it a little longer, grate in half a tea-spoonful of ginger, dip the cloth in boiling water, butter it well, and flour it, put in the pudding and tie it close up, and boil it an hour; it requires great care when you turn it out; pour over it thick melted butter.

HERB PUDDING:

OF spinage, beets, parsley, and leeks take each a handful, wash them and give them a scald in boiling water, then shred them very fine, have ready a quart of groats steeped in warm water half an hour, and a pound of hog's-lard cut in little bits, three large onions chopped small, and three sage leaves hacked fine, put in a little salt, mix all well together, and tie it close up; it will require to betaken up in boiling to slacken the string a little.

To make a YAM PUDDING.

TAKE a middling white yam, and either boil or roast it, then pare off the skin and pound it very fine, with three quarters of a pound of butter, half a pound of sugar, a little mace, cinnamon, and twelve eggs, leaving out half the whites, beat them with a little rose water. You may put in a little citron cut small, if you like it, and bake it nicely.

GOOSEBERRY PUDDING.

SCALD half a pint of green gooseberries in water till they are soft, put them into a sieve to drain, when cold work them through an hair sieve with the back of a clean wooden spoon, add to them half a pound of sugar, and the same of butter, four ounces of Naples biscuits, beat six eggs very well, then mix all together, and beat them a quarter of an hour, pour it in an earthen dish without paste; half an hour will bake it.

To make RASPBERRY DUMPLINGS.

MAKE a good cold paste, roll it a quarter of an inch thick, and spread over it raspberry jam to your own liking, roll it up, and boil it in a cloth one hour at least, take it up, and cut it in five slices, and lay one in the middle and the other four round it, pour a little good melted butter in the dish, and grate fine sugar round the edge of the dish. — It is proper for a corner or side for dinner.

To make DAMSON DUMPLINGS.

MAKE a good hot paste crust, roll it pretty thin, lay it in a bason, and put in what quantity of damsons you think proper, wet the edge of the paste, and close it up, boil it in a cloth one hour and send it up whole, pour over it melted butter, and grate sugar round the edge of the dish: Note, you may make any kind of preserved fruit the same way.

To make APPLE DUMPLINGS.

PARE your apples, take out the core with an apple scraper, fill the hole with quince or orange marmalade, or sugar, which suits you, then take a piece of cold paste, and make a hole in it, as if you was going to make a pye, lay in your apple, and put another piece of paste in the same form, and close it up round the side of your apple, it is much better than gathering it in a lump at one end, tie it in a cloth, and boil it three quarters of an hour, pour melted butter over them, and serve them up, five is enough for a dish.

To make a SPARROW DUMPLING.

MIX half a pint of good milk, with three eggs, a little salt, and as much flour as will make it a thick batter, put a lump of butter rolled in pepper and salt in every sparrow, mix them in the batter, and tie them in a cloth, boil them one hour and a half, pour melted butter over them and serve them up.

To make a BARM PUDDING.

TAKE a pound of flour, mix a spoonful of harm in it, with a little salt, and make it into a light paste with warm water, let it lie one hour, then make it up into round balls, and tie them up in little nets, and put them in a pan of boiling water, do not cover them, it will make them sad, nor do not let them boil so fast as to let the water boil over them, turn them when they have been in six or seven minutes, and they will rise through the nets and look like diamonds, twenty minutes will boil them; serve them up and pour sweet sauce over them.

To make a HANOVER CAKE or PUDDING.

TAKE half a pound of almonds blanched, and beat fine with a little rose water, half a pound of fine sugar, pounded and lifted, fifteen eggs, leaving out half the whites, the rind of a lemon grated very fine; put a few almonds in the mortar at a time, and put in by degrees about a tea-cupful of rose water; keep throwing in the sugar; when you have done the almonds and sugar together a little at a time till they are all riled up, then put it into your pan with the eggs: beat them very well together. Half an hour will bake it; it must be a light brown.

PART II.

CHAP. VII

Observations On making DECORATIONS *for a* TABLE

When you spin a silver web, or a dessert, always take particular care your fire is clear, and a pan of water upon the fire, to keep the heat from your face and stomach, for fear the heat should make you faint; you must not spin it before a kitchen fire, for the smaller the grate is, so that the fire be clear and hot, the better able you will be to sit a long time before it, for if you spin a whole desert, you will be several hours in spinning it; be sure to have a tin box to put every basket in as you spin them, and cover them from the air, and keep them warm, until you have done the whole as your receipt directs you.

If you spin a gold web, take care your chafing dish is burnt clear, before you set it upon the table where your mould is, set your ladle on the fire, and keep stirring it with a wood skewer till it just boils, then let it cool a little, for it will not spin when it is boiling hot, and if it grows cold it is equally as bad, but as it cools on the sides of your ladle, dip the point of your knife in, and begin to spin round your mould as long as it will draw, then heat it again; the only art is to keep it of a proper heat, and it will draw out like a fine thread, and of a gold colour; it is a great fault to put in too much sugar at a time, for often heating takes the moisture out of the sugar, and burns it, therefore the best way is to put in a little at a time, and clean out your ladle.

When you make a hen or bird nest, let part of your jelly be set in your bowl, before you put on your flummery, or straw, for if your jelly is warm, they will settle to the bottom, and mix together.

If it be a fish pond, or a transparent pudding, put in your jelly at three different times, to make your fish or fruit keep at a proper distance, one from another, and be sure your jelly is very clear and stiff, or it will not shew the figures, nor keep whole; when you turn them out, dip your bason in warm water, as your receipt directs, then turn your dish or salver upon the top of your bason, and turn your bason upside down.

When you make flummery, always observe to have it pretty thick, and your moulds wet in cold water, before you put in your flummery, or your jelly will settle to the bottom, and the cream swim at the top, so that it will look to be two different colours.

If you make custards, do not let them boil after the yolks are in, but stir them all one way, and keep them of a good heat till they be thick enough, and the rawness of the eggs is gone off.

When you make whips, or syllabubs, raise your froth with a chocolate mill, and lay it upon a sieve to drain, it will be much prettier, and will lie upon your glasses, without mixing with your wine, or running down the sides of your glasses; and when you have made any of the before-mentioned things, keep them in a cool, airy place, for a close place will give them a bad taste, and soon spoil them.

To spin a SILVER WEB *for covering* SWEET- MEATS.

TAKE a quarter of a pound of treble-refined sugar, in one lump, and set it before a moderate fire on the middle of a silver salver, or pewter plate, set it a little aslant, and when it begins to run like clear water to the edge of the plate or salver, have ready a tin cover, or china bowl set on a stool, with the mouth downward, close to your sugar, that it may not cool by carrying too far, then take a clean knife, and take up as much of the syrup as the point of the knife will hold, and a fine thread will come from the point, which you must draw as quick as possible back wards and forwards and also round the mould, as long as it will spin from the knife; be very careful you do not drop the syrup on the web, if you do it will spoil it, then dip your knife into the syrup again, and take up more, and so keep spinning till your sugar is done, or your web is thick enough; be sure you do not let the knife touch the lump on the plate that is not melted, it will make it brittle, and not spin at all, if your sugar is spent before your web is done, put fresh sugar on a clean plate or salver, and do not spin from the same plate again; if you do not want the web to cover the sweetmeats immediately, set it in a deep pewter dish, and cover it with a tin cover and lay a cloth over it, to prevent the air from getting to it, and set it before the fire (it requires to be kept warm, or it will fall) when your dinner or supper is dished, have ready a plate or dish the size of your web, filled with different coloured sweetmeats, and set your web over it. It is pretty for a middle, where the dishes are few, or corner where the number is large.

To spin a GOLD WEB *for covering* SWEET MEATS.

BEAT four ounces of treble-refined sugar in a marble mortar, and sift it through a hair sieve, then put it in a silver or brass ladle, but silver makes the colour better, set it over a chafing-dish of charcoal, that is burnt clear, and set it on a table, and turn a tin cover or china bowl upside down upon the same table, and when your sugar is melted, it will be of a gold colour, take your ladle off the fire, and begin to spin it with a knife, the same way as the silver web ; when the sugar begins to cool and set, put it over the fire to warm, and spin it as before, but do not warm it too often, it will turn the sugar a bad colour; if you have not enough sugar, clean the ladle before you put in more, and spin it till your web is thick enough, then take it off and set it over the sweetmeats, as you did the silver web.

To make GUM PASTE for DESERT BASKETS OR COVERS.

TAKE one ounce of gum dragon, steep it in a tea-cupful of cold water all night, the next morning have ready a pound of treble-refined sugar, beat and sift it through a silk sieve, rub your gum through a hair sieve, then mix your sugar and gum together with a strong hand, and in working it will become as white as snow; then take a little fine hair powder, and make it into a very stiff paste, and cut it into baskets, or crocrans, swans, or any kind of mould or figure you please; dry it in a very cool stove or oven, or before the fire, and it will be quite white and hard and fit for use, either to cover sweetmeats or to set off a desert.

To make a CHINESE TEMPLE or OBELISK.

TAKE four ounces of fine flour, half an ounce of butter, one ounce of fine sugar, boil the sugar and butter in a little water, when it is cold beat an egg and put to the water, sugar, and butter, mix it with the flour, and make it into a very stiff paste, then roll it as thin as possible, have a set of tins the form of a temple, and put the paste upon them, and cut it in what form you please, upon the separate parts of your tins, keeping them separate till baked, but take care to have the paste exactly the size of the tins ; when you have cut all the parts, bake them in a flow oven, when cold take them out of the tins and join the parts with strong isinglass and water with a camel's-hair brush, and set them one upon the other, and the forms of the tin moulds will direct you; if you cut it neat, and the paste be rolled very thin, it is a beautiful corner for a large table; if you have obelisk moulds you may make them the same way for an opposite corner. Take care to make the pillars stronger than the top, so as to bear the weight; you may cut the form of covers with this paste for wet or dry sweetmeats, or creams for supper dishes

To make a DESERT *of* SPUN SUGAR.

Spin two large webs, and turn one upon the other to form a globe, and put in the inside of them a few sprigs of small flowers and myrtle, and spin a little more round to bind them together, and set them covered close up before the fire, then spin two more on a lesser bowl and put in a sprig of myrtle, and a few small flowers, and bind them as before, set them by, and spin two more less than the last, and put in a few flowers, bind them and set them by, then spin twelve couple on tea-cups of three different sizes in proportion to the globes, to represent baskets, and bind them two and two as the globes with spun sugar; set the globes on a silver salver, one upon another, the largest at the bottom, and smallest at the top; when you have fixed the globes, run two small wires through the middle of the largest globes, across each other; then take a large darning needle and silk, and run it through the middle of the largest baskets, cross it at the bottom, and bring it up to the top, and make a loop to hang them on the wire, and do so with the rest of your baskets, hang the largest baskets on the wires, then put two more wires a little shorter across, through the middle of the second globes, and put the ends of the wires out betwixt the baskets, and hang on the four middle ones, then run two more wires shorter than the last, through the middle of the top globes, and hang the baskets over the lowest; stick a sprig of myrtle on the top of your globes, and set it in on the middle of the table. — Observe you do not put too much sugar down at a time for a silver web, because the sugar will lose its moisture, and run in lumps instead of drawing out; nor too much in the ladle, for the gold web will lose its colour by heating too oft. — You may make the baskets a silver, and the globes a gold colour, if you choose them. — It is a pretty desert for a grand table.

To make CALF'S FOOT JELLY.

PUT a gang of calves feet well cleaned into a pan, with six quarts of water, and let them boil gently till reduced to two quarts, then take out the feet, scum off the fat, clean, and clear the jelly from the sediment, beat the whites of five eggs to a froth, then add one pint of Lisbon, Madeira, or any pale made wine, if you choose it, then squeeze in the juice of three lemons; when your stock is boiling, take three spoonfuls of it, and keep stirring it with your wine and eggs to keep it from curdling, then add a little more stock, and still keep stirring it, and then put it in the pan, and sweeten it with loaf sugar to your taste, a glass of French brandy will keep the jelly from turning blue in frosty air, put in the outer rind of two lemons, and let it boil one minute all together, and pour it into a flannel bag, and let it run into a bason, and keep pouring it back gently into the bag till it runs clear and bright, then set your glasses under the bag, and cover it lest dust gets in. — If you would have the jelly for a fish-pond, transparent pudding, or hen's nest, to be turned out of the mould, boil half a pound of isinglass in a pint of water, till reduced to one quarter, and put it into the stock before it is refined..

To make SAVOURY JELLY.

SPREAD some slices of lean veal and ham, in the bottom of a stew-pan, with a carrot and turnip or two or three onions; cover it, and let it sweat on a slow fire, till it is as deep a brown as you would have it, then put to it a quart of very clear broth, some whole pepper, mace, a very little isinglass, and salt to your taste; let this boil ten minutes, then strain it through a French strainer, scum off all the fat and put it to the whites of three eggs, run it several times through a jelly bag as you do other jellies.

To make SAVOURY JELLY for cold Meat.

BOIL beef and mutton to a stiff jelly, season it with a little pepper and salt, a blade or two of mace, and an onion, then beat the whites of four eggs, put it to the jelly, and beat it a little, then run it through a jelly bag, and when clear pour it on your meat or fowls in the dish you send it up on.

To make HARTSHORN JELLY *a second Way.*

TAKE half a pound of hartshorn and put to it two quarts of water, let it stand in the oven all night, then strain it from the hartshorn, and put to it a pint of Rhenish wine, the whites of four eggs, a little mace, the juice of three lemons, and sugar to your taste; boil them together, and strain it through a jelly bag; when it is fine put it in your glasses for use. N. B. — If you have no Rhenish wine, white wine will do.

To make FLUMMERY.

PUT one ounce of bitter and one of sweet almonds into a bason, pour over them some boiling water, to make the skins come off, which is called blanching, strip off the skins, and throw the kernels into cold water, then take them out, and beat them in a marble mortar, with a little rose water to keep them from oiling, when they are beat, put them into a pint of calf's foot stock, set it over the fire, and sweeten it to your taste with loaf sugar, as soon as it boils strain it through a piece of muslin or gauze, when a little cold put it into a pint of thick cream, and keep stirring it often till it grows thick and cold, wet your moulds in cold water, and pour in the flummery, let it stand five or six hours at least before you turn them out; if you make the flummery stiff, and wet the moulds, it will turn out without putting it into warm water, for water takes off the figures of the mould, and makes the flummery look dull. — N. B. Be careful to keep stirring it till cold or it will run in lumps when you turn it out of the mould.

To make COLOURING *for* FLUMMERY *and* JELLIES

TAKE two penny-worth of cochineal, bruise it with the blade of a knife, and put it into half a tea-cupful of the best French brandy, and let it stand a quarter of an hour; filter it through a fine cloth, and put in as much as will make the jelly or flummery a fine pink; if yellow, take a little saffron, and tie it in a rag, dissolve it in cold water; if green, take some spinage, boil it, take off the froth, and mix it with the jelly; if white, put in some cream.

To make a FISH POND

FILL four large fish moulds with flummery, and six small ones, take a china bowl, and put in half a pint of stiff clear calf's foot jelly, let it stand till cold, then lay two of the small fishes on the jelly, the right side down, put in half a pint more jelly, let it stand till cold, then lay in the four small fishes across one another, that when you turn the bowl upside down the heads and tails may be seen, then almost fill your bowl with jelly, and let it stand till cold, then lay in the jelly four large fishes, and fill the bason quite full with jelly, and let it stand till the next day; when you want to use it, set your bowl to the brim in hot water for one minute, take care that you do not let the water go into the bason, lay your plate on the top of the bason, and turn it upside down, if you want it for the middle, turn it out upon a salver; be sure you make your jelly very stiff and clear.

To make a HEN'S NEST.

TAKE three or five of the smallest pullet eggs you can get, fill them with flummery, and when they are stiff and cold peel off the shells, pare off the rinds of two lemons very thin, and boil them in sugar and water, to take off the bitterness, when they are cold, cut them in, long shreds to imitate straws, then fill a bason one third full of stiff calf's foot jelly, and let it stand till cold, then lay in the shred of the lemons, in a ring about two inches high in the middle of your bason, strew a few corns of sago to look like barley, fill the basin to the height of the peel, and let it stand till cold, then lay your eggs of flummery in the middle of the ring that the straw may be seen round, fill the bason quite full of jelly, and let it stand, and turn it out the same way as the fish-pond.

To make BLANC-MANGE of ISINGLASS.

BOIL one ounce of isinglass in a quart of water till it is reduced to a pint, then put in the whites of four eggs, with two spoonfuls of rice water, to keep the eggs from poaching, and sugar to your taste, and run it through a jelly- bag, then put to it two ounces of sweet and one ounce of bitter almonds, give them a scald in your jelly, and put them through a hair sieve, put it in a China bowl, the next day turn it out, and stick it all over with almonds, blanched and cut lengthways: garnish with green leaves or flowers.

GREEN BLANC-MANGE of ISINGLASS.

DISSOLVE your isinglass, and put to it two ounces of sweet and two ounces of bitter almonds, with as much juice of spinage as will make it green, and a spoonful of French brandy, set it over a stove fire till it is almost ready to boil, then strain it through a gauze sieve, when it grows thick, put it into a lemon mould, and the next day turn it out — garnish it with red and white flowers.

CLEAR BLANC-MANGE.

TAKE a quart of strong calf's foot jelly, skim off the fat and strain it, beat the whites of four eggs, and put them to your jelly, set it over the fire, and keep stirring it till it boils, then pour it into a jelly bag, and run it through several times till it is clear, beat one ounce of sweet almonds, and one of bitter, to a paste, with a spoonful of rose water squeezed through a cloth, then mix it with the jelly, and three spoonfuls of very good cream, set it over the fire again, and keep stirring it till it is almost boiling, then pour it into a bowl, and stir it very often till it is almost cold, then wet your moulds and fill them.

YELLOW FLUMMERY.

TAKE two ounces of isinglass, beat it and open it, put it into a bowl, and pour a pint of boiling water upon it, cover it up till almost cold, and add a pint of white wine, the juice of two lemons, with the rind of one, the yolks of eight eggs beat well, sweeten it to your taste, put it in a tossing-pan and keep stirring it, when it boils strain it through a fine sieve, when al most cold, put it into cups and moulds.

A *good* GREEN

LAY an ounce of gambouge in a quarter of a pint of water, put an ounce and a half of good stone blue in a little water, when they are both dissolved, mix them together, add a quarter of a pint more water, and a quarter of a pound of fine sugar, boil it a little, then put it into a galli pot, cover it close, and it will keep for years; be careful not to make it too deep a green, for a very little will do at a time.

FRUITS *in* JELLY,

PUT half a pint of clear stiff calf's foot jelly into a bason, when it is set and stiff lay in three fine ripe peaches, and a bunch of grapes with the stalks up, put a few vine leaves over them, then fill up your bowl with jelly, and let it stand till the next day; then set your bason to the brim in hot water, and as soon as, you find it leaves the bason, lay your dish over it, and turn your jelly carefully upon it — garnish with flowers.

GREEN MELON *in* FLUMMERY.

MAKE a little stiff flummery, with a good deal of bitter almonds in it, add to it it as much juice of spinage as will make it a fine pale green, when it is as thick as good cream wet your melon mould and put it in, then put a pint of clear Calf's foot jelly into a large bason, and let them stand till the next day, then turn out your melon, and lay it the right side down in the middle of your bason of jelly; then fill up your bason with jelly that is beginning to set, let it stand all night, and turn it out the same way as the fruit in jelly: make a garland of flowers, and put it in your jelly. — It is a pretty dish for middle at supper, or corner for a second course at dinner.

GILDED FISH in JELLY.

MAKE a little clear blanc-mange as is directed in the receipt, then' fill two large fish moulds with it and when it is cold turn it out, and gild them with gold leaf, or strew them over with gold and silver bran mixed, then lay them on a soup dish, and fill it with clear thin calf's foot jelly, it must be so thin as they will swim in it; if you have no jelly, Lisbon wine, or any kind of pale made wines will do.

HEN and CHICKENS in JELLY.

MAKE some flummery with a deal of sweet almonds in it, colour a little of it brown with chocolate, and put it in a mould the shape of a hen; then colour some more flummery with the yolk of a hard egg beat as fine as possible, leave part of your flummery white, then fill the moulds of seven chickens, three with white flummery, and three with yellow, and one the colour of the hen; when they are cold turn them into a deep dish ; put under and round them lemon peel, boiled tender and cut like straw, then put a little clear calf's foot jelly under them, to keep them in their places, and let it stand till it is stiff, then fill up your dish with more jelly. — They are a pretty decoration for a grand table

To make a TRANSPARENT PUDDING.

MAKE your calf's foot jelly very stiff, and when it is quite fine put a gill into a china basin, let it stand till it is quite set; blanch a few Jordan Almonds, cut them and a few jar raisins lengthways, cut a little citron and candied lemon in little thin slices, stick them all over the jelly, and throw in a few currants, then pour more jelly on till it is an inch higher; when your jelly is set, stick in your almonds, raisins, citron, and candied lemon, with a few currants strewed in, then more jelly as before, then more almonds, raisins, citron, and lemon in layers, till your bason is full let it stand all night, and turn it out the same way as the fish-pond.

To make a DESERT ISLAND,

TAKE a lump of paste, and form it into a rock three inches broad at the top, colour it, and set it in the middle of a deep China dish, and set a cast figure on it, with a crow on its head, and a knot of rock candy at the feet; then make a roll of paste an inch thick, and stick it on the inner edge of the dish, two parts round, and cut eight pieces of eringo roots, about three inches long, and fix them upright to the roll of paste on the edge; make gravel walks of mot comfits, from the middle of the end of the dish, and set small figures in them, roll out some paste, and cut it open like Chinese rails; bake it, and fix it on either side of one of the gravel walks with gum, have ready a web of spun sugar, and set it on the pillars of eringo root, and cut part of the web off, to form an entrance where the Chinese rails are. — It is a pretty middle dish for a second course at a grand table, or a wedding supper, only set two crowned figures on the mount instead of one.

To make a FLOATING ISLAND.

GRATE the yellow rind of a large lemon into a quart of cream, put in a large glass of Madeira wine, make it pretty sweet with loaf sugar, mill it with a chocolate mill to a strong froth, take it off as it riles, then lay it upon a sieve to drain all night, then take a deep glass dish, and lay in your froth, with a Naples biscuit in the middle of it, then beat the white of an egg to a strong froth, and roll a sprig of myrtle in it to imitate snow, stick it in the Naples biscuit, then lay all over your froth currant jelly cut in very thin slices, pour over it very fine strong calf's foot jelly, when it grows thick lay it all over, till it looks like a glass, and your dish is full to the brim; let it stand till it is quite cold and stiff, then lay on rock candied sweet-meats upon the top of your jelly, and sheep and swans to pick at the myrtle; stick green sprigs in two or three places on the top of your jelly, amongst your shapes; it looks very pretty in the middle of a table for supper. You must not put the shapes on the jelly till you are going to send it to the table.

To make a FLOATING ISLAND *a second Way.*

TAKE calf's foot jelly that is set, break it a little, but not too much, for it will make it frothy, and prevent it from looking clear, have ready a middle sized turnip, and rub it over with gum water, or the white of an egg, then strew it thick over with green shot comfits, and stick on the top of it a sprig of myrtle, or any other pretty green sprig, then put your broken jelly round it, set sheep or swans upon your jelly, with either a green leaf, or a knot of apple paste under them, to keep the jelly from dissolving; there are sheep and swans made for that purpose, you may put in snakes, or any wild animals of the same fort.

To make a ROCKY ISLAND.

MAKE a little stiff flummery, and put it into five fish moulds, wet them before you put it in, when it is stiff, turn it out, and gild them with gold leaf, then take a deep China dish, fill it near full of clear calf's foot jelly, and let it stand till it is set, then lay on your fishes, and a few slices of red currant jelly cut very thin round them, then rasp a small French roll, and rub it over with the white of an egg, and strew all over it silver bran and glitter mixed together, stick a sprig of myrtle in it, and put it into the middle of your dish, beat the white of an egg to a very high froth, then hang it on your sprig of myrtle like snow, and fill your dish to the brim with clear jelly; when you send it to table, put lambs and ducks upon your jelly, with either green leaves or moss under them, with their heads towards the myrtle.

To make MOONSHINE.

TAKE the shapes of half a moon, and five or seven stars, wet them, and fill them with flummery, let them stand till they are cold, then turn them into a deep China dish, and pour lemon cream round them, made thus: Take a pint of spring water, put to it the juice of three lemons, and the yellow rind of one lemon, the whites of five eggs well beaten, and four ounces of loaf sugar, then set it over a slow fire, and stir it one way till it looks white and thick, if you let it boil it will curdle, then strain it through a hair sieve, and let it stand till it is cold, beat the yolks of five eggs, mix them with your whites, set them over the fire, and keep stirring it till it is almost ready to boil, then pour it into a bason ; when it is cold pour it among your moon and stars: garnish with flowers. — It is a proper dish for a second course, either for dinner or supper.

To make MOON and STARS in JELLY.

TAKE a deep China dish, turn the mould of a half moon, and seven' stars, with the bottom side upward in the dish, lay a weight upon every mould to keep them down, then make some flummery, and fill your dish with it; when it is cold and stiff, take your moulds carefully out, and fill the vacancy with clear calf's foot jelly; you may colour your flummery with cochineal and chocolate to make it look like the sky, and your moon and stars will show more clear: garnish with rock candy sweet meats. — It is a pretty corner dish, or a proper decoration for a grand table.

To make EGGS *and* BACON *in* FLUMMERY.

TAKE a pint of stiff flummery, and make part of it a pretty pink colour with the colouring for the flummery, dip a potting-pot in cold water, and pour in red flummery the thickness of a crown piece, then the same of white flummery, and another of red, and twice the thickness of white flummery at the top; one layer must be stiff and cold before you pour on another, then take five tea-cups, and put a large spoonful of white flummery into each tea-cup, and let them stand all night, then turn your flummery out of your potting pots on the back of a plate, with cold water, cut your flummery into thin slices; and lay it on a China dish, then turn your flummery out of the cups on the dish, and take a bit out of the top of every one, and lay in half a preserved apricot; it will confine the syrup from discolouring the flummery, and make it like the yolk of a poached egg; garnish with flowers. — It is a pretty corner dish for dinner, or side for supper.

SOLOMON'S TEMPLE *in* FLUMMERY.

MAKE a quart of stiff flummery, divide it it into three parts, make one part a pretty thick colour, with a little cochineal bruised fine, and steeped in French brandy, scrape one ounce of chocolate very fine, dissolve it in a little strong coffee, and mix it with another part of your flummery, to make it a light stone colour, the last part must be white, then whet your temple mould, and fix it in a pot to stand even, then fill the top of the temple with red flummery for the steps, and the four points with white, then fill it up with chocolate flummery ; let it stand till the next day, then loosen it round with a pin, and shake it loose very gently, but do not dip your mould in warm water, it will take off the gloss, and spoil the colour when you turn it out stick a small sprig or a flower stalk, down from the top of every point, it will strengthen them, and make it look pretty, lay round it rock candy sweet-meats. — It is proper for a corner dish for a large table.

To make OATMEAL FLUMMERY.

TAKE a pint of bruised groats, and put three pints of fair water to them early in the morning, and let it stand till noon, then pour all the water off, and put in the same quantity of water as before upon them, stir it well, and let it stand till four o'clock, then run it through a sieve or cloth, then boil it, and keep stirring it all the while, put in a spoonful of water now and then as it boils, when it begins to thicken drop a little on a plate; when it leaves the plate it is enough : put it in glasses to turn out.

To make CRIBBAGE CARDS *in* FLUMMERY.

FILL five square tins the size of a card with very Riff flummery, when you turn them out have ready a little cochineal dissolved in brandy, and strain it through a muslin rag, then take a camel's hair pencil, and make hearts and diamonds with your cochineal, then rub a little cochineal with a little eating oil upon a marble flab till it is very fine and bright, then make clubs and spades; pour a little Lisbon wine into the dish, and send it up.

To make a DISH *of* SNOW.

TAKE twelve large apples, put them in cold water, and set them over a very slow fire, and when they are soft pour them upon a hair sieve, take off the skin, and put the pulp into a bason, then beat the whites of twelve eggs into a very strong froth, beat and sift half a pound of double refined sugar, and strew it into the eggs, beat the pulp of your apples to a strong froth, then beat them all together till they are like a stiff snow, then lay it upon a China dish, and heap it up as high as you can, and set round it green knots of paste in imitation of Chinese rails, stick a sprig of myrtle in the middle of the dish, and serve it up.— It is a pretty corner dish for a large table.

To make BLACK CAPS.

TAKE six large apples, and cut a slice off the blossom end, put them in a tin, and set them in a quick oven till they are brown, then wet them with rose water, and grate a little sugar over them, and set them in the oven again till they look bright, and very black, then take them out, and put them into a deep China dish or plate, and pour round them thick cream custard, or white wine and sugar.

To make GREEN CAPS.

TAKE codlings just before they are ripe, green them as you would for preserving, then rub them over with a little oiled butter, grate double refined sugar over them, and set them in the oven till they look bright, and sparkle like frost, then take them out, and put them into a deep China dish, make a very fine custard, and pour it round them; stick single flowers in every apple and serve them up. — It is a pretty corner dish for either dinner or supper.

To stew PEARS.

PARE the largest stewing pears, and stick a clove in the bottom end, then put them in a well tinned saucepan, with a new pewter spoon in the middle, fill it with hard water, and set it over a slow fire for three or four hours, till your pears are soft, and the water reduced to a small quantity, then put in as much loaf sugar as will make it a thick syrup, and give the pears a boil in it, then cut some lemon peel like straws and hang them about your pears, and serve them up with the syrup in a deep dish.

To make LEMON SYLLABUBS.

TO a pint of cream put a pound of double refined sugar, the juice of seven lemons, grate the rinds of two lemons into a pint of white wine, and half a pint of sack, then put them all into a deep pot, and whisk them for half an hour, put it into glasses the night before you want it: it is better for standing two or three days, but it will keep a week if required.

To make LEMON SYLLABUBS *a second way*

PUT a pint of cream to a pint of white wine, then rub a quarter of a pound of loaf sugar upon the out rind of two lemons, till you have got out all the essence, then put the sugar to the cream, and squeeze in the juice of both lemons, let it stand for two hours, then mill them with a chocolate mill, to raise the froth, and take it off with a spoon as it rises, or it will make it heavy, lay it upon a hair sieve to drain, then fill your glasses with the remainder, and lay on the froth as high as you can, let them stand all night and they will be clear at the bottom ; send them to the table upon a salver, with jellies.

To make SOLID SYLLABUBS.

TAKE a quart of rich cream, and put in a pint of white wine, the juice of four lemons, and sugar to your taste, whip it up very well, and take off the froth as it rises, put it upon a hair sieve, and let it stand till the next day in a cool place, fill your glasses better than half full with the thin, then put on the froth, and heap it as high as you can; the bottom will look clear, and keep several days.

To make WHIP SYLLABUBS.

TAKE a pint of thin cream, rub a lump of loaf sugar on the outside of the lemon, and sweeten it to your taste, then put in the juice of a lemon, and a glass of Madeira wine, or French brandy, mill it to a froth with a chocolate mill, and take it off as it rises, and lay it upon a hair sieve, then fill one half of your posset glasses a little more than half full with white wine, and the other half of your glasses a little more than half full of red wine, then lay on your froth as high as you can, but observe that it is well drained on your sieve, or it will mix with your wine, and spoil your syllabubs.

To make a SYLLABUB under the COW.

PUT a bottle of strong beer and a pint of cyder into a punch-bowl, grate in a small nut meg, and sweeten it to your taste; then milk as much milk from the cow as will make a strong froth, and the ale look clear, let it stand an hour, then strew over it a few currants, well washed, picked, and plumped before the fire, then send it to the table.

CHAP. VIII

Observations on PRESERVING

WHEN you make any kind of jelly, take care you don't let any of the seeds from the fruit fall into your jelly, nor squeeze it too near, for that will prevent your jelly from being so clear; pound your sugar, and let it dissolve in the syrup before you set it on the fire, it makes the scum rise well, and the jelly a better colour: It is a great fault to boil any kind of jellies too high, it makes them a dark colour; you must never keep green sweetmeats in the first syrup longer than the receipt directs, lest you spoil their colour; you must take the same care with the oranges and lemons, as to cherries, damsons, and most sorts of stone fruit, put over them either mutton suet rendered, or a board to keep them down, or they will rise out of the syrup and spoil the whole jar, by giving them a sour bad taste; observe to keep all wet sweetmeats in a dry cool place, for a wet damp place will make them mould, and a hot place will dry up the virtue, and make them candy; the best direction I can give, is to dip writing paper in brandy, and lay it close to your sweetmeats, tie them well down with white paper, and two fold of thick cap paper to keep out the air, for nothing can be a greater fault than bad tieing down, and leaving the pots open.

To make ORANGE JELLY.

TAKE half a pound of hartshorn shavings, and two quarts of spring water, let it boil till it be reduced to a quart, pour it clear off, let it stand till it is cold, then take half a pint of spring water, and the rind of three oranges pared very thin, and the juice of six, let them stand all night, strain them through a fine hair sieve, melt the jelly and pour the orange liquor to it, sweeten it to your taste with double refined sugar, put to it a blade or two of mace, four or five cloves, half a small nutmeg, and the rind of a lemon, beat the whites of five eggs to a froth, mix it well with your jelly, set it over a clear fire, boil it three or four minutes, run it through your jelly bags several times till it is clear, and when you pour it into your bag, take great care you do not shake it.

To make HARTSHORN JELLY.

PUT two quarts of water into a clean pan, with half a pound of hartshorn shavings, let it simmer till near one half is reduced, strain it off, then put in the peel of four oranges, and two lemons pared very thin, boil them five minutes, put to it the juice of the before-mentioned lemons and oranges, with about ten ounces of double refined sugar, beat the whites of six eggs to a froth, mix them carefully with your jelly, that you do not poach the eggs, just let it boil up, and run it through a jelly bag till it is clear.

To make RED CURRANT JELLY.

GATHER your currants when they are dry and full ripe, strip them off the stalks, put them , in a large stew-pot, tie the paper over them, and let them stand an hour in a cool oven, strain them through a cloth, and to every quart of juice add a pound and a half of loaf sugar, broken in small lumps, stir it gently over a clear fire till your sugar is melted, skim it well, let it boil pretty quick twenty minutes, pour it hot into your pots; if you let it stand it will break the jelly, it will not set so well as when it is hot ; put brandy papers over them, and keep them in a dry place for use. N. B. You may make jelly of half red and half white currants the same way.

To make BLACK CURRANT JELLY.

GET your currants when they are ripe and dry, pick them off the stalks, and put them in a large stew-pot; to every ten quarts of currants put a quart of water, tie a paper over them, and set them in a cool oven for two hours, then squeeze them through a very thin cloth ; to every quart of juice add a pound and a half of loaf sugar broken in small pieces, stir it gently till the sugar is melted; when it boils skim it well, let it boil pretty quick for half an hour over a clear fire, then pour it into pots; put brandy papers over them, and keep them for use.

To make APRICOT JAM

PARE the ripest apricots you can get, cut them thin, infuse them in an earthen pan till they are tender and dry ; then to every pound and a half of apricots put a pound of double refined sugar, and three spoonfuls of water; boil your sugar to a candy height then put it upon your apricots, stir them over a flow fire till they look clear and thick, but do not let them boil, only simmer; put them in glasses for use.

To make RED RASPBERRY JAM

GATHER your raspberries when they are ripe and dry, pick them very carefully from the stalks and dead ones, crush them in a bowl with a silver or wooden spoon, pewter is apt to turn them a purple colour ; as soon as you have crushed them, strew in their own weight of loaf sugar, and half their weight of currant juice, baked and strained as for jelly, then set them over a clear flow fire, boil them half an hour, skim them well, and keep stirring them at the time, then put them into pots or glasses with brandy papers over them and keep them for use. — N. B. As soon as you have got your berries, strew in your sugar, do not let them stand long before you boil them; it will preserve their flavour.

To make WHITE RASPBERRY JAM.

GET your raspberries dry and full ripe, crush them fine, and strew in their own weight of loaf sugar, and half their weight of the juice of white currants, boil them half an hour over a clear slow fire, skim them well, and put them into pots or glasses, tie them down with brandy papers, and keep them dry for use. — N. B. Strew in your sugar as in the red raspberry jam.

To make RED STRAWBERRY JAM,

GATHER the scarlet strawberries very ripe, bruise them very fine, and put to them a little juice of strawberries, beat and lift their weight in sugar, strew it among them, and put them in the preserving pan, set them over a clear slow fire, skim them, and boil them twenty minutes, then put them in pots or glasses for use.

To make GREEN GOOSEBERRY JAM.-

TAKE the green walnut gooseberries when they are full grown, but not ripe, cut them in two and pick out the seeds, then put them in a pan of water, green them as you do the gooseberries, in imitation of hops, and lay them on a sieve to drain, then beat them in a marble mortar, with their weight in sugar, then take a quart of gooseberries, boil them to mash in a quart of water, then squeeze them, and to every pint of liquor put a pound of fine loaf sugar, boil and skim it, then put in you green gooseberries, boil them till they are very thick, clear, and a pretty green, then put them in glasses for use.

To make BLACK CURRANT JAM.

GET your black currants when they are full ripe, pick them clear from the stalks, and bruise them in a bowl with a wooden mallet, to every two pounds of currants put a pound and a half of loaf sugar beat fine, put them into a preserving pan, boil them full half an hour, skim it and stir it all the time, then put it in the pots, and keep it for use.

To preserve RED CURRANTS in Bunches.

STONE your currants, and tie six or seven bunches together with a thread to a piece of split deal, about the length of your finger, weigh the currants, and put their weight of double refined sugar in your preserving pan, with a little water, and boil it till the sugar flies, then put the currants in, and just give them a boil up, and cover them till next day, then take them out, and either dry them or put them in glasses, with the syrup boiled up with a little of the juice of red currants; put brandy paper over them and tie them close down with another paper, and set them in a dry place.

To preserve WHITE CURRANTS in Bunches.

STONE your currants, and tie them in bunches as before, and put them in the preserving- pan with their weight of double refined sugar, beat and sifted fine, let them stand all night, then take some pippens, pare, core, and boil them, but do not stir the apples, only press them down with the back of your spoon, when the water is strong of the apple, add to it the juice' of a lemon, strain it through a jelly bag till it runs quite clear, to every pint of your liquor put a pound of double refined sugar, boil it up to a strong jelly, put it to your currants, and boil them till they look clear, cover them in the preserving-pan with paper till they are almost cold, then put a bunch of currants in your glasses, and fill it up with jelly ; when they are cold, Wet papers in brandy, and lay over them, tie another on, and set them in a dry place.

To preserve CURRANTS for TARTS.

GET your currants when they are dry, and pick them; to every pound and a quarter of currants, put a pound of sugar into a preserving-pan, with as much juice of currants as will dissolve it, when it boils skim it, and put in your currants, and boil them till they are clear; put them into a jar, lay brandy paper over, tie them down, and keep them in a dry place.

To preserve CUCUMBERS.

TAKE small cucumbers and large ones that will cut into quarters, the greenest and most free from seeds you can get, put them in a strong salt and water, in a strait mouth jar, with a cabbage leaf to keep them down, tie a paper over them, set them in a warm place till they are yellow, wash them out, and set them over the fire in fresh water, with a little salt in, and a fresh cabbage leaf over them, cover the pan very Close, but take care they do not boil ; if they are not it fine green, change your water (and it will help them) and make them hot, and cover them as before ; when they are a good green, take them off the fire, let them stand till they are cold, then cut the large ones in (quarters, take out the seeds and soft part, then put. them in cold water, and let them stand two days but change the water twice each day to take out the salt, take a pound of single refined sugar, and half a pint of water, set it over the fire ; when you have skimmed it clear, put in the rind of a lemon, one ounce of ginger, with the outside scraped off : when your syrup is pretty thick, take it off, and when it is cold, wipe the cu cumbers dry, and put them in, boil the syrup once in two or three days for three weeks, and strengthen the syrup, if required, for the greatest danger of spoiling them is at first The syrup is to be quite cold when you put it to your cucumbers.

To preserve GRAPES in BRANDY.

TAKE some close bunches of grapes, but not too ripe, either red or white, put them into ajar, with a quarter of a pound of sugar-candy, and fill the jar with common brandy, tie it close with a bladder, and set them in a dry place. Morello cherries are done the same way.

To preserve KENTISH or GOLDEN PIPPINS,

BOIL the rind of an orange very tender, then lay it in water for two or three days, take a quart of golden pippins, pare, core, quarter, and boil them to a strong jelly, and run it through a jelly bag, then take twelve pippins, pare them and scrape out the cores; put two pounds of loaf sugar into a slew-pan with near a pint of water, when it boils skim it, and put in your pippins, with the orange rind in thin slices, let them boil fast till the sugar is very thick and will almost candy, then put in a pint of the pippin jelly, boil them fast till the jelly is clear, then squeeze in the juice of a lemon, give it one boil, and put them into pots or glasses with the orange peel.

To preserve GREEN CODLINGS that will keep all the Year.

TAKE codlings about the size of a walnut, with the stalks and a leaf or two on, put a handful of vine leaves into a brass pan of spring water, then a lay of codlings, then vine leaves, do so till the pan is full, cover it close, that no steam can get out, set it on a slow fire; when they are soft take off the skins with a penknife, then put them in the same water with the vine leaves; it must be quite cold or it will be apt to crack them, put a little roach allum, and let them over a very slow fire till they are green (which will be in three or four hours) then take them out and lay them on a sieve to drain.— Make a good syrup, and give them a gentle boil once a day for three days, then put them in small jars; put brandy paper over them, and keep them for use,

To preserve GREEN APRICOTS.

GATHER your apricots before the stones are hard, put them into a pan of hard water, with plenty of vine leaves, set them over a slow fire till they are quite yellow, then take them out and rub them with a flannel and salt to take off the lint, put them into the pan to the same water and leaves, cover them close, set them a great distance from the fire till they are a fine light green, then take them carefully up pick out all the bad coloured and broken ones, boil the best gently for two or three times in a thin syrup, let them be quite cold every times when they look plump and clear, make a syrup of double refined sugar, but not too thick, give your apricots a gentle boil in it, then put them into pots or glasses, dip paper in brandy, lay it over them, and keep them for use, then take all the broken and bad coloured ones and boil them in the first syrup for tarts.

To preserve GOOSEBERRIES *green*.

TAKE green walnut gooseberries when they are full grown, and take out the seeds, put them in cold water, cover them close with vine leaves, and set them over a slow fire; when they are hot take them off, and let them stand, and when they are cold set them on again till they are pretty green, then put them on a sieve to drain, and have ready a syrup made of a pound of double refined sugar, and half a pint of spring water; the syrup is to be cold when the gooseberries are put in, and boil them till they are clear, then set them by for a day or two, then give them two or three scalds, and then put them into pots, or glasses for use.

To preserve GREEN GOOSEBERRIES *in Imitation of* HOPS.

TAKE the largest green walnut gooseberries you can get, cut them at the stalk end in four quarters, leave them whole at the blossom end, then take out all the seeds, and put five or six one in another, take a needleful of strong thread, with a large knot at the end, run the needle through the bunch of gooseberries, and tie a knot to fasten them together (they resemble hops) and put cold spring water in your pan, a large handful of vine haves in the bottom, and three or four lays of gooseberries, with plenty of vine leaves between every lay, and over the top of your pan, cover it so that no steam can get out, and set them on a flow fire; when they are scalding hot take them off, and let them stand till they are cold, then let them on again till they are a good green, then take them off and let them stand till they are quite cold, then put them in a sieve to drain, make a thin syrup; to every pint of water put in a pint of common loaf sugar, boil it and skim it well: when it is about half cold, put in your gooseberries, and let them stand till the next day, then give them one boil a day for three days, then make a syrup, to every pint of water, put in a pound of fine sugar, a slice of ginger, and a little lemon peel cut length, ways exceeding fine, boil and skim-it well, give your gooseberries, a boil in it; when they are cold put them into glasses or pots, lay papers dipped in brandy over them, tie them up, and keep them for use.

To preserve SPRIGS *green.*

GATHER the sprigs of mustard when it is going to seed, put them in a pan of spring Water, with a great many vine leaves under and over them, put to them one ounce of roach allum, set it over a gentle fire, when it is hot, take it off, and let it stand till it is quite cold, then cover it very close, and hang it a great height over a slow fires when they are green, take out the sprigs, and lay them on a sieve to drain, then make a good syrup, boil your sprigs in it once a day for three days, put them in, and keep them for use. — They are very pretty to stick in the middle of a preserved orange, or garnish a set of servers. — You may preserve young peas when they are just come into pod the same way.

To preserve GREEN GAGE PLUMS.

TAKE the finest plums you can get just before they are ripe, put them in a pan with a lay of vine leaves at the bottom of your pan, then a lay of plums, do so till your pan is almost full, then fill it with water, set them on a slow fire; when they are hot, and their skins begin to rise, take them off, and take the skins carefully off, put them on a sieve as you do them, then lay them in the same water, with a lay of leaves betwixt, as you did at the first, cover them very close so that no steam can get out, and hang them a great distance from the fire till they are green, which will be five or six hours at least, then take them carefully up, lay them on a hair sieve to drain, make a good syrup, give them a gentle boil in it twice a day, for two days, take them out and put them into a fine clear syrup; put paper dipped in brandy over them, and keep them for use.

To preserve WALNUTS black.

TAKE the small kind of walnuts, put them in fait and water, change the water every day for nine days, then put them into a sieve, let them stand in the air until they begin to turn black, then put them into a jug, and pour boiling water over them, and let them stand till the next day, then put them in a sieve to drain, stick a clove into each end of your walnut, put them into a pan of boiling water, let them boil five minutes, then take them up; make a thin syrup, scald them in it three or four times a day till your walnuts are black and bright, then make a thick syrup with a few cloves and a little ginger cut in slices, skim it well, put in your walnuts, boil them five or six minutes, and then put them in your jar; wet your paper with brandy, lay it over them, and tie them down with bladders. The first year they are a little bitter, but the second year they will be very good.

To preserve WALNUTS *green.*

TAKE large French walnuts when they are a little larger than a good nutmeg, wrap every walnut in vine leaves, tie it round with a string, then put them into a large quantity of salt and water, let them lie in it for three days, then put them in fresh, salt and water, and let them lie in that for three days longer, then take them out, and lay a large quantity of vine leaves in the bottom of your pan, then a lay of walnuts, then vine leaves, do so till your pan is full, but take great care the walnuts do not touch one another; fill your pan with hard water, with a little bit of roach allum, set it over the fire till, the water is very hot, but do not let it boil, take it off, let them stand in the water till it is quite cold, then set them over the fire again ; when they are green take the pan off the fire, and when the water is quite cold take out the walnuts, lay them on a sieve a good distance from each other, have ready a thin syrup boiled and skimmed; when it is pretty cool put in your walnuts, let them stand all night, the next day give them several scalds, but do not let them boil, keep your preserving pan close covered, and when you see that they look bright, and a pretty colour, have ready made a rich syrup, of fine loaf sugar, with a few slices of ginger, and two or three blades of mace, scald your walnuts in it, put them in small jars, with paper dipped in brandy over them, tie them down with bladders, and keep them for use.

To preserve WALNUTS *white.*

TAKE the large French walnuts full grown, but not shelled, pare them till you see the white appear, put them in salt and water as you do them, have ready boiling a large saucepan full of soft water, boil them in it five minutes, take them up, and lay them betwixt two cloths till you have made a thin syrup, boil them gently in it for four or five minutes, then put them in a jar, stop them up close that no steam can get out, if it does it will spoil the colour, the next day boil them again, when they are cold, make a fresh thick syrup, with two or three slices of ginger and a blade of mace, boil and skim it well, then give your walnuts a. boil in it, and put them in glass jars, with papers dipped in brandy laid over them, and tie bladders over them to keep out the air.

To make ORANGE MARMALADE.

TAKE the clearest Seville oranges you can get, cut them in two, then takeout all the pulp and juice into a bason, pick all the seeds and skins out of it, boil the rinds in hard water till they are tender (change the water two or three times while they are boiling) then pound them in a marble mortar, add to it the juice and pulp, and put them in the preserving pan, with double its weight of loaf sugar, set it over a flow fire, boil it a little more than half an hour, then put it into pots with brandy papers over them.

To make TRANSPARENT MARMALADE.

TAKE very pale Seville oranges, cut them in quarters, take out the pulp, and put it into a bason, pick the skins and seeds out, put the peels in a little salt and water, let them stand all night, then boil them in a good quantity of spring water till they are tender, then cut them in very thin slices, and put them to the pulp; to every pound of marmalade put a pound and a half of double refined sugar beaten fine, boil them together gently for twenty minutes; if it is not clear and transparent, boil it five or six minutes longer, keep stirring it gently all the time, and take care you do not break the slices ; when it is cold, put it into jelly or sweetmeat glasses, tie them down with brandy papers over them..-- They are pretty for a desert of any kind.

To make QUINCE MARMALADE.

GET your quinces when they are full ripe, pare them and cut them into quarters, then take out the core, and put them into a saucepan that is well tinned, cover them with the parings, fill the saucepan near full of spring water, cover it close, and let them stew over a slow fire till they are soft, and of a pink colour, then pick out all your quinces from the parings, beat them to a pulp in a marble mortar, take their weight of fine loaf sugar, put as much water to it as will dissolve it, boil and skim it well, then put in your quinces and boil them gently three quarters. of an hour, keep stirring it all the time, or it will stick to the pan and burn ; when it is cold put it into flat sweetmeat pots, and tie it down with brandy paper.

To make APRICOT MARMALADE.

WHEN you preserve your apricots, pick out all the bad ones, and those that are too ripe for keeping, boil them in the syrup till they will math, then beat them in a marble mortar to a paste; take half their weight of loaf sugar, and put as much water to it as will dissolve it, boil and skim it well, boil them till they look clear, and the syrup thick like a fine jelly, then put it into your sweetmeat glasses, and keep them for use.

To preserve GREEN PINE APPLES.

GET your pineapples before they are ripe, and lay them in strong salt and water five days, then put a large handful of vine leaves in the bottom of a large saucepan, and put in your pine apples, fill your pan with vine leaves, then pour on the salt and water it was laid in, cover it up very close, and set it over a flow fire, let it stand till it is a fine light green, have ready a thin syrup, made of a quart of water and a pound of double refined sugar; when it is almost cold put it into a deep jar, and put in the pineapple with the top on, let it stand a week, and take care that it is well covered with the syrup, then boil your syrup again, and pour it carefully into your jar, lest you break the top of your pine apple, and let it stand eight or ten weeks, and give the syrup two or three boils to keep it from moulding, let your syrup stand till it is near cold, before you pour it on; when your pine apple looks quite full and green, take it out of the syrup, and make a thick syrup of three pounds of double refined sugar, with as much water as will dissolve it, boil and skim it well, put a few slices of white ginger in it; when it is near cold pour it upon your pine apple, tie it down with a bladder, and the pine apple will keep many years, and not shrink, but if you put it into thick syrup at the first, it will shrink, for the strength of the syrup draws out the juice and spoils it. N. B. It is a great fault to put any kind of fruit that is preserved whole into thick syrup at first.

To preserve RED GOOSEBERRIES.

TO every quart of rough red gooseberries, put a pound of loaf sugar, put your sugar into a preserving pan with as much water as will dissolve it, boil and skim it well, then put in your gooseberries, let them boil a little, and set them by till the next day, then boil them till they look clear, and the syrup thick, then put them into pots or glasses, cover them with brandy papers, and keep them for use.

To preserve STRAWBERRIES *whole.*

GET the finest scarlet strawberries with their stalks on, before they are too ripe, then lay them separately oh a china dish, beat and sift twice their weight of double refined sugar, and strew it over them, then take a few ripe scarlet straw berries, crush them, and put them into a jar, With their weight of double refined sugar beat small, cover them close, and let them stand in a kettle of boiling water till they are soft, and the syrup is come out of them, then strain them through a muslin rag into a tossing pan, boil and skim it well, when it is cold put in your whole strawberries, and set them over the fire till they are milk warm, then take them off, and let them stand till they are quite cold, then set them on again, and make them a little hotter, do so several times till they look clear, but do not let them boil, it will fetch the stalks off, when the strawberries are cold, put them into jelly glasses, with the stalks downwards, and fill up your glasses with the syrup; tie them down with brandy papers over them. — They are very pretty amongst jellies and creams, and proper for set ting out a defect of any kind.

To preserve WHITE RASPBERRIES *whole.*

GET your raspberries when they are turning white, with the stalks on about an inch long, lay them single on a dish, beat and sift their weight of double refined sugar, strew it over them, to every quart of raspberries take a quart of white currant juice, put to it its weight of double refined sugar, boil and slum it well, then put in your raspberries and give them a scald, take them off and let them stand for two hours, then set them on again and make them a little hotter, do so for two or three times, till they look clear, but do not let them boil, it will make the stalks come off ; when they are pretty cool, put them into jelly glasses with the stalks down, and keep them for use. — N. B. You may preserve red raspberries the same way, only take red currant juice instead of white.

To preserve MORELLO CHERRIES.

GET- your cherries when they are full ripe, take out the stalks and prick them with a pin; to every two pounds of cherries put a pound and a half of loaf sugar, beat part of your sugar and strew it over them; let them stand all night, dissolve the rest of your sugar in half a pint of the juice of currants, set it over a flow fire, and put in the cherries with the sugar, and give them a gentle scald, let them stand all night again, and give them another scald, then take them care fully out, and boil your syrup till it is thick, then pour it upon your cherries, if you find it be too thin boil it again.

To preserve BARBERRIES in Bunches.

TAKE the female barberries, pick out all the largest bunches, then pick the rest from the stalks, put them in as much water as will make a syrup of your bunches, boil them till they are soft, then strain them through a sieve; to every pint of the juice put a pound and a half of loaf sugar, boil and skim it well, and to every pint of syrup put half a pound of barberries in bunches, boil them till they look very fine and clear, then put them carefully into pots and glasses ; tie brandy papers over, and keep them for use.

To preserve BARBERRIES for TARTS.

PICK the female barberries clean from the stalks, then take their weight in loaf sugar, put them in a jar and set them in a kettle of boiling water till the sugar is melted, and the barberries quite soft, the next day put them in a preserving pan, and boil them fifteen minutes, then put them in jars, and keep them in a dry cool place.

To preserve DAMSONS.

TAKE the small long damsons, pick off the stalks, and prick them with a pin, then put them into a deep pot, with half their weight of loaf sugar pounded, set them in a moderate oven till they are soft, then take them off, and give the syrup a boil, and pour it upon them, do so two or three times, then take them care fully out, and put them into the jars you intend to keep them in, and pour over them rendered mutton suet; tie a bladder over them and keep them for use in a very cool place.

To preserve MAGNUM BONUM PLUMS.

TAKE the large yellow plums, put them in a pan full of spring water, set them over a slow fire, keep putting them down with a spoon till you find the skin will come off, then take them up and peel the skin off with a penknife, put them in a fine thin syrup and give them a gentle boil, then take them off, and turn them pretty often. in the syrup, or the outside will turn brown ; when they are quite cold, set them over the fire again, let them boil five or six minutes, then take them off and turn them very often in the syrup till they are near cold, then take them out and lay them separately on a flat china dish, strain the syrup through a muslin rag, add to it the weight of the plums of fine loaf sugar, boil and skim it very well, then put in your plums, boil them till they look clear, then put them carefully into jars or glasses, cover them well with the syrup, or they will loose their colour, put brandy papers and a bladder over them.

To preserve WINE SOURS.

TAKE the finest wine sours you can get, pick off the stalks, run down the seam with a pin only skin deep, then take half their weight of loaf sugar pounded, and lay it betwixt your plums in layers till your jar is full, set them in a kettle of boiling water till they are soft, then drain the syrup from them, and give it a boil, and pour it on them, do so for several times, till you see the skin look hard and the plums clear, let them stand a week, then take them out one by one, and put them into glasses, jars, or pots, give your syrup a boil, if you have not syrup enough, boil a little clarified sugar with your syrup and fill up your glasses, jars, or pots, with it, and put brandy papers over, and tie a bladder over them to keep out the air, or they will lose: their colour and grow a purple.- They are pretty with either steeple cream, any kind of flummeries, or under a silver web.

To preserve APRICOTS,

PARE your apricots, and thrust out the stones with a skewer, to every pound of apricots put a pound of loaf sugar, strew part of it over them, and let them stand till the next day, then give them a gentle boil three or four different times, let them go cold betwixt every time; take them out of the syrup one by one, the last time as you boil them, skim your syrup well, boil it till it looks thick and clear, then pour it over your apricots, and put brandy papers over them,

To preserve PEACHES.

GET the largest peaches before they are too ripe, rub off the lint with a cloth, then run them down the seam with a pin, skin deep, cover them with French brandy, tie a bladder over them, and let them stand a week, then take them out, and make a strong syrup for them, boil and skim it well, put in your peaches, and boil them till they look clear, then take them out, and put them into pots or glasses; mix the syrup with the brandy, when it is cold pour it on your peaches; tie them close down with a bladder that the air cannot get in, or the peaches will turn black,

To preserve QUINCES *whole*.

PARE your quinces very thin and round, that they may look like a screw, then put them into a well tinned saucepan, with a new pewter spoon in the middle of them, and fill your sauce pan with hard water, and lay the parings over your quinces, to keep them down; cover your saucepan so close that the steam cannot get out; set them over a slow fire till they are soft, and a fine pink colour, let them stand till they are cold, and make a good syrup of double refined sugar, boil and skim it well, then put in your quinces, let them boil ten minutes, take them off, and let them stand two or three hours, then boil them till the syrup looks thick, and the quinces clear, then put them into deep jars, with brandy papers and leather over them; keep them in a dry place for use. -N. B. You may preserve quinces in quarters the same way.

To preserve ORANGES *carved.*

TAKE the fairest Seville oranges you can get, cut the rinds with a penknife in what form you please, draw out the part of your peel as you cut them, and put them into salt and hard water, let them stand for three days to take out the bitter, then boil them an hour in a large saucepan of fresh water, with salt in it, but do not cover them, it will spoil the colour, then, take them out of the salt and water, and boil them ten minutes in a thin syrup for four or five days together, then put them into a deep jar, let them stand two months, and then make a thick syrup, and just give them a boil in it, let them stand till the next day, then put them in your jar, with brandy papers over; tie them down with a bladder, and keep them for use. N. B. You may preserve whole oranges with out carving the lame way, only do not let them boil so long, and keep them in a very thin syrup at first, or it will make them shrink and weather. — Always observe to put salt in the water for either oranges preserved, or any kind of orange chips.

To preserve ORANGES *in* JELLY.

TAKE Seville oranges, and cut a hole out at the stalk as large as a sixpence, and scoop out the pulp quite clean, tie them separately in muslin, and lay them in spring water for two days, change the water twice a day, then boil them in the muffin till tender upon a slow fire, as the water wasteth put hot water into the pan, and keep them covered, weigh the oranges before you scoop them, and to every pound put two pounds of double refined sugar, and one pint of water, boil the sugar and water with the juice of the oranges to a syrup, skim it very well, let it stand till cold, then put in the oranges and boil them half an hour, if they are not quite clear, boil them once a day for two or three days, pare and core some green pippins, and boil them till the water is strong of the apple, but do not stir the apples, only put them down in the water, with the back of a spoon, strain the water through a jelly bag till quite clear, then to every pint of water, put one pound of double refined sugar, and the juice of a lemon strained fine, boil it up to a strong jelly, drain the oranges out of the syrup, put them into glass jars, or pots of the size of an orange, with the holes upward, and pour the jelly over them, cover them with brandy papers, and tie them close down with bladders. — N. B. You may do lemons the same way.

To preserve LEMONS

CARVE or pare your lemons very thin, and make a round hole on the top the size of a shilling, takeout all the pulp and stains, rub them with salt, and put them in spring water as you do them, to prevent them from turning black, let them lie in for five or six days, then boil them in fresh salt and water fifteen minutes, have ready made a thin syrup of a quart of water, and a pound of loaf sugar, boil them in it five minutes, once a day, for four or five days, then put them in a large jar, let them stand for six or eight weeks, and it will make them look clear and plump, then take them out of that syrup, or they will mould; make a syrup of fine sugar, put as much water to it as will dissolve it, boil and skim it, then put in your lemons, and boil them gently till they are clear, then put them into a jar with brandy papers over; tie them close down, and keep them in a dry place for use.

To preserve ORANGES with MARMALADE.

PARE your oranges as thin as you can, then cut a hole in the stalk end, the size of a sixpence, take out all the pulp, then put your oranges in salt and water, boil them a little more than an hour, but do not cover them, it will turn them a bad colour, have ready made a syrup of a pound of fine loaf sugar, with a pint of water, put in your oranges, boil them till they look clear, then pick out all the skins and pippins out of your pulp, and cut one of your oranges into it, as thin as possible, and take its weight of double refined sugar, boil it in a clean tossing- pan over a flow clear fire, till it looks quite clear and transparent, when it is cold take your oranges out and fill them with your marmalade, and put on your top, and put them in your syrup again, let them stand for two months, then make a syrup of double refined sugar, with as much water as will dissolve it, boil and skim it well, then give your oranges a boil in it; put brandy papers over, and tie them down with a ladder ; they will keep for several years.

To make BULLACE CHEESE.

TAKE your bullace when they are full ripe, put them into a pot, and to every quart of bullace put a quarter of a pound of loaf sugar beat small, bake them in a moderate oven till they . are soft, then rub them through a hair sieve; to every pound of pulp add half a pound of loaf sugar beat fine, then boil it an hour and a half over a slow fire, and keep stirring it all the time, then pour it into potting pots, and tie brandy papers over them, and keep them in a dry place; when it has stood a few months it will cut out very bright and fine. — N. B. You may make sloe cheese the same way.

To make ELDER ROB.

GATHER your elder berries when they are full ripe, pick them clean from the stalks, put them in large stew pots, and tie a paper over them, put them in a moderate oven, let them stand two hours, then take them out, and put them in a thin coarse cloth and squeeze out all the juice you can get, then put eight quarts into a well-tinned copper, set it over a flow fire, let it boil till it be reduced to one quart, when it grows near done, keep stirring it to prevent its burning to the bottom, then put it into potting pots, let if stand two or three days in the fun, then dip a paper in sweet oil the size of your pot, and lay it on, tie it down with a bladder, and keep it in a very dry place for use.

To make BLACK CURRANT ROB.

GET your currants when they are ripe, pick, bake, and squeeze them the same as you did the elderberries, then put six quarts of the juice into a large tossing pan, boil it over a flow fire, till it is pretty thick, keep stirring it till it is reduced to one quart, pour it into flat pots, dry it, and tie it down the same way as you did your elder rob.

To Stew PIPPINS whole.

PARE and core your pippins and throw them into fair water as you pare them, then take the weight of the fruit of double refined sugar, and dissolve it in a quart of water, then boil it up, and scum it clean, then put in the fruit, let them stew gently till they are tender, and look clear, then take them out and squeeze in the juice of a large lemon and let it boil up, scum it and run it through a jelly bag upon the fruit; you may stick the pippins with candied oranges and lemons cut in thin slices, if you please.

CHAP. IX

Directions for DRYING *and* CANDYING

Before you candy any sort of fruit, preserve them first, and dry them in a stove or before the fire, till the syrup is run out of them, then boil your sugar, candy height, dip in the fruit, and lay them in dishes in your stove till dry, then put them in boxes, and keep them in a dry place.

To make APRICOT PASTE

PARE and stone your apricots, boil them iii water till they will mash quite small, put a pound of double refined sugar in your preserving pan, with as much water as will dissolve it, and boil it to sugar again, take it off the stove, and put in a pound of apricots, let it, stand till the sugar is melted, then make it scalding hot, but do not let it boil, pour it into China dishes, or cups, set them in a stove, when they are stiff enough to turn out, put them on glass plates, turn them as you see occasion till they are dry.

To make RASPBERRY PASTE.

MASH a quart of raspberries, strain one half, and put the juice to the other half, boil them a quarter of an hour, put to them a pint of red currant juice, let them boil all together till your berries are enough, put a pound and a half of double refined sugar into a clean pan, with as much water as will dissolve it, and boil it to a sugar again, then put in your berries and juice, give them a scald, and pour it into glasses of plates, then put them into a stove to dry, and turn them as you see occasion.

To make GOOSEBERRY PASTE.

TAKE a pound of red gooseberries when they are full grown and turned, but not ripe, cut them in halves, pick out all the seeds, have ready a pint of currant juice, boil your gooseberries in it till they are tender, put a pound and a half of double refined sugar into your pan, with as much water as will dissolve it, and boil it to sugar again, then put all together and make it scalding hot, but it must not boil, pour it into plates or glasses, the thickness you like, then dry it in a stove.

To make CURRANT PASTE *either red or white,*

STRIP your currants, put a little juice to them to keep them from burning, boil them well and rub them through a hair sieve, then boil it a quarter of an hour: to a pint of juice put a pound and a half of double refined sugar, sifted, shake in your sugar, when it is melted, pour it on plates, dry it as the other pastes, and turn it into what form you please.

To make CURRANT CLEAR CAKE.

STRIP and wash your currants, to four quarts of currants put one quart of water, boil them very well, then run it through a jelly bag, to a pint of jelly put a pound and a half of double refined sugar, pounded and sifted through a hair sieve, set your jelly on the fire, when it has just boiled up, shake in the sugar, stir it well, then set it on the fire again, make it scalding hot to melt the sugar, but do not let it boil, then pour it on clear cake glasses or plates, when it is jellied, before it is candied, cut it in rounds or half rounds, this will not knot; and dry them the same way as you did the apricot paste. White currant clear cakes are made the same way, but observe that as soon as the jelly is made, you must put the sugar to it, or it will change the colour.

To make VIOLET CAKES.

TAKE the finest violets you can get, pick off the leaves, beat the violets fine in a mortar, with the juice of a lemon, beat and sift twice their weight of double refined sugar, put your sugar and violets into a silver sauce-pan, or tankard, set it over a flow fire, keep stirring it gently till all your sugar is dissolved, if you let it boil it will discolour your violets, drop them in china plates; when you take them off, put them in a box with paper betwixt every layer.

To dry CHERRIES.

TAKE Morello cherries, stone them, and to every pound of cherries put a pound and a quarter of fine sugar, beat and sift it over your cherries, let them stand all night, take them out of your sugar, and to every pound of sugar put two spoonfuls of water, boil and scum it well, then put in your cherries, let your sugar boil over them, the next morning strain them, and to every pound of the syrup put half a pound more sugar, let it boil a little thicker, then put in your cherries, and let them boil gently, the next day strain them, and dry them in a stove, and turn them every day.

A second way to dry CHERRIES.

STONE a pound and a half of cherries, put them in a preserving pan, with a little water, when they are scalding hot, put them in a sieve, or on a cloth to dry, then put them in your pan again, beat and sift half a pound of double refined sugar, strew it betwixt every lay of cherries, when it is melted set them on the fire, and make them scalding hot, let them stand till they are cold, do so twice more, then drain them from the syrup, and lay them separately to dry; dip them in cold water, and dry them with a cloth, set them in the hot sun to dry as before, and keep them in a dry place till you want to use them.

To dry GREEN GAGE PLUMS.

MAKE a thin syrup of half a pound of single refined sugar, skim it well, flit a pound of plums down the seam, and put them in the syrup, keep them scalding hot till they are tender, they must be well covered with syrup, or they will lose their colour, let them stand all night, then make a rich syrup ; to a pound of double refined sugar put two spoonfuls of water, skim it well, and boil it almost to a candy, when it is cold, drain your plums out of the first syrup, and put them in the thick syrup, be sure let the syrup cover them, set them on the fire to scald till they look clear, then put them in a china bowl, when they have stood a week take them out, and lay them on china dishes, dry them in a stove, and turn them once a day till they are dry. — If you would have them green, scald them with vine leaves, the same way as the green gages are done.

To make APRICOT CAKES.

TAKE a pound of nice ripe apricots, scald them, and as soon as you find the stuff will come off, peel them and take out the stones, beat them in a marble mortar to a pulp, boil half a pound of double refined sugar, with a spoonful of water, skim it exceeding well, then put in the pulp of your apricots, let them simmer a quarter of an hour over a slow fire, stir it softly all the time, then pour it into shallow flat glasses, turn them out upon glass plates, put them in a stove, and turn them once a day till they are dry.

To burn ALMONDS.

TAKE two pounds of loaf sugar, two pounds of almonds, put them in a stew-pan with a pint of water, set them over a clear coal fire, let them boil till you hear the almonds crack, take them off and stir them about till they are quite dry, then put them in a wine sieve and sift all the sugar from them, put the sugar into the pan again with a little water, give it a boil, put four spoonfuls of scraped cochineal to the sugar to colour it, put the almonds into the pan, keep stirring them over the fire till they are quite dry, put them into a glass and they will keep twelve months.

To dry DAMSONS.

GET your damsons when they are full ripe, spread them on a coarse cloth, set them in a very cool oven, let them stand a day or two; if they are not as dry as a fresh prune, put them in an other cool oven for a day or two longer, till they are pretty dry, then take them out, and lay them in a dry place, they will eat like fresh plums in the winter.

To candy GINGER.

BEAT two pounds of fine loaf sugar, put one pound in a tossing pan, with as much water as will dissolve it, with one ounce of race ginger grated fine, stir them well together over a very slow fire till the sugar begins to boil, then stir in the other pounds and keep stirring it till it grows thick, then take it off the fire, and drop it in cakes upon earthen dishes, set them in a warm place to dry, and they will look white, and be very hard and brittle.

To make ORANGE CHIPS.

TAKE the best Seville oranges, pare them aslant, a quarter of an inch broad, if you can keep the paring whole it looks much prettier, when you have pared them all, put them in salt and spring water for a day or two, then boil them in a large quantity of spring water till they are tender, then drain them on a sieve, have ready a thin syrup, made of a quart of water, and a pound of fine sugar, boil them (a few at a time to keep them from breaking) till they look clear, then put them into a syrup made of fine loaf sugar, with as much water as will dissolve it, and boil them to a candy height, when you take them up, lay them on sieves, and grate double refined sugar all over them, and put them in a stove, or by the fire to dry, and keep them in a dry place for use.

To dry CURRANTS in bunches.

WHEN the currants are stoned and tied up in bunches, to every pound of currants take a pound and a half of sugar, and to every pound of sugar put half a pint of water, boil the syrup very well, lay your currants in it, set them on the fire, and let them just boil, take them off, cover it close with paper, let them stand till the next day, then make them scalding hot, let them stand for two or three days, with a paper close to them, then lay them on earthen plates, and lift them well over with sugar, put them in a stove to dry, the next day lay them on sieves, but do not turn them till the upper side is dry, then turn them, and lift the other side well with sugar; when they are quite dry, lay them be twixt papers.

To dry APRICOTS.

TAKE a pound of apricots, pare and stone them, put them in your tossing pan, pound and fifty half a pound of double refined sugar, strew a little amongst them, and lay the rest over them; let them stand twenty-four hours turn them three or four times in the syrup, then boil them pretty quick till they look clear, when they are cold take them out, and lay them on glasses, put them into a stove, and turn them every half hour, the next day every hour, and after as you see occasion.

To make LEMON DROPS.

DIP a lump of treble refined loaf sugar in water, boil it stiffish, take it off, rub it with the back of a silver spoon to the side of your pan, then grate in some lemon-peel, boil it up, and drop it on paper; if you want it red put in a little cochineal.

To make LEMON DROPS a second Way.

TAKE the juice of three fresh lemons strained fine, and mix it with a pound of treble refined sugar beaten and sifted through a lawn sieve, beat them together for an hour, it will make them white and bright, then drop them upon writing paper, and dry them before the fire or in the sun. They are a pretty ornament for a desert.

To make PEPPERMINT DROPS to carry in the Pocket.

TAKE one pound of treble refined sugar, beat it fine and sift it through a lawn sieve, then mix it with the whites of two eggs, beat it to a thick froth, then add sixty drops of the oil of peppermint and beat them all well together, then with a tea-spoon drop it upon fine cap paper, the size of half a nutmeg, and put them upon the hearth to dry, the next day take them off, and they are fit for use.

To make RASPBERRY or CURRANT DROPS.

TAKE the juice of raspberries or red cur rants, add as much treble refined sugar beaten and finely sifted as will make it into a thin paste, drop them upon fine cap paper with a tea-spoon, dry them before the fire, the next day take them off, and keep them in a glass jar, it will preserve the flavour. They are a great ornament to a desert.

To dry PEACHES.

PARE and stone the largest Newington peaches, have ready a saucepan of boiling water, put in the peaches, let them boil till they are tender, lay them or a sieve to drain, then weigh them, and put them in the pan they were boiled in, and cover them with their weight of sugar, let them lie two or three hours, then boil them till they are clear, and the syrup pretty thick, let them stand all night covered close, scald them very well, then take them off to cool, then set them on again till the peaches are thoroughly hot; do this for three days, lay them on plates to dry, and turn them every day.

To candy ANGELICA.

TAKE it when young, cut it in lengths, cover it close, and boil it till it is tender, peel it, and put it in again, let it simmer and boil till it is green, then take it up, and dry it with a cloth; to every pound of stalks put a pound of sugar; put your stalks into an earthen pan, beat the sugar and strew over them, let it stand two days, then boil it till it is clear and green, put it in a cullender to drain; beat a pound of sugar to powder again, strew it on your angelica, lay it on plates to dry, and set them in the oven after the pies are drawn. — Three pounds and a half of sugar is enough to four pounds of stalks.

To candy LEMON *or* ORANGE PEEL.

CUT your lemons or oranges long-ways, and take out all the pulp, and put, the rinds into a pretty strong salt and hard water six days, then boil them in a large quantity of spring water till they are tender, then take them out and lay them on a hair sieve to drain, then make a thin syrup of fine loaf sugar, a pound to a quart of water; put in your peels and boil them half an hour, or till they look clear, have ready a thick syrup made of fine loaf sugar, with as much water as will dissolve it, put in your peels, and boil them over a slow fire, till you see the syrup candy about the pan and peels, then take them out, and grate fine sugar all over them, lay them on a hair sieve to drain, and set them in a stove, or before the fire to dry, and keep them in a dry place for use. — N. B. Do not cover your sauce pan when you boil either lemons or oranges.

To boil SUGAR *candy height.*

PUT a pound of sugar into a clean tossing pan, with half a pint of water, set it over a very clear slow fire, take off the scum as it rises, boil it till it looks fine and clear, then take out a little with a silver spoon; when it is cold, if it will draw a thread from your spoon, it is boiled high enough for any kind of sweetmeat, then boil your syrup, and when it begins to candy round the edge of your pan, it is candy height. N. B. It is a great fault to put any kind of sweetmeats into too thick a syrup, especially at the first, for it withers your fruit, and takes off both the beauty and flavour.

CHAP. X

Observations upon CREAMS, CUSTARDS and CHEESECAKES

When you make any kind of creams and custards, take great care your tossing pan be well tinned, put a spoonful of water in it, to prevent the cream from sticking to the bottom of your pan, then beat your yolks of eggs, and strain out the threads, and follow the directions of your receipt.—As to cheese-cakes they should not be made long before you bake them, particularly almond or lemon cheese-cakes, for standing makes them oil and grow sad, a moderate oven bakes them best, if it is too hot it burns them and takes off the beauty, and a very slow oven makes them sad and look black; make your cheese-cakes up just when the oven is of a proper heat, and they will rise well and be of a proper colour.

To make PISTACHIO CREAM.

TAKE half a pound of pistachio nuts, take out the kernels, beat them m a mortar with a spoonful of brandy, put them into a tossing pan, with a pint of good cream, and the yolks of two eggs beat fine, stir it gently over a very flow fire till it grows thick, then put it into a china soup plate, when it grows cold stick it all over with small pieces and serve it up.

To make CHOCOLATE CREAM

SCRAPE fine a quarter of a pound of the best chocolate, put to it as much water as will dissolve it, put it in a marble mortar, beat it half an hour, put in as much fine sugar as will sweeten it and a pint and a half of cream, mill it, and as the froth rises lay it on a sieve, put the remainder part of your cream in posset glasses, and lay the frothed cream upon them. — It makes a pretty mixture upon a set of servers.

To make SPANISH CREAM.

DISSOLVE in a quarter of a pint of rose water three quarters of an ounce of isinglass cut small, run it through a hair sieve, add to it the yolks of three eggs, beat and mixed with half a pint of cream, two sorrel leaves, and sugar to your taste, dip the dish in cold water before you put in the cream, then cut it out with a jigging iron, and lay it in rings round different coloured sweetmeats.

To make ICE CREAM.

PARE, stone, and scald twelve ripe apricots, beat them fine in a marble mortar, put to them six ounces of double refined sugar, a pint of scalding cream, work it through a hair sieve, put it into a tin that has a close cover, set it in a tub of ice broken small, and a large quantity of salt put amongst it, when you see your cream grow thick round the edges of your tin, stir it, and set it in again till it grows quite thick, when your cream is all froze up, take it out of your tin, and put it into the mould you intend it to be turned out of, then put on the lid, and have ready another tub with ice and salt in as before, put your mould in the middle, and lay your ice under and over it, let it stand four or five hours, dip your tin in warm water when you turn it out ; if it be summer, you must not turn it out till the moment you want it; you may use any sort of fruit if you have not apricots, only ob serve to work it fine.

To make CLOTTED CREAM.

PUT one tea-spoon of earning into a quart of good cream, when it comes to a curd break it very carefully with a silver spoon, lay it upon a sieve to drain a little, put it into a china soup plate, pour over it some good cream, with the juice of raspberries, damsons, or any kind of fruit to make it a fine pink colour, sweeten it to your taste, and lay round it a few strawberry leaves. — It is proper for a middle at supper, or a corner at dinner,

To make HARTSHORN CREAM.

TAKE four ounces of hartshorn shavings, boil them in three pints of water till it is reduced to half a pint, run it through a jelly bag, put to it a pint of cream, let it just boil up, then ,put it into jelly glasses, let it stand till it is cold, by dipping your glasses into scalding water it will slip out whole, then stick them all over with slices of almonds cut length-ways: it eats well with white wine and sugar, like flummery.

To make RIBBAND CREAM.

TAKE eight quarts of new milk, set it on the fire, when it is ready to boil put in a quart of good cream, earn it, and pour it into a large bowl, let it stand all night, then take off the cream, and lay it on a sieve to drain, cut it to the size of your glasses, and lay red, green, or coloured sweetmeats between every layer of cream.

To make LEMON CREAM.

TAKE a pint of spring water, the rinds of two lemons pared very thin, and the juice of three, beat the whites of six eggs very well, mix the whites with the water and lemon, put sugar so your taste, then set it over the fire, and keep stirring it till it thickens, but do not let it boil, strain it through a cloth, beat the yolks of six eggs, put it over the fire till it be quite thick, then put it into a bowl to cool, and put it in your glasses.

To make STEEPLE CREAM with WINE SOUR,

TAKE one pint of strong clear calf 's-foot jelly, the yolks of 'four hard eggs, pounded in a mortar exceeding fine, with the juice of a Seville orange, and as much double refined sugar as will make it sweet, when your jelly is warm put it in, and keep stirring it till it is cold and grows as thick as cream, then put it into jelly glasses, the next day turn it out into a dish with preserved wine sours, stick a sprig of myrtle in the top of every cream, and serve it up with flowers round it.

To make RASPBERRY CREAM.

TAKE a quart of raspberries, or raspberry jam, rub it through a hair sieve to take out the feeds, mix it well with your cream, put in as much loaf sugar as will make it pleasant, they'd put it into a milk pot to raise a froth with a chocolate mill; as your froth rises take it off with a spoon, lay it upon a hair sieve, when you have got what froth you have occasion for, put the remainder of your cream into a deep china dish or punch bowl, put your frothed cream upon it, as high as it will lie on, then stick a light flower in the middle and send it up,— It is proper for a middle at supper, or a corner at dinner, ,

LEMON CREAM *with* PEEL.

BOIL a pint of cream, when it is half cold put in the yolks of four eggs, stir it till it is cold, then set it over the fire, with four ounces of loaf sugar, a teaspoonful of grated lemon peel, stir them till it is pretty hot, take it off the fire and put it in a basin to cool, when it is cold put it in sweetmeat glasses, lay paste knots, or lemon peel cut like long straws over the tops of your glasses. — It is proper to be put upon a bottom salver amongst jellies and whips.

ORANGE CREAM,

TAKE the juice of four Seville oranges, and the out-rind of one pared exceeding fine, put them into a tossing-pan with one pint of water, and eight ounces of sugar, beat the whites of five eggs, set it over the fire, stir it one way till it grows thick and white, strain it through a gauze sieve, stir it till it is cold, then beat the yolks of five eggs exceeding well, put it in your tossing pan with the cream, stir it over a very slow fire till it is ready to boil, put it into a bason to cool and stir it till it is quite cold, then put it into jelly glasses: send it in upon a salver with whips and jellies.

To make BURNT CREAM.

BOIL a pint of cream with sugar, and a little lemon peel shred fine, then beat the yolks of six and the whites of four eggs separately, when your cream is cooled, put in your eggs, with a spoonful of orange flower water, and one of fine flour, set it over the fire, keep stirring it till it is thick, put it into a dish; when it is cold sift a quarter of a pound of sugar all over, hold a hot salamander over it till it is very brown, and looks like a glass plate put over your cream.

To make LA POMPADOUR CREAM.

BEAT the whites of five eggs to a strong froth, put them into a tossing pan, with two spoonfuls of orange flower water, two ounces of sugar, stir it gently for three or four minutes, then pour it into your dim, and pour good melted butter over it, and send it in hot. It is a pretty corner dish for a second course at dinner.

To make TEA CREAM.

TO half a pint of milk put a quarter of an ounce of fine hyson tea, boil them together, strain the leaves out, and put to the milk half a pint of cream, and two spoonfuls of rennet; set it over some hot embers in the dish you send it to table in, and cover it with a tin plate; when it is thick it is enough. Garnish with sweetmeats and send it up.

To make KING WILLIAM'S CREAM.

BEAT the whites of three eggs very well, then squeeze out the juice of two large or three small lemons; take two ounces more than the weight of the juice of double refined sugar, and mix it together with two or three drops of orange flower water ; and five or six spoonfuls of fair spring water; when all the sugar is melted, put in the whites of the eggs into the pan and the juice, set it over a flow fire, and keep stirring it till you find it thicken, then strain it through a coarse cloth quick into the dish.

SNOW and CREAM, a pretty Supper Dish.

MAKE a rich boiled custard and put it in the bottom of your china or glass dish, then take the whites of eight eggs beat with rose water and a spoonful of treble refined sugar, till it is a strong froth; put some milk and water into a broad stew-pan, and when it boils take the froth off the eggs and lay it on the milk and water, and let it boil once up; take it off carefully, and lay it on your custard.

To make CREAM CHEESE.

PUT one large spoonful of steep to five quarts of afterings, break it down light, put it upon a cloth in a sieve bottom, and let it run till dry, break it, cut and turn it in a' clean cloth, then put it into the sieve again, and put on it a two pound weight, sprinkle a little salt on it and let it stand all night, then lay it on a board to dry, when dry lay a few strawberry leaves on it, and ripen it between two pewter dimes in a warm place, turn it, and put on fresh leaves every day.

To make a TRIFLE.

PUT three large maccaroons in the middle of your dish, pour as much white wine over them as they will drink, then take a quart of cream, put in as much sugar as will make it sweet, rub your sugar upon the rind of a lemon to fetch out the essence, put your cream into a pot, mill it to a strong froth, lay as much froth upon a sieve as will fill the dish you intend to put your trifle in, put the remainder of your cream into a tossing pan, with a stick of cinnamon, the yolks of four eggs well beat, and sugar to your taste, set them over a gentle fire, stir it one way till it is thick, then take it off the fire, pour it upon your maccaroons, when it is cold put on your frothed cream, lay round it different coloured sweetmeats, and small shot comfits in, and figures or flowers.

ALMOND CUSTARDS.

PUT a quart of cream into a tossing pan, d stick of cinnamon, a blade or two of mace, boil it and set it to cool, blanch two ounces of almonds, beat them fine in a marble mortar with rose water, if you like a ratafia taste, put in a few apricot kernels or bitter almonds, mix them with your cream, sweeten it to your taste, set it on a slow fire, keep stirring it till it is pretty thick, if you let it boil it will curdle, pour it into cups, &c.

To make LEMON CUSTARDS

TAKE a pint of white wine, half a pound of double refined sugar, the juice of two lemons, the out-rind of one pared very thin, the inner- rind of one boiled tender and rubbed through a sieve, let them boil a good while, then take out the peel and a little of the liquor, set it to cool, pour the rest into the dish you intend for it; beat four yolks and two whites of eggs, mix them with your cool liquor, strain them into your dish, stir them well up together, set them on a slow fire, or boiling water to bake as a custard, when it is enough, grate the rind of a lemon all over the top; you may brown it over with a hot salamander. It may be eat either hot or cold.

To make ORANGE CUSTARDS.

BOIL the rind of half a Seville orange very tender, beat it in a marble mortar till it is very fine, put to it one spoonful of the best brandy, the juice of a Seville orange, four ounces of loaf sugar, and the yolks of four eggs, beat them all together ten minutes, then pour in by degrees a pint of boiling cream, keep beating them till they are cold, put them in custard cups, and set them in an earthen dish of hot water, let them stand till they are set, then take them out, and stick preserved orange on the top, and serve them up either hot or cold. — It is a pretty corner dish for dinner, or a side dish for supper.

To make a common CUSTARD.

TAKE a quart of good cream, set it over a slow fire, with a little cinnamon, and four ounces of sugar ; when it has boiled take it off the fire; beat the yolks of eight eggs, put to them a spoonful of orange flower water, to prevent the cream from cracking, stir them in by degrees as your cream cools, put the pan over a very slow fire, stir them carefully one way till it is al most boiling, then put it into cups, and serve them up.

To make a BEEST CUSTARD.

TAKE a pint of beest, set it over the fire, with a little cinnamon, or three bay leaves, let it be boiling hot, then take it off, and have ready mixed one spoonful of flour, and a spoonful of thick cream, pour your hot beast upon it by degrees, mix it exceeding well together, and sweeten it to your taste you may either put it in crafts or cups, or bake it.

To make an APPLE FLOATING ISLAND.

BAKE six or eight very large apples, when they are cold peel and core them, rub the pulp through a sieve with the back of a wooden spoon, then beat it up light with fine sugar, well sifted, to your taste; beat the whites of four eggs with orange flower water in another bowl till it is a light froth, then mix it with your apple a little at a time till all is beat together, and exceeding light; make a rich boiled custard, and put it in a china or glass dish, and lay the apples all over it. Garnish with currant jelly, or what you please.

To make FAIRY BUTTER.

TAKE the yolks of four eggs boiled hard, a quarter of a pound of butter, beat two ounces of sugar in a large spoonful of orange flower water, beat them all together to a fine paste, let it stand two or three hours, then rub it through a cullendar upon a plate; it looks very pretty.

To make ALMOND CHEESE CAKES-,

TAKE four ounces of Jordan almonds, blanch them and put them into cold water, beat them with rose water in a marble mortar, or wooden bowl, with a wooden pestle, put to it four ounces of sugar, and the yolks of four eggs beat fine, work it in the mortar or bowl till it becomes white and frothy, then make a rich puff paste, which must be made thus: Take half a pound of flour, a quarter of a pound of butter, rub a little of the butter into the flour, mix it stiff with a little cold water, then roll your paste straight out, strew over a little flour, and lay over it in thin bits one third of your butter, throw a little more flour over the butter, do so for three times, then put your paste in your tins, fill them, and grate sugar over them, and bake them in a gentle oven.

To make BREAD CHEESE CAKES.

SLICE a penny loaf as thin as possible, pour on it a pint of boiling cream, let it stand two hours, then take eight eggs, half a pound of butter, and a nutmeg grated, beat them well together, put in halt a pound of currants well washed, and dried before the fire, and a spoonful of brandy, or white wine, and bake them in raised crusts, or petty pans.

To make CITRON CHEESE CAKES.

BOIL a quart of cream, beat the yolks of four eggs, mix them with your cream when it is cold, then set it on the fire's let it boil till it curds, blanch some almonds, beat them with orange flower water, put them into the cream, with a few Naples biscuits, and green citron shred fine, sweeten it to your taste, and bake them in tea-cups;

To make RICE CHEESE CAKES.

BOIL four ounces of rice till tender, put it upon a sieve to drain, put in four eggs well beaten, half a pound of butter, half a pint of cream, six ounces of sugar, a nutmeg grated, and a glass of ratafia water, or brandy: beat them all together, and bake them in raised crusts.

To make CURD CHEESE-CAKES.

TAKE half a pint of good curds, beat them with four eggs, three spoonfuls of rich cream, half a nutmeg grated, one spoonful of ratafia, rose, or orange water, put to them a quarter of a pound of sugar, half a pound of currants well washed and dried before the fire, mix them all well together, and bake it in petty pans, with a good crust under them.

To make ORANGE CRUMPETS.

TAKE a pint of cream, and a pint of new milk, warm it, and put in it a little rennet, when it is broke, stir it gently, lay it on a cloth to drain all night, and then take the rinds of three oranges, boiled as for preserving in three different waters, pound them very fine, and mix them with the curd, and eight eggs, in a mortar, a little nutmeg, juice of lemon, or orange, and sugar to your taste, bake them in tin pans rubbed with butter, when they are baked turn them out, and put sack and sugar over them. — Some put sliced pressed oranges among them.

To make CHEESE-CAKES.

SET a quart of new milk near the fire, with a spoonful of rennet, let the milk be blood warm, when it is broke, drain the curd through a coarse sloth, now and then break the curd gently with your fingers, rub into the curd a quarter of a pound of butter, a quarter of a pound of sugar, a nutmeg, and two Naples biscuits grated, the yolks of four eggs, and the white of one egg, one ounce of almonds well beat, with two spoonfuls of rose water, and two of sack, clean six ounces of currants very well, put them into your curd, and mix them all well together.

To make CURD PUFFS.

TAKE two quarts of milk, put a little rennet in it, when it is broke, put it in a coarse cloth to drain, then rub the curd through a hair sieve, with four ounces of butter beat, ten ounces of bread, half a nutmeg, and a lemon peel grated, a spoonful of wine, and sugar to your taste, rub your cups with butter, and bake them a little more than half an hour.

To make EGG CHEESE,

BEAT six eggs well, put them into three gills of new milk, sugar, cinnamon, and lemon peel to your taste, let it over the fire, keep stirring it, and squeeze a quarter of a lemon in it to turn it to cheese, let it run into what shape you would have it, when it is cold, turn it out, pour over it a little almond cream, made of sweet almonds beat fine with a little cream, then put them into a pint of cream, let it boil and strain it, put to it the yolks of three eggs well beat, set it over the fire, and make it like a custard.

To make a LOAF ROYAL.

TAKE a French roll, grasp it, cut off the bottom crust, lay it in a pan, with the, bottom upwards, boil a pint of cream, put to it the yolks of two eggs, a little cinnamon, orange flower water, and sugar to your taste, when it is cold pour it upon the roll, let it stand in all night to steep, then make a very good custard of cream, a little sack, orange slower water, and sugar, put the roll into a dish, with some good paste round the edge, and pour your custard upon it; you may lay lumps of marrow in the custard, and stick long slips of citron and orange peel in the loaf, then send it to the oven, a little time will bake it.

To make a PRINCE LOAF.

TAKE small French rolls, about the size of an egg, cut a small round hole in the top, take put all the crumb, fill them, with almond custard, layover it currant jelly, in thin slices, beat the white of an egg, and double refined sugar to a froth, and ice them all over with it; five is a pretty dish.

To make a DRUNKEN LOAF.

TAKE a French roll hot out of the oven, grasp it, and pour a pint of red wine upon it, and cover it close up for half an hour, boil one ounce of maccaroni in water till it is soft, and lay it upon a sieve to drain, then put the size of a walnut of butter into it, and as much thick cream as it will take, then scrape in six ounces of Parmesan cheese, shake it about in your tossing- pan, with the maccaroni till it be like a fine custard, then pour it hot upon your loaf: brown it with a salamander, and serve it up. — It is a pretty dish for supper.

To make SNOW BALLS.

PARE five large baking apples, take out the cores with a scoop, fill the holes with orange or quince marmalade, then make a little good hot paste, and roll your apples in it, and make your crust of an equal thickness, and put them in a tin dripping-pan, bake them in a moderate oven, when you take them out, make iceing for them the same way as for the plum-cake, and ice them all over with it, about a quarter of an inch thick, set them a good distance from the fire till they are hardened, but take care you do not let them brown, put one in the middle of a China dish, and the other five round it. Garnish them with green sprigs and small flowers. - They are proper for a corner either for dinner or supper.

To make FRIED TOAST,

CUT a slice of bread about half an inch thick, steep it in rich cream, with sugar and nutmeg to your taste, when it is quite soft, put a good lump of butter into a tossing-pan, fry it a fine brown, lay it on a dish, pour wine sauce over it, and serve it up.

CHAP. XI

Observations On CAKES

When you make any kind of cakes, be sure that you get your things ready before you begin, then beat your eggs well and don't leave them 'till you have finished the cakes, or else they will go back again, and your cakes will not be light; if your cakes are to have butter in, take care you beat it to a fine cream before you put in your sugar, for if you beat it twice the time, it will not answer as well: as to plum-cake, seed-cake, or rice cake, it is best to bake them in wood garths for if you bake them in either pot or tin, they burn the outside of the cakes, and confine them so that the heat cannot penetrate into the middle of your cake, and prevents it from rising: bake all kinds of cake in a good oven, according to the size of your cake, and follow the directions of your receipt, for though care hath been taken to weigh and measure every article belonging to every kind of cake, yet the management and the oven must be left to the maker's care.

To make a BRIDE CAKE.

TAKE four pounds of fine flour well dried, four pounds of fresh butter, two pounds of loaf sugar, pound and sift fine a quarter of an ounce of mace, the same of nutmegs, to every pound of flour put eight eggs, wash four pounds of currants, pick them well, and dry them before the fire, blanch a pound of sweet almonds, and cut them lengthways very thin, a pound of citron, one pound of candied orange, the same of candied lemon, half a pint of brandy; first work the butter with your hand to a cream, then beat in your sugar a quarter of an hour, beat the whites of your eggs to a very strong froth, mix them with your sugar and butter, beat your yolks half an hour at least, and mix them with your cake, then put in your flour, mace, and nutmeg, keep beating it well till your oven is ready, put in your brandy, and beat your currants and almonds lightly in, tie three sheets of paper round the bottom of your hoop to keep it from running out, rub it well with butter, put in your cake, and lay your sweetmeats in three lays, with cake betwixt every lay, after it is risen and coloured, cover it with paper before your oven is stopped up, it will take three hours baking.

To make ALMOND-ICING For the BRIDE CAKE.

BEAT the whites of three eggs to a strong froth, beat a pound of Jordan almonds very fine with rose-water, mix your almonds with the eggs lightly together, a pound of common loaf sugar beat fine, and put in by degrees; when your cake is enough, take it out, and lay your icing on, then put it in to brown.

To make SUGAR ICING for the BRIDE CAKE.

BEAT two pounds of double refined sugar, with two ounces of fine starch, sift it through a gauze sieve, then beat the whites of five eggs with a knife upon a pewter dish half an hour to beat in your sugar a little at a time, or it will make the eggs fall, and will not be so good a colour when you have put in all your sugar, beat it half an hour longer, then lay it on your almond iceing, and spread it even with a knife; if it be put on as soon as the cake comes out of the oven it will be hard by the time the cake is cold.

To make a good PLUM CAKE.

TAKE a pound and a half of fine flour well dried, a pound and a half of butter, three quarters of a pound of currants washed and well picked, stone half a pound of raisins, and slice them, eighteen ounces of sugar beat and sifted, fourteen eggs, leave out the whites of half of them, shred the peel of a large lemon exceeding fine, three ounces of candied orange, the same of lemon, a teaspoonful of beaten mace, half a nutmeg grated, a teacupful of brandy, or white wine, four spoonfuls of orange flower water ; first work the butter with your hand to a cream, then beat your sugar well in, whist; your eggs for half an hour, then mix them with your sugar and butter, and put in your flour and spices, when your oven is ready, mix your brandy, fruit, and sweetmeats lightly in, then put it in your hoop, and send it to the oven; it will require two hours and a half baking. — it will take an hour and a half beating.

To make a rich SEED CAKE.

TAKE a pound of flour well dried, a pound of butter, a pound of loaf sugar beat and sifted, eight eggs, two ounces of carraway seeds, one nutmeg grated, and its weight of cinnamon ; first beat your butter to a cream, then put in your sugar, beat the whites of your eggs half an hour, mix them with your sugar and butter, then beat the yolks half an hour, put to it the whites, beat in your flour, spices, and seeds, a little before it goes to the oven, put it in the hoop and bake it two hours in a quick oven, and let it stand two hours. — It will take two hours beating.

To make a WHITE PLUM CAKE.

TO two pounds of flour well dried, take a pound of sugar beat and sifted, one pound of butter, a quarter of an ounce of mace, the same of nutmegs, sixteen eggs, two pounds and a half of currants, picked and warned, half a pound of candied lemon, the same of sweet almonds, half a pint of sack or brandy, three spoonfuls of orange flower water, beat your butter to a cream, put in your sugar, beat the whites of your eggs half an hour, mix them with your sugar and butter, then beat your yolks half an hour, mix them with your whites, it will take two hours beating, put in your flour a little be fore your oven is ready, mix your currants and all your other ingredients lightly in, just when you put it in your hoop,— Two hours will bake it

To make little PLUM CAKES.

TAKE a pound of flour, rub it into half a pound of butter, the same of sugar, a little beaten mace, beat four eggs very well (leave out half the whites) with three spoonfuls of yeast, put to it a quarter of a pint of warm cream, strain them into your flour, and make it up light, set it before the fire to rise; just before you send it to the oven, put in three quarters of a pound of currants.

To make ORANGE CAKES;

TAKE Seville oranges that have very good rinds, quarter them, and boil them in two or three waters until they are tender, and the bitterness is gone off, scum them, then lay them on a clean napkin to dry, take all the seeds and skins out of the pulp with a knife, shred the peels fine, put them to the pulp, weigh them, and put rather more than their weight of fine sugar into a tossing pan, with just as much water as will dissolve it, boil it till it becomes a perfect sugar, then by degrees put in your orange peels and pulp, stir them well before you let them on the fire, boil it very gently till it looks clear and thick, then put it into flat-bottomed glasses, set them in a stove, and keep a constant moderate heat to them, when they are candied on the top, turn them out upon glasses. N. B. You may make lemon cakes the same way.

To make LEMON CAKE a second Way.

BEAT the whites of ten eggs with a whisk for one hour with three spoonfuls of rose or orange flower water, then put in one pound of loaf sugar beat and sifted, with the yellow rind of a lemon grated into it ; when it is well mixed put in the juice of half a lemon and the yolks of ten eggs beat smooth, and just before you put it into the oven stir in three quarters of a pound of flour; butter your pan, and one hour will bake it in a moderate oven.

To make RICE CAKE.

TAKE fifteen eggs, leave out one half of the whites, beat them exceeding well near an hour with a whisk, then beat the yolks half an hour, put to your yolks ten ounces of loaf sugar sifted fine, beat it well in, then put in half a pound of rice flour, a little orange water or brandy, the rinds of two lemons grated, then put in your whites, beat them all well together for a quarter of an hour, then put them in a hoop and set them in a quick oven for half an hour.

To make RATAFIA CAKES.

TAKE half a pound of sweet almonds, the same quantity of bitter, blanch and beat them fine in orange, rose, or clear water, to keep them from oiling, pound and sift a pound of fine sugar, mix it with your almonds, have ready very well beat, the whites of four eggs, mix them lightly with the almonds and sugar, put it in a preserving pan, and set it over a moderate fire, keep stirring it quick one way until it is pretty hot, when it is a little cool roll it in small rolls, and cut it in thin cakes, dip your hands in flour and shake them on it, give them each a light tap with your finger, put them on sugar papers, and sift a little fine sugar over them just as you are putting them into a flow oven.

To make RATAFIA CAKES *a second Way.*

TAKE one pound and a half of sweet almonds, and half a pound of bitter almonds, beat them as fine as possible with the whites of two eggs, then beat the whites of five eggs to a strong froth, shake in lightly two pounds and a half of fine loaf sugar beat and sifted very fine, drop them in little drops the size of a nutmegs on cap paper, and bake them in a slack oven.

To make SHREWSBURY CAKES.

TAKE half a pound of butter, beat it to at cream, then put in half a pound of flour, one egg, six ounces of loaf sugar beat and sifted, half an ounce of carraway seeds mixed into a paste, roll them thin, and cut them round with a small glass, or little tins, prick them, and lay them on sheets of tin, and bake them in a slow oven.

To make SHREWSBURY CAKES a second Way.

TO a pound of butter, beat and sift a pound of double refined sugar, a little mace, and four eggs, beat them all together with your hand till it is very light and looks curdling, then shake in a pound and a half of fine flour, roll it thin and cut it into little cakes with a tray and bake them.

To make BATH CAKES.

RUB half a pound of butter into a pound of flour, and one spoonful of good barm, warm some cream, and make it into a light paste, set it to the fire to rise, when you make them up, take four ounces of carraway comfits, work part of them in, and strew the rest on the top, make them into a round cake, the size of a French roll, bake them on meet tins, and send them in hot for breakfast.

To make QUEEN CAKES.

TAKE a pound of loaf sugar, beat and sift it, a pound of flour well dried, a pound of butter, eight eggs, half a pound of currants washed and picked, grate a nutmeg, the same quantity of mace and cinnamon, work your butter to a cream, then put in your sugar, beat the whites of your eggs near half an hour, mix them with your sugar and butter, then beat your yolks near half an hour, and put them to your butter, beat them exceeding well together, then put in your flour, spices, and the currants, when it is ready for the oven, bake them in tins, and dust a little sugar over them.

To make a common SEED CAKE.

TAKE two pounds of flour, rub it into half a pound of powdered sugar, one ounce of carraway seeds beaten, have ready a pint of milk, with half a pound of butter melted in it, and two spoonfuls of new barm, make it up into a paste, set it to the fire to rise, flour your tin, and bake it in a quick oven.

To make CREAM CAKES.

BEAT the whites of nine eggs to a stiff froth, then stir it gently with a spoon, for fear the froth should fall, and grate the rinds of two lemons, to every white of an egg, shake in softly a spoonful of double refined sugar lifted fine, lay a wet sheet of paper on a tin, and drop the froth in little lumps on it with a spoon, a small distance from each other, and sift a good quantity of sugar over them, set them in an oven after brown bread, make the oven close up, and the froth will rise, when they are just coloured they are baked enough, take them out and put two bottoms together, and lay them on a sieve, then set them in a cool oven to dry. — You may lay raspberry jam, or any other sorts of sweet meats betwixt them before you close the bottoms together to dry.

To make little CURRANT CAKES.

TAKE one pound and a half of fine flour, dry it well before the fire, a pound of butter, half a pound of fine loaf sugar well beat and sifted, four yolks of eggs, four spoonfuls of rose water, four spoonfuls of sack, a little mace, and one nutmeg grated: beat the eggs very well, and put them to the rose water and sack, then put to it the sugar and butter; work them all together, strew in the currants and the flour, being both made warm together before. — This quantity will make six or eight cakes; bake them pretty crisp, and a fine brown.

To make PRUSSIAN CAKE.

TAKE a pound of sugar beat and sifted, half a pound of flour dried, seven eggs, beat the yolks and whites separately, the juice of one lemon, the peel of two grated very fine, half a pound of almonds beat fine with rose water; as soon as the whites are beat to a froth, put in all the things except the flour, and beat them together for half an hour, just before you set it in the oven, fluke in the flour. — N. B. The whites and yolks must be beat separate, or it will be quite heavy.

To make a CAKE *without butter.*

BEAT eight eggs half an hour, have ready pounded and sifted a pound of loaf sugar, shake it in, and beat it half an hour more, put to it a quarter of a pound of sweet almonds beat fine, with orange flour water, grate the rind of a lemon into the almonds, and squeeze in the juice of the lemon, mix them all together, and keep beating them till the oven is ready, and just before you set it in, put to it three quarters of a pound of warm dry fine flour ; rub your hoop with butter: an hour and a half will bake it.

To make BARBADOES JUMBALLS.

BEAT very light the yolks of four eggs and the whites of eight, with a spoonful of rose water, and dust in a pound of treble refined sugar, then put in three quarters of a pound of the best fine flour, stir it lightly in, grease your tin sheets, and drop them in the shape of a macaroon, and bake them nicely.

To make CHACKNELS.

To a pint of blue milk put about two ounces of butter and a good spoonful of yeast, make it just warm, and mix into it as much fine flour as will make it a light dough, roll it out very thin, and cut it into long pieces two inches broad, prick them well, and bake them in a flow oven upon tin plates.

To make LIGHT WIGS.

TO three quarters of a pound of fine flour, put half a pint of milk made warm, mix in it two or three spoonfuls of light barm, cover it up, set it half an hour by the fire to rise, work in the paste four ounces of sugar, and four ounces of butter, make it into wigs with as little flour as possible, and a few seeds, set them in a quick oven to bake.

To make MACAROONS.

TO one pound of blanched and beaten sweet almonds, put one pound of sugar, and a little rose water, to keep them from oiling, then beat the whites of seven eggs to a froth, put them in and beat them well together, drop them on wafer paper, grate sugar over them, and bake them.

To make SPANISH BISCUITS.

BEAT the yolks of eight eggs near half an hour, then beat in eight spoonfuls of sugar, beat the whites to a strong froth, then beat them very well with your yolks and sugar near half an hour, put in four spoonfuls of flour, and a little lemon cut exceeding fine, and bake them on papers.

To make SPONGE BISCUITS.

BEAT the yolks of twelve eggs half an hour, put in a pound and a half of sugar beat and sifted, whisk it well till you see it rise in bubbles, beat the whites to a strong froth, whisk them well with your sugar and yolks, beat in fourteen ounces of flour, with the rinds of two lemons grated, bake them in tin moulds buttered, or coffins; they require a hot oven, the mouth must not be stopped ; when you put them into the oven dust them with sugar ; they will take half an hour baking.

To make LEMON BISCUITS.

BEAT very well the yolks of ten eggs, and the whites of five, with four spoonfuls of orange flower water till they froth up, then put in a pound of loaf sugar sifted, beat it one way for half an hour or more, put in half a pound of flour with the raspings of two lemons, and the pulp of a small one, butter your tin, and bake it in a quick oven, but do not stop up the mouth at first for fear it should scorch, dust it with sugar before you put it in the oven, it is soon baked.

To make DROP BISCUITS.

BEAT the yolks of ten eggs and the whites of six, with one spoonful of rose water, half an hour, then put in ten ounces of loaf sugar beat and sifted, whisk them well for half an hour, then add one ounce of carraway seeds crushed a little, and six ounces of fine flour, whisk in your flour gently, drop them on wafer papers, and bake them in a moderate oven.

To make common BISCUITS.

BEAT eight eggs half an hour, put in a pound of sugar beat and sifted, with the rind of a lemon grated, whisk it an hour till it looks light, then put in a pound of flour, with a little rose water, and bake them in tins, or on papers, with sugar over them.

To make WAFERS.

TAKE two spoonfuls of cream, two of sugar, the same of flour, and one spoonful of orange flower water, beat them well together for half an hour, then make your wafer tongs hot, and pour a little of your batter in to cover your irons, bake them on a stove fire, as they are baked roll them round a stick like a piggot, as soon as they are cold, they will be very crisp ; they are proper for tea, or to put upon a salver to eat with jellies.

To make LEMON PUFFS.

BEAT a pound of double refined sugar, sift it through a fine sieve, put it in a bowl, with the juice of two lemons, beat them well together, then beat the white of an egg to a very high froth, put it in your bowl, beat it half an hour; then put in three eggs, with two rinds of lemons grated, mix it well up, dust your papers with sugar, drop on the puffs in small drops, and bake them in a moderate oven.

To make CHOCOLATE PUFFS.

BEAT and sift half a pound of double refined sugar, scrape into it one ounce of chocolate very fine, mix them together, beat the white of an egg to a very high froth, then strew in your sugar and chocolate; keep beating it till it is as stiff as paste, sugar your papers, and drop them on about the size of a sixpence, and bake them in a very slow oven.

To make ALMOND PUFFS.

BLANCH two ounces of sweet almonds, beat them fine with orange flower water, beat the whites of three eggs to a very high froth, then strew in a little sifted sugar, mix your almonds with your sugar and eggs, then add more sugar till it is as stiff as a paste, lay it in cakes, and bake it on paper in a cool oven.

To make PICKLETS.

TAKE three pounds of flour, make a hole in the middle with your hand, then mix two-spoonfuls of barm, with as much milk and a little salt as will make it into a light paste, pour your milk and harm into the middle of your flour and stir a little of your flour into it, then let it stand all night, and the next morning work all the flour into the barm, and beat it well for a quarter of an hour, then let it stand an hour; after that take it out with a large spoon, and lay it on a board well dusted with flour, and dredge flour over them; pat it with your hand, and bake them upon your bake stone.

To make FRENCH BREAD.

TAKE a quarter of a peck of flour, one ounce of butter melted in milk and water, mix two or three spoonfuls of barm with it, strain it through a sieve, beat the white of an egg, put it in your water with a little salt, work it up to a light paste, put it into a bowl, then pull it into pieces, let it stand all night, then work it well up again, cover it, and lay it on a dresser for half an hour, then work all the pieces separate and make them into rolls, and set them in the oven.

To make WHITE BREAD.

TO a gallon of the best flour, put six ounces of butter, half a pint of good yeast, a little salt, break two eggs into a bason, but leave out one of the whites, put a spoonful or two of water to them, and beat them up to a froth, and put them in the flour, have as much new milk as will wet it, make it just warm and mix it up, lay a handful of flour and drive it about, holding one hand in the dough, and driving it with the other band till it is quite light, then put it in your pan again, and put it near the tire and cover it with a cloth, and let it stand an hour and a quarter; make your rolls ten minutes before you set them in the oven, and prick them with a fork; if they are the bigness of a French roll, three quarters of an hour will bake them.

To make TEA CRUMPETS,

BEAT two eggs very, well, put to them a quart of warm milk and water, and a large spoonful of barm; beat in as much fine flour as will make them rather thicker than a common batter pudding, then make your bake-stone very hot, and rub it with a little butter wrapped in a clean linen cloth, then pour a large spoonful of batter upon your stone, and let it run to the size of a tea saucer; turn it, and when you want to use them toast them very crisp and hotter them.

CHAP. XII

LITTLE SAVORY DISHES

To ragoo PIGS FEET *and* EARS.

BOIL your feet and ears, then split your feet down the middle, and cut the ears in narrow slices, dip them in batter, and fry them a good brown, put a little beef gravy in a tossing- pan, with a tea spoonful of lemon pickle, a large one of mushroom catchup, the same of browning, and a little salt, thicken it with a lump of butter rolled in flour, and put in your feet and ears, give them a gentle boil, and then lay your feet in the middle of your dish, and the ears round them; strain your gravy and pour it over: Garnish with curled parsley _ It is a pretty corner dish for dinner,

To make a SOLOMON-GUNDY.

TAKE the white part of a roasted chicken, the yolks of four boiled eggs, and the whites of the same, two pickled herrings, and a handful of parsley, chop them separately exceeding small, take the same quantity of lean boiled ham scraped fine, turn a china basin upside down in the middle of a dish, make a quarter of a pound of butter in the shape of a pine apple and set it on the bason bottom, lay round your bason a ring of shred parsley, then a ring of yolks of eggs, then whites, then ham, then chicken, then herring, till you have covered your bason and used all the ingredients, lay the bones of the pickled herrings upon it with the tails up to the butter, and the heads lie on the edge of the dish ; lay a few capers, and three or four pickled oysters round your dish, and send it up.

SOLOMON-GUNDY *a second way.*

CHOP all the ingredients, as for the first, mix them well together, and put in the middle of your dish a large Seville orange, and your ingredients round it, rub a little cold butter through a sieve, and it will curl, lay it in lumps on the meat; stick a sprig of curled parsley on your butter and serve it up.

To roast a CALF'S HEART.

MAKE a forcemeat with the crumbs of half a penny loaf, a quarter of a pound of beef suet shred small, or butter, chop a little parsley, sweet marjoram, and lemon peel, mix it up with a little nutmeg, pepper, salt, and the yolk of an egg, fill your heart, and lay over the stuffing a caul of veal, or writing paper, to keep it in the heart, lay it in a Dutch oven, keep turning it and roast it thoroughly; when you dish it up, pour over it good melted butter, and lay slices of lemon round it, and send it to table.

To dress a Dish of LAMBS BITS,

SKIN the stones and split them, lay them on a dry cloth with the sweetbreads and liver, and dredge them well with flour, and fry them in boiling lard, or butter, a light brown, then lay them on a sieve to drain, fry a good quantity of parsley, lay your bits on the dish, and the parsley in lumps over it, pour melted butter round them.

To fricassee CALF'S-FEET.

BOIL your feet, take out the bones and cut the meat in thin slices, and put it into a tossing- pan, with half a pint of good gravy, boil them a little, and then put in a few morels, a tea spoonful of lemon pickle, a little mushroom powder, or pickled mushrooms, the yolks of four eggs boiled hard, and a little salt, thicken with a little butter rolled in flour, mix the yolk of an egg with a tea cupful of good cream, and half a nutmeg grated, put it in, and shake it over the fire, but do not let it boil, it will curdle the milk : garnish with lemon, and curled parsley.

CHICKENS in SAVORY JELLY.

ROAST two chickens, then boil a gang of calf's-feet to a strong jelly, take out the feet, skim off the fat, beat the whites of three eggs very well, then mix them with half a pint of white wine vinegar, the juice of three lemons, a blade or two of mace, a few pepper corns, and a little salt, put them to your jelly; when it has boiled five or six minutes, run it through a jelly bag several times till it is very clear, then put a little in the bottom of a bowl that will hold your chickens, when they are cold, and the jelly quite set, lay them in with their breasts down, then fill up your bowl quite full with the rest of your jelly, which you must take care to keep from setting (so that when you pour it into your bowl it will not break) let it stand all night, the next day put your bason into warm water, pretty near the top; as soon as you find it loose in the bason, lay your dish over it, and turn it out upon it.

PIGEONS in SAVORY JELLY.

ROAST your pigeons with the head and feet on, put a sprig of myrtle in their bills, make a jelly for them the same way as for the chickens, pour a little into a bason, when it is set lay in the pigeons with their breasts down, fill up your bowl with your jelly, and turn it out as before.

9 Small BiRDS in Savory Jelly.

TAKE eight small birds with their heads and feet on, put a good lump of butter in them and sew up their vents, put them in a jug, cover it close with a cloth, set them in a kettle of boiling water till they are enough, drain them, make your jelly as before, put a little into a bason, when it is set, lay in three birds with their breasts down, cover them with- the jelly, when it is set put the other five with the heads in the middle, fill up your bowl with jelly as before, and turn it out the same way.

SMELTS in SAVORY JELLY.

GUT and wash your smelts, season them with mace and fait, lay them in a pot with butter over them, tie them down with paper, and bake them half an hour, take them out, and when they are a little cool, lay them separately on a board to drain, when they are quite cold, lay them on a deep plate in what form you please, pour cold jelly over them, and they will look like live fish. — Make your jelly as before,

CRAW-FISH in SAVORY JELLY.

BOIL your craw- fish, then put a little jelly in a bowl, made as for the chickens, when it is set, put in a few craw-fish, then cover them with jelly, when it is cold, put in more lays till your bowl is full, let it stand all night, and turn them out the same as the chickens.

CRAW-FISH in JELLY.

BOIL half a dozen large craw-fish, and let them cool, wipe them clean, lay them in a punch-bowl with their backs downwards, pour in them some nice calf's-foot jelly, when it is cold turn it out upon a glass dish; it makes a very pretty side dish for either dinner or supper.

To dress MACCARONI with PARMESAN CHEESE.

BOIL four ounces of maccaroni till it be quite tender, and lay it on a sieve to drain, then put it in a tossing pan, with about a gill of good cream, a lump of butter rolled in flour, boil it five minutes, pour it on a plate, lay all over it Parmesan cheese, toasted ; send it to table on a water plate for it soon goes cold.

To stew CHEESE with LIGHT WIGS.

CUT a plateful of cheese, pour on it a glass of red wine, stew it before the fire, toast a light wig, pour over it two or three spoonfuls of hot red wine, put it in the middle of your dish, lay the cheese over it, and serve it up.

To Stew CHEESE.

CUT your cheese very thin, lay it in a toaster, set it before the fire, pour a glass of ale over it, let it stand till it is all like a light custard, then pour it on toasts or wigs, and send it in hot.

To Stew CHARDOONS.

TAKE the inside of your chardoons, wash them well, boil them in salt and water, put them into a tossing pan with a little veal gravy, a tea-spoonful of lemon pickle, a large one of mushroom catchup, pepper and salt to your taste, thicken it with flour and butter, boil it a little, and serve it up in a soup plate.

To fry CHARDOONS.

BOIL your chardoons as you did for stewing, then dip them in batter made of a spoonful of flour and ale, fry them in a pan of boiling lard, pour melted butter over them, and serve them up.

To ragoo CELERY.

TAKE off all the outsides of your heads of celery, cut them in pieces, put them in a tossing pan, with a little veal gravy or water, boil them till they are tender, put to it a tea- spoonful of lemon pickle, a meat spoonful of white wine, and a little salt; thicken it with flour and butter, and serve them up with sippets.

To fry CELERY.

BOIL your celery as for a ragoo, then cut it and dip it in batter, fry it a light brown in hog's- lard; put it on a plate, and pour melted butter upon it.

To stew CELERY

TAKE off the outside and the green ends of your heads of celery, boil them in water till they are very tender, put in a slice of lemon, a little beaten mace, thicken it with a good lump of butter and flour, boil it a little, beat the yolks of two eggs, grate in half a nutmeg, mix them with a tea-cupful of good cream, put it to your gravy, shake it over the fire till it be of a fine thickness, but do not let it boil ; serve it up hot.

Hot *scollop* POTATOES.

BOIL your potatoes, then beat them fine in a bowl with good cream, a lump of butter and salt, put them into scollop shells, make them smooth on the top, score them with a knife, lay thin slices of butter on the top of them, put them in a Dutch oven to brown before the fire. Three shells is enough for a dish.

To *Stew* MUSHROOMS.

TAKE large buttons, wipe them with a wet flannel, put them in a stew-pan with a little water, let them stew a quarter of an hour, then put in a little salt, work a little flour and butter to make it as thick as cream, let it boil five minutes, when you dish it up put two large spoonfuls of cream mixed with the yolk of an egg, shake it over the fire about a minute or two, but do not let it boil for fear of curdling ; put sippets round the inside of the rim of the dish, but not toasted, and serve it up. — It is proper for a side-dish for supper, or a corner for dinner.

Another Way to *Stew* MUSHROOMS.

PUT your mushrooms in salt and water, wipe them with a flannel, and put them again in salt and water, then throw them into a saucepan by them selves, and let them boil up as quick as possible, then put in a little Chyan pepper, a little mace if you like the flavour, let them stew in this a quarter of an hour, then add a tea-cupful of cream with a little flour and butter the size of a walnut; let them be served up as soon as done.

To make MUSHROOM LOAVES.

TAKE small buttons, wash them as for pickling, put them in a tossing pan, with a little white bread crumbs that have been boiled half an hour in water, then boil your mushrooms in the bread and water five minutes, thicken it with flour and butter, and two spoonfuls of cream, but no yolks of eggs, put in a little salt, then take five small French rolls, make holes in the tops of them about the size of a shilling, and scrape out all the crumb, and put in your mushrooms ; stick a bay leaf on the top of every roll. Five is a handsome dish for dinner, and three for supper.

To ragoo MUSHROOMS.

TAKE large mushrooms, peel, and take out the inside, broil them on a gridiron, when the outside is brown put them, into a tossing pan, with as much water as will cover them, let them stand ten minutes, then put to them a spoonful of white wine, the same of browning, a very little allegar, thicken it with flour and butter, boil it a little, lay sippets round your dish, and serve it up.

To stew PEAS *with* LETTUCES;

SHELL your peas, boil them in hard water with salt in it, drain them in a sieve, then cut your lettuces in slices, and fry them in fresh butter, put your peas and lettuces into a tossing pan, with a little good gravy, pepper, and salt, thicken it with flour and butter, put in a little shred mint, and serve it up in a soup dish.

To poach EGGS *with* TOASTS.

PUT your water on in a flat bottom pan, with a little salt, when it boils break your eggs carefully in, and let them boil two minutes, then take them up with an egg spoon, and lay them on buttered toasts.

To dress EGGS and SPINAGE.

PICK and wash your spinage in several waters, set a pan over the fire with a large quantity of water, throw a handful of salt in, when it boils put your spinage in, and let it boil two minutes, take it up with a fish slice, and lay it on the back of a hair sieve, squeeze the water out, and put it in a tossing pan, with a quarter of a pound of butter, keep turning and chopping it with a knife, till it is quite dry, then press it a little betwixt two pewter plates, cut it in the shape of sippets, and some in diamonds, poach your eggs as before, and lay them on your spinage, and serve them up hot. — N. B. You may boil brocoli instead of spinage, and lay it in bunches betwixt every egg.

To dress EGGS with ARTICHOKE BOTTOMS.

BOIL your artichoke bottoms in hard water, if dry ones in soft water, put in a good lump of butter in the water, it will make them boil in half the time, and they will be white and plump; when you put them up put the yolk of an hard egg in the middle of every bottom, and pour good melted butter upon them, and serve them up; you may lay asparagus, or brocoli, betwixt every bottom.

To make a fricassee of EGGS.

BOIL your eggs pretty hard, cut them in round slices, make a white sauce the same way as for boiled chickens, pour it over your eggs, lay sippets round them, and put a whole yolk in the middle of your plate. — It is proper for a corner dish at supper.

To fry SAUSAGES.

CUT them in single links, and fry them in fresh butter, then take a slice of bread and fry it a good brown in the butter you fried the sausages in, and lay it in the bottom of your dish, put the sausages on the toast, in four parts, and lay poached eggs betwixt them pour a little good melted butter round them, and serve them up.

To stew CUCUMBERS.

PEEL off the out-rind, slice the cucumbers pretty thick, fry them in fresh butter, and lay them on a sieve to drain, put them into a tossing pan with a large glass of red wine, the same of strong gravy, a blade or two of mace, make it pretty thick with flour and butter, and when it boils up put in your cucumbers, keep making them, and let them boil five minutes, be careful you do not break them pour them into a dish, and serve them up.

To make an AMULET

PUT a quarter of a pound of butter into a frying pan, break six eggs and beat them a little, strain them through a hair sieve, put them in when your butter is hot, and strew in a little shred parsley and boiled ham scraped fine, with nutmeg, pepper, and salt, fry it brown on the underside, lay it on your dish, but do not turn it, hold a hot salamander half a minute over it to take off the raw look of the eggs: stick curled parsley in it, and serve it up. — N. B. You may put in clary and chives, or onions if you like it.

To make an AMULET of ASPARAGUS.

TAKE six eggs, beat them up with cream, boil some of the largest and finest asparagus, when boiled cut off all the green in small pieces, and mix them with the eggs, and some pepper and salt; make your pan hot, and put in a slice of butter, then put them in, and send them up hot. — You may serve them up hot on buttered toasts.

To make CANADA.

GRATE the crumb of a penny loaf, and boil it in a pint of water, with one onion and a few pepper corns, till quite thick and soft, then put in two ounces of butter, a little salt, and half a pint of thick cream, keep stirring it till it is like a fine custard, pour it into a soup plate, and serve it up. — N. B. You may use sugar and currants, instead of onions and pepper corns if you please.

To make a RAMEQUIN OF CHEESE.

TAKE some old Cheshire cheese, a lump of butter, and the yolk of a hard boiled egg, and beat it very well together in a marble mortar, spread it on some slices of bread toasted and buttered; hold a salamander over them, and send them up.

PART III

CHAP. XIII

Observations on POTTING AND COLLARING

Cover your meat well with butter, and tie over it strong paper, and bake it well, when it comes out of the oven pick out all the skins quite clean, and drain the meat from the gravy, or the skins will hinder it from looking well, and the gravy will soon turn it sour, beat your seasoning well before you put in your meat, and put it in by degrees, as you are beating; when you put it into your pots, press it well, and let it be quite cold before you pour the clarified butter over it. --In collaring be careful you roll it up, and bind it close, boil it 'till it is thoroughly enough, when quite cold, put it into pickle with the binding on, next day take off the binding when it will leave the skin clear; make fresh pickle often, and your meat will keep good a long time.

To pot BEEF.

RUB twelve pounds of beef with half a pound of brown sugar, and one ounce of saltpetre, let it lie twenty-four hours, then wash it clean and dry it well with a cloth, season it with a little beaten mace, pepper and salt, to your taste, cut it in five or six pieces, and put it in an earthen pot, with a pound of butter in lumps upon it, set it in an hot oven, and let it stand three hours; then take it out, cut off the hard outsides, and beat it in a mortar; add to it a little more mace, pepper and salt: oil a pound of butter in the gravy and fat that came from your beef, and put it in as you see it requires it, and beat it exceeding fine, then put it into your pots, and press it close down; pour clarified butter over it, and keep it in a dry place,.

To pot BEEF to eat like VENISON.

PUT ten pounds of beef into a deep dish, pour over it a pint of red wine, and let it lie in it for two days, then season it with mace, pepper, and salt, and put it into a pot with the wine it was steeped in, add to it a large glass more of wine, tie it down with paper, and bake it three hours in a quick oven; when you take it out beat it in a mortar or wooden bowl, clarify a pound of butter, and put it in as you see it requires it, keep beating it till it is a fine paste, then put it into your pots, lay a paper over it, and set on a weight to press it down; the next day pour clarified butter over it, and keep it in a dry place for use

.

To pot OX CHEEK,

WHEN you stew an ox cheek, take some of the fleshy part and season it well with salt and pepper, and beat it very fine in a mortar with a little clear fat skimmed off the gravy, then put it close into your potting pots, and pour over it clarified butter, and keep it for use.

To pot VENISON.

IF your venison be stale rub it with vinegar, and let it lie one hour, then dry it clean with a cloth and rub it all over with red wine, season it with beaten mace, pepper, and. salt, put it on an earthen dish, and pour over it half a pint of red wine, and a pound of butter, and set it in the oven ; if it be a shoulder put a coarse paste, over it, and bake it all night in a brown bread oven; when it comes out, pick it clean from the bones, and beat it in a marble mortar, with the fat from your gravy ; if you find it not seasoned enough, add more seasoning and clarified butter, and keep beating it till it is a fine paste, then press it hard down into your pots, and pour clarified butter over it, and keep it in a dry place.

To pot VEAL.

CUT a fillet of veal in three or four pieces, season it with pepper, salt, and a little mace, put it into pots with half a pound of butter, tie a paper over it, and set it, in a hot oven, and bake it three hours, when you take it out cut off all the outsides, then put the veal in a marble mortar, and beat it with the fat from your gravy, then oil a pound of fresh butter, and put it in, a little at a time, and keep beating it till you see it is like a fine paste, then put it close down into your potting pots, put a paper upon it, and set on a weight to press it hard; when your veal is cold and stiff, pour over it clarified butter, the thickness of a crown piece, and tie it down.

To pot MARBLE VEAL.

BOIL a dried tongue, skin it, and cut it as thin as possible, and beat it exceeding well with near a pound of butter and a little beaten mace, till it is like a paste, have ready veal stewed and beat the same way as before, then put some veal into your potting pots, then some tongue in lumps over the veal: fill your pot close up with veal, and press it very hard down, and pour clarified butter over it, and keep it in a dry place. N. B. Do not lay on your tongue, in any form, but in lumps, and it will cut like marble; when you send it to the table cut it out in slices, and garnish it with curled parsley.

To pot TONGUES.

TAKE a neat's tongue, and rub it with an ounce of salt-petre, and four ounces of brown sugar, and let it lie two days, then boil it till it is quite tender, and take off the skin and side-bits, then cut the tongue in very thin slices, and beat it in a marble mortar, with one pound of clarified butter, mace, pepper, and salt to your taste, beat it exceeding fine, then put it close down into small potting pots, and pour clarified butter over them.

To pot a HARE.

HANG up your hare four or five days with the skin on, then case it, and cut it up as for eating, put it in a pot, and season it with mace, pepper, and salt, put a pound of butter upon it, tie it down, and bake it in a bread oven, when it comes out, pick it clean from the bones, and pound it very fine in a mortar, with the fat from your gravy, then put it close down into your pots, and pour clarified butter over it, and keep it in a dry place.

To pot HAM with CHICKENS.

TAKE as much lean of a boiled ham as you please, and half the quantity of fat, cut it as thin as possible, beat it very fine in a mortar, with a little oiled butter, beaten mace, pepper, and salt, put part of it into a china pot, then beat the white part of a fowl with a very little seasoning; it is to qualify the hams put a lay of chicken, then one of ham, then chicken at the top, press it hard down, and when it is cold, pour clarified butter over it; when you send it to the table cut out a thin slice in the form of half a diamond, and lay it round the edge of your pot.

To pot WOODCOCKS.

PLUCK six woodcocks, draw out the train, skewer their bills through their thighs, and put the legs through each other, and their feet upon their breasts, season them with three or four blades of mace, and a little pepper and salt, then put them into a deep pot, with a pound of butter over them, tie a strong paper over them, and bake them in a moderate oven; when they are enough, lay them on a dish, to drain the gravy from them, then put them into potting pots, and take all the clear butter from your gravy, and put it upon them, and fill up your pots with clarified butter, and keep them in a dry place.

To pot MOOR GAME.

PICK and draw your moor game, wipe them clean with a cloth, and season them pretty well with mace, pepper, and salt, put one leg through the other, roast them till they are quite enough, and a good brown; when they are cold put them into potting pots, and pour over them clarified butter, and keep them in a dry place. — N. B. Observe to leave their heads uncovered with butter.

To pot PIGEONS,

PICK your pigeons, cut off the pinions, wash them clean, and put them into a sieve to drain, then dry them with a cloth, and season them with pepper and salt, roll a lump of butter in chopped parsley, and put it into the pigeons, sew up the vent, then put them into a pot with butter over them, tie them down, and set them in a moderate oven; when they come out, put them into potting pots, and cover them well with clarified buttter.

To pot all Kinds of small BIRDS.

PICK and gut your birds, dry them well with a cloth, season them with mace, pepper, and salt, then put them into a pot with butter, tie your pot down with paper, and bake them in a moderate oven; when they come out, drain the gravy from them, and put them into potting pots, and cover them with clarified butter.

To make a cold PORCUPINE of BEEF.

SALT a flank of beef the same way as you did the round of beef, and turn it every day for a fortnight at least, then lay it flat upon a table, beat it an hour, or till it is soft all over, then rub it over with the yolks of three eggs, strew over it a quarter of an ounce of beaten mace, the same of nutmeg, pepper, and salt to your taste, the crumb of two penny loaves, and two large handfuls of parsley shred small, then cover it with thin slices of fat bacon, and roll your beef up very tight, and bind it well with pack-thread, boil it four hours, when it is cold, lard it all over, one row with the lean of ham, a second with cucumbers, a third with fat bacon, cut them in pieces about the thickness of a pipe, shank and lard it so that it may appear red, green, and white; send it to the table with pickles and scraped horse-radish round it, keep it in salt and water, and a little vinegar. — You may keep it four or five days without pickle.

To collar a BREAST of VEAL.

BONE your veal, and beat it a little, then rub it over with the yolk of an egg, strew over it a little beaten mace, nutmeg, pepper, and salt, a large handful of parsley chopped small, with a few sprigs of sweet marjoram, a little lemon peel cut exceeding fine, one anchovy warmed, boned, and chopped very small, and mixed with a few bread crumbs, then roll it up very tight, bind it hard with a fillet, and wrap it in a clean cloth, then boil it two hours and a half in soft water, when it is enough, hang it up by one end, and make a pickle for it; to one pint of salt and water, put half a pint of vinegar; when you send it to the table, cut a slice off one end: garnish with pickles and parsley.

To collar a CALF'S HEAD.

TAKE a calf's head with the skin on, and dress off the hair, then rip it down the face, and take out all the bones carefully from the meat, and steep it in warm blue milk, till it is white, then lay it flat, and rub it with the white of an egg, and strew over it a teaspoonful of white pepper, two or three blades of beaten mace, and one nutmeg, a spoonful of malt, two score of oysters chopped small, half a pound of beef marrow, and a large handful of parsley, lay them all over the inside of the head, cut off the ears, and by them in a thin part of the head, then roll it up tight, bind it up with a fillet, and wrap it up in a clean cloth, boil it two hours, and when it is almost cold, bind it up with a fresh fillet, and put it in a pickle made as above, and keep it for use.

To collar a BREAST of MUTTON.

BONE your mutton, and rub it over with the yolk of an egg, then grate over it a little lemon peel, and a nutmeg, with a little pepper and salt, then chop small one tea-cupful of capers, two anchovies, shred fine a handful of parsley, a few sweet herbs, mix them with the crumb of a penny loaf, and strew it over your mutton, and roll it up tight, boil it two hours, then take it up, and put it in a pickle made as for the calf's-head.

To collar PIG.

KILL your pig, dress off the hair, and draw out the entrails, and wash it clean, take a sharp knife, rip it open, and take out all the bones, then rub it all over with pepper and salt beaten fine, a few sage leaves, and sweet herbs chopped small, then roll up your pig tight, and bind it with a fillet, then fill your boiler with soft water, one pint of vinegar, and a handful of salt, eight or ten cloves, a blade or two of mace, a few pep per corns, and a bunch of sweet herbs; when it boils put in your pig, and boil it till it is tender, then take it up, and when it is almost cold, bind it over again, and put it into an earthen pot, and pour the liquor your pig was boiled in upon it, keep it covered, and it is fit for use.

To collar SWINE'S FACE.

CHOP the face in many places, and wash it in several waters, then boil it till the meat will leave the bones, take out the bones, cut open the ears, and take out the ear roots, cut the meat in pieces, and season it with pepper and salt ; while it is hot put it into an earthen pot, but put the ears round the outside of the meat, put a board on that will goon the inside of the pot, and set a heavyweight upon it, and let it stand all night, the next day turn it out, cut it round-ways, and it will look close and bright.

To make MOCK BRAWN

TAKE a piece of the belly part, and the head of a young porker, rub it with salt-petre, and let it lie three days, then wash it clean, split the head and boil it, then take out the bones, and cut it in pieces, then take four ox feet boiled tender and cut in thin pieces, lay them in your belly piece with the head cut small, then roll it up tight with sheet tin, that a trencher will go in at each end, boil it four or five hours ; when it comes out, set it upon one end and press the trencher down with a large lead weight, let it stand all night, and in the morning take it out of your tin, and bind it with a white fillet, put it into cold salt and water, and it will be fit for use. N. B. You must make fresh salt and water every four days, and it will keep a long time.

To collar FLAT RIBS of BEEF.

BONE your beef, lay it flat upon a table, and beat it half an hour with a wooden mallet till it is quite soft, then rub it with six ounces of brown sugar, four ounces of common salt, and one ounce of salt-petre beat fine, let it lie then for ten days, and turn it once every day, take it out, then put it in warm water for eight or ten hours, then lay it flat upon a table, with the outward skin down, and cut it in rows, and across, about the breadth of your finger, but take care you do not cut the outside skin; then fill one nick with chopped parsley, the second with fat pork, the third with crumbs of bread, mace, nutmeg, pepper, and salt, then parsley, and so on till to have filled all your nicks; then roll it up tight you and bind it round with coarse broad tape, wrap it in a cloth and boil it four or five hours; then take it up, and hang it up by one end of the string to keep it round, save the liquor it was boiled in, the next day skim it, and add to it half the quantity of allegar as you have liquor, and a little mace, long pepper, and salt, then put in your beef, and keep it for use. N. B. When you send it to the table cut a little off both ends, and it will be in diamonds of different colours, and look very pretty, set it upon a dish as you do brawn; if you make a fresh pickle every week it will keep a long time.

To collar BEEF

SALT your beef, and beat it as before, then rub it over with the yolks of eggs, strew over it two large handfuls of parsley shred small, half an ounce of mace, black pepper and salt to your taste, roll it up tight, and bind it about with a coarse broad tape, and boil it till it is tender; make a pickle for it the same way as before.

To force a ROUND of BEEF.

TAKE a good round of beef, and rub over it a quarter of an hour with two ounces of salt petre, the same of bay salt, half a pound of brown sugar, and a pound of common salt, let it lie in it for ten or twelve days, turn it once every day in the brine, then warn it well, and make holes in it with a penknife about an inch one from another, and fill one hole with shred parsley, a second with fat pork cut in small pieces, and a third with bread crumbs, beef marrow, a little mace, nutmeg, pepper, and salt, mixed together, then parsley, and so on till you have filled all the holes, then wrap your beef in a cloth, and bind it with a fillet, and boil it four hours; when it is cold, bind it over again, and cut a thin slice off before you send it to the table: garnish with parsley and red cabbage.

To souse a TURKEY.

KILL your turkey and let it hang four or five days in the feathers, then pick it and lit it up the back, and take out the entrails, bone it, and bind it with a piece of matting like sturgeon or Newcastle salmon, set over the fire a clean saucepan, with a pint of strong allegar, a score of cloves, three or four blades of mace, a nutmeg sliced, a few pepper corns, and a handful of salt, when it boils put in the turkey, and boil it one hour, then take it up, and when cold, put it into an earthen pot, and pour the liquor over it, and keep it for use; when you send it to table lay sprigs of fennel over it.

To souse PIGS FEET and EARS.

CLEAN your pigs feet and ears, and boil them till they are tender, then split the feet, and put them into salt and water with the ears; when you use them dry them well with a cloth, and dip them in batter made of flour and eggs, fry them a good brown, and send them up with good melted butter. — N. B. You may eat them cold; make fresh pickle every two days, and they will keep some time.

To souse TRIPE;

WHEN your tripe is boiled, put it into salt and water, change the salt and water every day till you use it, dip it in batter, and fry it as the pigs feet and ears, or boil it in fresh salt and water, with an onion sliced, and a few sprigs of parsley, and send melted butter for sauce.

To hang a SIRLOIN of BEEF to roast.

TAKE the suet out of a sirloin, and rub it half an hour with one ounce of salt-petre four ounces of common salt, and half a pound of brown sugar, hang it up ten or twelve days, then wash it, and roast it; you may eat it either hot or cold.

To salt HAMS.

AS soon as your hams are cut out, rub them very well with one ounce of salt-petre, half an ounce of salt prunella pounded, and one pound of common salt to every ham, lay them in lead or earthen salt pans for ten days, turn them once in the time, then rub them well with more common salt, let them lie ten days longer, and turn them every day, then take them out, and scrape them exceeding clean, and dry them well with a clean cloth, and rub it slightly over with a little salt, and, hang them up to dry.

To smoke HAMS.

WHEN you take your hams out of the pickle, and have rubbed them dry with a coarse cloth, hang them in a chimney, and make a fire of oak shavings, and lay over it horse litter, and one pound of juniper berries, keep the fire smothered down for two or three days, and then hang them up to dry.

To salt CHOPS.

THROW over your chops a handful of salt, and lay them skin-side down aslant on a board, to let all the blood, run from them ; the next day pound to every pair of chops one ounce of bay salt, the same of salt-petre, two ounces of brown sugar, and half a pound of common salt, mix them together, and rub them exceeding well, let them lie ten days in your salting cistern, then rub them with common salt, and let them lie a week longer, and rub them clean, and hang them to dry in a dry place.

To salt BACON

WHEN your pig is cut down, cut off the hams and head, if it be a large one cut out a chine, but leave in the spare ribs, it keeps the bacon from rusting, and the gravy in, salt it with common salt, and a little salt-petre, (but neither bay salt nor sugar) let it lie ten days on a table, that will let all the brine run from it, then salt it again ten or twelve days, turning it every day after the second salting, then scrape it very clean, rub a little dry salt on it, and hang it up. — N. B. Take care to scrape the white froth off very clean that is on it, which is caused by the salt to work out of your pork, and rub on a little dry salt, it keeps the bacon from rusting ; the dry salt will candy and mine like diamonds on your bacon.

To salt TONGUES.

SCRAPE your tongues, and dry them clean with a cloth, and salt them well with common salt, and half an ounce of salt-petre to every tongue, lay them in a deep pot, and turn them every day for a week or ten days, salt them again, and let them lie a week longer, take them up, dry them with a cloth, flour them, and hang them up.

To salt a LEG of MUTTON.

POUND one ounce of bay salt, and half an ounce of salt-petre, and rub it all over your leg of mutton, and let it lie all night ; the next day salt it well with common salt, and let it lie a week or ten days, then hang it up to dry.

To pickle PORK.

CUT your pork in such pieces as will be most convenient to lie in your powdering tub, rub every piece all over with salt-petre, then take one part bay salt, and two parts common salt, and rub every piece well, lay the pieces as close as possible in your tub, and throw a little salt over.

To pickle BEEF.

TAKE sixteen quarts of cold water and put to it as much salt as will make it bear an egg, then add two pounds of bay salt, half a pound of salt-petre pounded small, and three pounds of brown sugar ; mix all together, then put your beef into it, and keep it in a dry cool place.

CHAP. XIV

Observations On POSSETS AND GRUELS &c.

In making possets, always mix a little of the hot cream or milk with your wine, it will keep the wine from curdling the rest, and take the cream off the fire before you mix altogether.—observe in making gruels, that you boil them in well-tined sauce pans, for nothing will fetch the verdigrease out of copper sooner than acids or wines, which are the chief ingredients in gruels, sagos, and wheys; don't let your gruel or sago skim over, for it boils into them, and makes them a muddy colour.

To make a SACK POSSET.

GRATE two Naples biscuits into a pint of thin cream, put in a stick of cinnamon, and set it over a slow fire, boil it till it is of a proper thickness; then add half a pint of sack, a slice of the end of a lemon, with sugar to your taste; stir it gently over the fire, but do not let it boil lest it curdle, serve it up with dry toast.

To make a BRANDY POSSET.

BOIL a quart of cream over a slow fire, with a stick of cinnamon in it, take it off to cool, beat the yolks of six eggs very well, and mix them with the cream, add nutmeg and sugar to your taste, set it over a slow fire, and stir it one way ; when it is like a fine thin custard, take it off, and pour it into your turene or bowl, with a glass of brandy, stir it gently together, and serve it up with tea wafers round it.

To make a LEMON POSSET.

GRATE the crumb of a penny loaf very fine, and put it into rather more than a pint of water, with half a lemon peel grated, or sugar rubbed upon it to take out the essence, boil them together till it looks thick and clear, then beat it very well; — to the juice of half a lemon, put in a pint of mountain wine, three ounces of Jordan almonds, and one ounce of bitter, beat fine with a little orange flower, or French brandy, and sugar to your taste, mix it well and put it in your posset, serve it up in a turene or bowl. — N. B. An orange posset is made the same way.

To make an ALMOND POSSET.

GRATE the crumb of a penny loaf very fine, pour a pint of boiling milk upon it, let it stand two or three hours, then beat it exceeding well, add to it a quart of good cream, four ounces of almonds blanched and beat as fine as possible, with rose water, mix them all well together, and set them over a very slow fire, and boil them a quarter of an hour, then set it to cool, and beat the yolks of four eggs, and mix them with your cream when it is cold, sweeten it to your taste; then stir it over a slow fire, till it grows pretty thick, but do not let it boil, it will curdle; then pour it into a china bowl ; when you send it to table, put in three macaroons to swim on the top, — It is proper for top at supper.

To make a WINE POSSET.

TAKE a quart of new milk, and the crumb of a penny loaf, and boil them till they are soft, when you take it off the fire, grate in half a nutmeg, and sugar to your taste, then put it into a china bowl, and put it in a pint of Lisbon wine carefully, a little at a time, or it will make the curd hard and tough; serve it up with toast and butter upon a plate.

To make an ALE POSSET.

PUT a little white bread in a pint of good milk, set it over the fire, then warm a little more than a pint of good strong ale, with nutmeg and sugar to your taste, then put it in a bowl, when your milk boils pour it upon your ale, let it stand a few minutes to clear, and the curd will rise to the top.

To mull WINE.

GRATE half a nutmeg into a pint of wine, and sweeten it to your taste with loaf sugar, set it over the fire, and when it boils take it off to cool, beat the yolks of four eggs exceeding well, add to them a little cold wine, then mix them carefully with your hot wine, a little at a time, then pour it backwards and forwards several times till it looks fine and bright, then set it on the fire, and heat it a little at a time for several times till it is quite hot and pretty thick, and pour it backwards and forwards several times ; then send it in chocolate cups, and serve it up with dry toast cut in long narrow pieces.

To mull ALE.

TAKE a pint of good strong ale, put it into a saucepan, with three or four cloves, nutmeg and sugar to your taste, set it over the fire, when it boils take it off to cool, beat the yolks of four eggs very well, and mix them with a little cold ale, then put it to your warm ale, and pour it in and out of your pan for several times, then set it over a slow fire and heat it a little, then take it off again and beat it two or three times till it is quite hot, then serve it up with dry toast.

To make mulled WINE.

BOIL a quart of new milk five minutes with a stick of cinnamon, nutmeg, and sugar to your taste, then take it off the fire and let it stand to cool, beat the yolks of six eggs very well, and mix them with a little cold cream, then mix them with your milk, and pour it backwards and forwards the same as you do mulled ale, and send it to the table with a plate of biscuits.

To make BEEF TEA,

TAKE a pound of lean beef, cut it in very thin slices, put it into a jar, and pour a quart of boiling water upon it, cover it very close to keep an the steam, let it stand by the fire, it is very good for a weak constitution, it must be drunk when it is new milk warm.

To make CHICKEN BROTH.

SKIN a small chicken, and split it in two, and boil one half in three half pints of water, with a blade or two of mace, a small crust of white bread, boil it over a slow fire till it is reduced to half the quantity, pour it into a bason, and take off the fat; and send it up with a dry toast.

To make CHICKEN WATER.

SKIN half a fowl, break the bones, and cut the flesh as thin as possible, then put it into a jar, and pour a pint of boiling water upon it, cover it close up, and set it by the fire for three hours, and it will be ready to drink.

To make MUTTON BROTH.

TAKE the scrag end of a neck of mutton, chop it into small pieces, put it into a saucepan, and fill it with water, set it over the fire, and when the scum begins to rise, take it clean off, and put in a blade or two of mace, a little French barley, or a crust of white bread to thicken it when you have boiled your mutton that it will shake to pieces, strain your broth through a hair sieve, scum off the fat, and send it up with dry toast.

To make WHITE WINE WHEY.

PUT a pint of skimmed milk, and half a pint of white wine into a bason, let it stand a few minutes, then pour over it a pint of boiling water, let it stand a little, and the curd will gather in a lump, and settle to the bottom, then pour your whey into a china bowl, and put in a lump of sugar, a sprig of balm, or a slice of lemon.

To make SCURVY GRASS WHEY.

BOIL a pint of blue milk, take it off to cool, then put in two spoonfuls of the juice of scurvy grass, and two spoonfuls of good old verjuice, set it over the fire, and it will turn to a fine whey; it is very good to drink in the spring for the scurvy.

To make CREAM OF TARTAR WHEY.

PUT a pint of blue milk over the fire, when it begins to boil, put in two tea spoonfuls of cream of tartar, then take it off the fire, and let it stand till the curd settles to the bottom of the pan, then pour it into a basin to cool, and drink it milk warm.

To make BARLEY WATER.

TAKE two ounces of barley, boil it in two quarts of water till it looks white, and the barley grows soft, then strain the water from the barley, add to it a little currant jelly or lemon.— N. B. You may put a pint more water to your barley, and boil it over again.

To make GROAT GRUEL

BOIL half a pint of groats in three pints of water or more, as you would have your gruel for thickness, with a blade or two of mace in it; when your groats are soft, put in it white wine and sugar to your taste, then take it off the fire, put to it a quarter of a pound of currants washed and picked, put it in a China bowl, with a toast: of bread round it, cut in long narrow pieces.

To make SAGO GRUEL,

TAKE four ounces of sago, give it a scald in hot water, then strain it through a hair sieve, and put it over the fire with two quarts of water and a stick of cinnamon, keep scumming it till it grows thick and clear, when your sago is enough, take out the cinnamon and put in a pint of red wine, if you would have it very strong put in more than a pint, and sweeten it to your taste, then set it over the fire to warm, but do not let it boil after the wine is put in, it weakens the taste, and makes the colour not so deep a red, pour it into a turene, and put in, a slice of lemon, when you are sending it to table. It is proper for a top dish for supper.

To make SAGO with MILK.

WASH your sago in warm water, and set it over the fire with a stick of cinnamon, and as much water as will boil it thick and soft, then put in as much thin cream or new milk as will make it a proper thickness, grate in half a nutmeg, sweeten it to your taste and serve it up in a China bowl or turene. — It is proper for a top dim for supper.

To make BARLEY GRUEL.

TAKE four ounces of pearl barley, boil it in two quarts of water with a stick of cinnamon in it, till it is reduced to one quart, add to it a little more than a pint of red wine, and sugar to your taste, wash and pick two or three ounces of currants very clean.

To make WATER GRUEL.

TAKE one spoonful of oatmeal, boil it in three pints of water for an hour and a half, or till it is fine and smooth, then take it off the fire -and let it stand to settle, then pour it in a china bowl, and add white wine, sugar, and nutmeg to your taste, serve it up hot with a toast buttered upon a plate,

To make a sweet PANADO.

CUT all the crust off a penny loaf, slice the rest very thin and put it into a saucepan with a pint of water, boil it till it is very soft and looks clear, then put in a glass of sack or Madeira wine, grate in a little nutmeg, and put in a lump of butter the size of a walnut, and sugar to your taste, beat it exceeding fine, then put it in a deep soup dish and serve it up.- N. B. You may leave out the wine and sugar, and put in a little good cream and a little salt, if you like it better.

To make CHOCOLATE.

SCRAPE four ounces of chocolate and pour a quart of boiling water upon it, mill it well with a chocolate mill, and sweeten it to your taste, give it a boil and let it stand all night, then mill it again very well, boil it two minutes, then mill it till it will leave a froth upon the top of your cups.

CHAP. XV

Observations on WINES, CATCHUP, and VINEGAR.

WINE is a very necessary thing in most families, and is often spoiled through mismanagement of putting together, for if you let it stand too long before you get it cold, and do not take great care to put your barm upon it in time, it summer-beams and blinks in the tub, so that it makes your wine fret in the cask, and will not let it fine; it is equally as great a fault to let it work too long in the tub, for that takes off all the sweetness and flavour of the fruit or flowers your wine is made from, so the only caution I can give, is to be careful in following the receipts, and to have your vessels dry, rinse them with brandy, and close them up as soon as your wine has done fermenting.

To make LEMON WINE *to drink like* CITRON WATER.
PARE five dozen of lemons very thin, put the peels into five quarts of French brandy, and let them stand fourteen days, then make the juice into a syrup with three pounds of single refined sugar; when the peels are ready, boil fifteen gallons of water with forty pounds of single refined sugar for half an hour, then put it into a tub, when cool add to it one spoonful of barm, let it work two days, then tun it, and put in the brandy, peels, and syrup, stir them all together, and close up your cask, let it stand three months, then bottle it, and it will be pale and as fine as any citron water; it is more like a cordial than wine.

To make LEMON WINE *a second Way.*
TO one gallon of water, put three pounds of powder sugar, boil it a quarter of an hour; scum it well, then pour it on the rinds of four lemons pared very thin, make the

juice into a thick syrup, with half a pound of the above sugar, take a slice of bread toasted and spread on it a spoonful of new barm, put it in the liquor when lukewarm, and let it work two days, then turn it into your cask, and let it stand three months, and then bottle it.

To make ORANGE WINE.

TO ten gallons of water, add twenty-four pounds of lump sugar, beat the whites of six eggs very well, and mix them when the water is cold, then boil it an hour, scum it very well, take four dozen of the roughest and largest Seville oranges you can get, pare them very thin, put them into a tub, and put the liquor on boiling hot, and when you think it is cold enough add to it three or four spoonfuls of new yest, with the juice of the oranges, and half an ounce of cochineal beat fine, and boiled in a pint of water, stir it all together, and let it work four days, then put it in the casks, and in six weeks time bottle it for use.

To make ORANGE WINE *a second Way.*

TO ten gallons of water, add twenty-seven pounds of lump sugar, boil it one hour, skim it all the time, then take the peels of five dozen of oranges, pared very thin, put them into a tub; when you take the liquor off the fire, pour it upon them, and when it is almost cold add to it three spoonfuls of good yest and free from being bitter, with the juice of all your oranges; let it work two or three days, stir it twice a day, then put it into a barrel with one quartos mountain wine, and four ounces of the syrup of citron; stir it well in the liquor; leave the barrel open till it has done working, then close it well up, let it stand six weeks, and then bottle it.

To make ORANGE WINE *a third Way.*

TAKE six gallons of water, and fifteen pounds of powder sugar, the whites of six eggs well beat, boil them all three quarters of an hour, and scum it well; when it is cold for working, take six spoonfuls of good yeast, and six ounces of the syrup of lemons, mix them well, and add it to the liquor, with the juice and peel of fifteen oranges; let it work two days and one night, then tun it, and in three months bottle it.

To make SMYRNA RAISIN WINE.

TO one hundred of raisins put twenty gallons of water, let it stand fourteen days, then put it into your cask; when it has been in six months, add to it one gallon of French brandy, and when it is fine then bottle it.

To make ELDER RAISIN WINE.

TO every gallon of water put six pounds of Malaga raisins shred small, put them into a vessel, pour the water on them boiling hot, and let it stand nine days, stirring it twice every day, get the elder berries when full ripe, pick them off the stalks, put them into an earthen pot, and set them in a moderate oven all night, then strain them through a coarse cloth, and to every gallon of liquor add one quart of this juice, stir it well together, then toast a slice of breads and spread three spoonfuls of yest on both sides, and put it in your wine, and let it work a day or two, then tun it into your cask, fill it up as it works over, when it has done working, close it up, and let it stand one year.

To make RAISIN WINE *another way*

BOIL ten gallons of spring water one hour, when it is milk warm, to every gallon add six pounds of Malaga raisins, clean picked and half chopped, stir it up together twice a day for nine or ten days, then run it through a hair sieve, and squeeze the raisins well with your hands, and put the liquor in your barrel, bung it close, up, and let it stand three months and then bottle it.

To make GINGER WINE.

TAKE four gallons of spring water, and seven pounds of Lisbon sugar, boil it a quarter of an hour, and keep scumming it well; when the liquor is cold squeeze in the juice of two lemons, then boil the peel with two ounces of ginger in three pints of water one hour; when it is cold put it all together into a barrel, with two spoonfuls of yeast, a quarter of an ounce of isinglass beat very thin, and two pounds of jar raisins, then close it up, and let it stand seven weeks, then bottle it; the best season to make it is the spring.

To make PEARL GOOSEBERRY WINE.

TAKE as many of the best pearl gooseberries when ripe as you please, bruise them with a wooden pestle in a tub, and let them stand all night, then press and squeeze them through a hair sieve, let the liquor stand seven or eight hours, then pour it clear from the sediments and to every three pints of liquor add a pound of double refined sugar, and stir it about till it is melted, then put to it five pints of water, and two pounds more of sugar, then dissolve half an ounce of isinglass in part of the liquor that has been boiled, put all in your cask, stop it well up for three months, then bottle it, and put in every bottle a lump of double refined sugar. This is excellent wine.

To make GOOSEBERRY WINE *a second Way.*

TO a gallon of water put three pounds of lump sugar, boil it a quarter of an hour, and scum it very well, then let it stand till it is al most cold, and take four quarts of gooseberries when full ripe, bruise them in a marble mortar, and put them in your vessels, then pour in the liquor and let it stand two days, and stir it every four hours, steep half an ounce of isinglass in a pint of brandy two days, strain the wine through a flannel bag into a case, then beat the isinglass in a marble mortar with five whites of eggs, then whisk them together half an hour, and put it in the wine and beat them all together, close up your cask and put clay over it, let it stand six months, then bottle it off for use, put in each bottle a lump of sugar and two raisins of the fun; this is a very rich wine, and when it has been kept in the bottles two or three years, will drink like champagne.

To make BLACKBERRY WINE.

GATHER your berries when they are full ripe, take twelve quarts, and crush them with your hand, boil six gallons of water with twelve pounds of brown sugar a quarter of an hour, scum it well, then pour it on the blackberries, and let it stand all night, then strain it through a hair sieve, put into your cask six pounds of Malaga raisins a little cut, then put the wine into the cask with one ounce of isinglass, which must be dissolved in a little cyder, stir it all up together, close it up, and let it stand six months, and then bottle it.

To make RASPBERRY WINE.

GATHER your raspberries when full ripe and quite dry, crush them directly and mix them with sugar, it will preserve the flavour which they would lose in two hours; to every quart of raspberries put a pound of fine powder sugar, when you have got the quantity you intend to make, to every quart of raspberries add two pounds more of sugar, and one gallon of cold water, stir it well together, and let it ferment three days, stirring it five or six times a day, then put it in your cask, and for every gallon put in two whole eggs, take care they are not broke in putting them in, close it well up, and at it stand three months, then bottle it. — N. B If you gather the berries when the sun is hot upon them, and be quick in making your wine, it will keep the virtue in the raspberries, and make the wine more pleasant.

To make RED CURRANT WINE.

GATHER the currants when full ripe, strip them from the stems, and squeeze out the juice; to one gallon of the juice put two gallons of cold water, and two spoonfuls of yeast, and let it work two days, then strain it through a hair sieve, at the same time put one ounce of isinglass to steep in cyder, and to every gallon of liquor add three pounds of loaf sugar, stir it well together, put it in a good cask: to every ten gallons of wine put two quarts of brandy, mix them all exceeding well in your cask, close it well up, let it stand four months, then bottle it.

To make CURRANT WINE *another way.*

TAKE an equal quantity of red and white currants, bake them an hour in a moderate oven, then squeeze them through a coarse cloth, what water you intend to use have ready boiling and to every gallon of water put in one quart of juice and three pounds of loaf sugar, boil it a quarter of an hour, scum it well, then put it in a tub, when cool toast a slice of bread and spread on both sides two spoonfuls of yeast, and let it work three days, stir it three or four times a day, then put it into a cask, and to every ten gallons of wine add a quartos French brandy and the whites of ten eggs well beat, make the cask close up, and let it stand three months, then bottle it. — N. B. This is a pale wine, but it is a very good one for keeping, and drinks pleasant.

To make SYCAMORE WINE.

TAKE two gallons of the sap and boil it half an hour, then add to it four pounds of fine powder sugar, beat the whites of three eggs to a froth, and mix them with the liquor, but if it be too hot, it will poach the eggs, scum it very well, and boil it half an hour, then strain it through a hair sieve, and let it stand till next day, then pour it clean from the sediments, put half a pint of good yest to every twelve gallons, cover it close up with blankets till it is white over, then put it into the barrel, and leave the bung-hole open till it has done working, then close it well up, let it stand three months, then bottle it, the fifth part of the sugar must: be loaf, and if you like raisins, they are a great addition to the wine. N. B. You may make birch wine the same way.

To make BIRCH WINE a second way

BOIL twenty gallons of birch water half an hour, then put in thirty pounds of bastard sugar, boil your liquor and sugar three quarters of an hour, and keep scumming it all the while, then put it into a tub and let it stand till it is quite cold, add to it three pints of yest, stir it three or four times a day for four or five days, then put it into a cask with two pounds of Malaga raisins, and one pound of loaf sugar, and half an ounce of isinglass, which must be dissolved in part of the liquor, then put to it one gallon of new ale that is ready for tunning, work it very well in the cask five or six days, then close it up and let it stand a year, then bottle it off.

To make WALNUT WINE.

TO every gallon of water put two pounds of brown sugar and one pound of honey, boil them half an hour, and take off the scum, put into the tub a handful of walnut leaves to every gallon and pour the liquor upon them, let it stand all night, then take out the leaves, and put in half a pint of yeast, and let it work fourteen days, beat it four or five times a day, which will take off the sweetness, then stop up the cask, and let it stand six months. — This is a good wine against consumptions, or any inward complaints.

To make COWSLIP WINE.

TO two gallons of water add two pounds and a half of powder sugar, boil them half an hour, and into a tub to cool, with the rinds of two lemons; when it is cold add four quarts of cowslip flowers to the liquor, with the juice of two lemons, let it stand in the tub two days, stirring it every two or three hours, and then put it in the barrel, and let it stand three weeks or a month, then bottle it, and put a lump of sugar into every bottle., N. B. It makes the best and strongest wine to have only the tops of the peeps,

A second Way to make COWSLIP WINE.

BOIL twelve gallons of water a quarter of an hour, then add two pounds and a half of loaf sugar to every gallon of water, then boil it as long as the scum rises till it clears itself, when almost cold pour it into a tub, with one spoonful of yeast, let it work one day, then put in thirty-two quarts of cowslip flowers, and let it work two or three days, then put it all into a barrel, with the parings of twelve lemons, the same of oranges, make the juice of them into a thick syrup, with two or three pounds of loaf sugar; when the wine has done working, add the syrup to it, then stop up your barrel very well and let it stand two or three months, then bottle it.

To make ELDER FLOWER WINE.

TAKE the flowers of elder, and be careful that you do not let any stalks in, to every quart of flowers put one gallon of water and three pounds of loaf sugar, boil the water and sugar a quarter of an hour, then pour it on the flowers, and let it work three days then strain the wine through a hair sieve, and put it into a cask; to every ten gallons of wine add one ounce of isinglass dissolved in cyder, and six whole eggs, close it up, and let it stand six months, and then bottle it.

To make BALM WINE.

TAKE nine gallons of water to forty pounds of sugar, boil them gently for two hours, scum it well, then put it into a tub to cool, then take two pounds and a half of the tops of balm, bruise it, and put it into a barrel with a little new yest, and when the liquor is cold, pour it on the balm, stir it well together, and let it stand twenty-four hours, and keep stirring it often, then close it up, and let it stand six weeks, then rack it off, and put a lump of sugar into every bottle, cork it well, and it will be better the second year than the first, N. B. Clary wine is made the same way

To make IMPERIAL WATER.

PUT two ounces of cream of tartar into a large jar, with the juice and peels of two lemons, pour on them seven quarts of boiling water, when it is cold, clear it through a gauze sieve, sweeten it to your taste, and bottle it. — It will be fit to use the next day.

To cure acid RAISIN WINE.

THE following ingredients must be proportioned to the degrees of acidity or sourness, if but small, you must use less, if a stronger acid, a larger quantity, it must be proportioned to the quantity of wine, as well as the degree of acidity or sourness; be sure that the cask be near full before you apply the ingredients, which will have this good effect, the acid part of the wine will rise to the top immediately, and issue out at the bung-hole, but if the cask be not full, the part that should fly off will continue in the cask, and weaken the body of the wine, but if your cask be full, it will be ready to have a body laid on it in three or four days time. — I shall here proportion the ingredients for a pipe; supposing it to be quite acid, that is just recoverable. Take two gallons of skimmed milk, and two ounces of isinglass, boil them a quarter of an hour, strain the liquor and let it stand until it is cold, then break it well with your whisk, add to it four pounds of alabaster, and three pounds of whiting, stir them well up together, then put in one ounce of salt of tartar, mix by degrees a little of the wine with it so as to dissolve it to a thin liquor, put these in your cask, and stir it well with a paddle, and it will immediately discharge the acid part from it as before mentioned; when it has done fermenting, bung it up for three days, then rack it off, and you will find part of its body gone off by the strong fermentation; to remedy this, you must lay a fresh body on in proportion to the degree to which it hath been lowered by the above method, always having a special care not to alter its flavour, and this must be done with clarified sugar, for no fluid will agree with it, but what will make it thinner, or confer its own taste, therefore the following is the best method for performing it: to lay a fresh body on wine, take three quarters of an hundred of brown sugar, and put it into your cop per, then put in a gallon of lime water to keep it from burning, stir it all the while till it boils, then mash three eggs and shells all together add them to the sugar, and keep it stirring about, and as 'the scum or filth rises take it off very clean, then put it in your can, and let it stand till it is cold before you use it, then break it with your whisk by degrees, with about ten gallons of the wine, and apply it to the pipe, work it with the paddle an hour, then put a quart of stum- forcing to it, which will unite their bodies, and make it fine and bright.

To make STUM.

TAKE a five gallon cask that has been well soaked in water, set it to drain, then take a pound of roll brimstone and melt it in a ladle, put as many rags to it as will suck up the melted brim stone, burn all those rags in the cask, cover the bung-hole but let it have a little air, so that it will keep burning; when it is burned out, put to it three gallons of the strongest cyder, and one ounce of common alum pounded, mix it with the cyder in the cask, and roll it about five or six times a day, for ten days, then take out the bung, and hang the remainder of the rags on a wire in the cask, as near the cyder as possible, and set them on fire as before, when it is burnt out bung the calk close, and roll it well about three or four times a day for two days, then let it stand seven or eight days, and this liquor will be so strong as to affect your eyes by looking at it. When you force a pipe of wine take a quart of this liquor, beat half an ounce of isinglass, and pull it in small pieces, whisk it together, and it will dissolve in four or five hours, break the jelly with your whisk, add a pound of alabaster to it and dissolve it in a little of the wine, then put it in the pipe and bung it close up, and in a day's time it will be fine and bright.

To refine MALT LIQUOR,

TO cure a hogshead of four ale : Take two ounces of isinglass, dissolve it in two quarts of new ale, and set it all night by the fire, then take two pounds of coarse brown sugar, and boil it in a quart of new wort, a quarter of an hour, then put it into a pail, with two gallons of new ale out of the kear, whisk the above ingredients very well for an hour or more till it be all of a white froth, beat very fine one pound of plaster of Paris, and put it into your caste, with the fermentation, and whisk it very well for half an hour in your castle with a strong hand, until you have brought all the filth and sediments from the bottom of your cask, and it will look white; if your cask be not full, fill it up with new ale, and the fermentation will have this good effect; the acid part of the ale will rise to the top immediately, and issue out at the bung hole, but, if the cask be not full, the part that should fly out will continue in, and weaken the body of the ale, be sure you do not fail filling up your cask four or five times a day, until it has done working, and all the sourness or white muddy part is gone, and when it begins to look like new tunned ale, put in a large handful of spent hops, close it up, and let it stand six weeks; if it be not fine, and cream like bottled ale, let it stand a month longer, and it will drink brisk like bottled ale; this is an excellent method, and I have used it to ale that has been both white and sour, and never found it to fail. If you have any malt that you suspect is not good, save out two gallons of wort, and a few hours before you want it, add to it half a pint of barm, and when you have tunned your drink into the barrel, and it hath quite done working, make the above fermentation, and when you have put it in the barrel whisk it very well for half an hour, and it will set your ale on working afresh, and when the two gallons is worked white over, keep filling up your barrel with it four or five times a day, and let it work four or five days, when it has done working close it up: if the malt has got any bad smack or take, or be of a fluid nature, this will take it off.

To make SACK MEAD.

TO every gallon of water add four pounds of honey, boil it three quarters of an hour, and scum it as before, to each gallon add half an ounce of hops, then boil it half an hour, and let it stand till the next day, then put it in your cask, and to thirteen gallons of the above liquor, add a quart of brandy or sack, let it be lightly closed till the fermentation is quite done, then make it up very close; if it be a large cask let it stand a year before you bottle it.

To make COWSLIP MEAD.

TO fifteen gallons of water put thirty pounds of honey, boil it till one gallon is wasted, scum it, then take it off the fire, have ready sixteen lemons cut in halves, take a gallon of the liquor, and put it to the lemons, put the rest of the liquor into a tub, with seven pecks of cowslips, and let them stand all night, then put in the liquor with the lemons, and eight spoonfuls of new zest, a handful of sweet briar, stir them all well together, and let it work three or four days, then strain it, and put it in your cask, and in six months time you may bottle it.

To make WALNUT MEAD.

To every gallon of water put three pounds and a half of honey, boil them together three quarters of an hour, to every gallon of liquor put about two dozen of walnut leaves, pour your liquor boiling hot upon them, let them stand all night, then take the leaves out and put in a spoonful of yeast, and let it work two or three days, then make it up, and let it stand three months, then bottle it.

To make OZYAT.

BLANCH a pound of sweet almonds, and the same of bitter, beat them very fine, with a spoonfuls of orange flower water, take three ounces of the four cold seeds, if you beat the almonds, but if you do not beat them, you must take six ounces of the four cold seeds, then with two quarts of spring water, rub your pounded seeds and almonds six times through a napkin, then add four pounds of treble refined sugar, boil it to a thin syrup, skim it well, and when it is cold, then bottle it.

To make OZYAT a second Way.

BOIL two quarts of milk with a stick of cinnamon in it, let it stand till it be quite cold; then blanch two ounces of the best sweet almonds, and about ten or twelve bitter almonds, pound them together in a marble mortar with a little rose water, then mix them well with the milk, sweeten it to your taste, and give it one boil, strain it through a very fine sieve till it is quite smooth and free from almonds. Send it up in ozyat glasses with handles, and quite cold; take great care you do not boil it too much, and that the almonds do not turn to oil.

LEMONADE *for the same Use.*

TO one quart of boiled water, add the juice of six lemons, rub the rinds of the lemons with loaf sugar to your own taste -, when the Water is near cold, mix the juice and sugar with it, then bottle it for use;

To make LEMONADE- *a second Way.*

PARE six or eight large lemons, put the peels into a pint of water, give them' a boil; when cold, squeeze your lemons into it, and put in one pound of sugar, then strain it through a lawn sieve to as much water as will make it pleasant; just before you send it up put in a pint of white wine and the juice of an orange if you like it.

To make LEMONADE *a third Way.*

TAKE the rinds of six lemons pared very thin, and put them in a pan with about twelve ounces of sugar, with a quart of pump water made not too hot; let it stand a night, then squeeze the juice of your lemons into it, with one spoonful of orange flower water, and run it through a bag till it looks clear.

To make a rich ACID for PUNCH

BAKE red currants and strain them as you do for jellies, take a gallon of the juice, put to it two quarts of new milk, crush pearl goose berries when full ripe, and strain them through a coarse cloth, add two quarts of the juice, and three pounds of double refined sugar, three quarts of rum and two of brandy, one ounce of isinglass dissolved in part of the liquor, mix it all up together, and put it in a little cask, and let it stand six weeks, and then bottle it for use. It will keep many years and save much fruit.

To make ORANGE JUICE *to keep.*

SQUEEZE your oranges into a pan, then strain them through a very coarse sieve, after that through a very fine sieve ; measure your juice, and to every pint put a pound of fine loaf sugar, let it stand together all night covered over, then take off the scum, stir it well in the pan, and put it in dry pint bottles, put in a spoonful of brandy, after they are filled tie it over the cork with leather; if you do not choose to put spirits in, a little oil will do, to be taken off clean before you use it keep it in a dry place, and it will be good for two years. The pulp that will be in your fine sieve will make marmalade.

To make SHRUB.

TAKE a gallon of new milk, put to it two quarts of red wine, pare six lemons and four Seville oranges very thin, put in the rinds, and the juice of twelve of each fort, two gallons of rum and one of brandy, let it stand twenty-four hours, add to it two pounds of double refined sugar, and stir it well together, then put it in a jug, cover it close up and let it stand a fortnight, then run it through a jelly bag, and bottle it for use.

To make SHERBET.

TAKE nine Seville oranges and three lemons, grate off the yellow rinds and put the raspings into a gallon of water and three pounds of double refined sugar and boil it to a candy height, then take it off the fire, and put in the juice the pulp of the above, and keep stirring it until it is almost cold, then put it in a pot for use.

To make fine SHERBET a second Way.

PARE four large lemons and boil the peels in six quarts of water and a little ginger cut fine, boil them a quarter of an hour, then add to it three pounds of sugar, and when it is cold put in the juice of the lemons and strain it, and it is fit for use.

To make SHERBET a third Way.

TAKE twelve quarts of water to six pounds of Malaga raisins, slice six lemons into it, with one pound of sixpenny sugar, put them all together into an earthen pan, let it stand three days, stirring it three times a day, then take them out, and let them drain in a flannel bag, then bottle it; do not fill the bottles too full lest they burst. It will be fit to drink in about a fortnight.

To make RASPBERRY BRANDY.

GATHER the raspberries when the sun is hot upon them, and as soon as ever you have got them, to every five quarts of raspberries put one quart of the best brandy, boil a quart of water five minutes with a pound of double refined sugar in it, and pour it boiling hot on the berries, let it stand all night, then add nine quarts more brandy, stir it about very well, put it in a stone bottle, and let it stand a month or six weeks; when fine bottle it.

To make BLACK- CHERRY BRANDY.

TAKE out the stones of eight pounds of black cherries, and put on them a gallon of the best brandy, bruise the stones in a mortar, then put them in your brandy, cover them up close and let them stand a month or six weeks, then pour it clear from the sediments and bottle it.

To make ORANGE BRANDY.

PARE eight oranges very thin, and steep the peels in a quart of brandy forty-eight hours in a close pitcher, then take three pints of water and three quarters of a pound of loaf sugar, boil it until it is reduced to half the quantity, then let it stand till it is cold, then mix it with the brandy; let it stand fourteen days, and then bottle it.

To make ALMOND SHRUB.

TAKE three gallons of rum or brandy, three quarts of orange juice, the peels of three lemons, three pounds of loaf sugar, then take four ounces of bitter almonds, blanch and beat them fine, mix them in a pint of milk, then mix them all well together, let it stand an hour to curdle, run it through a flannel bag several times till it is clear, then bottle it for use.

To make CURRANT SHRUB.

PICK your currants clean from the stalks when they are full ripe, and put twenty-four pounds into a pitcher, with two pounds of single refined sugar, close the jug well up, and put it into a pan of boiling water till they are soft, then strain them through a jelly bag, and to every quart of juice put one quart of brandy, a pint of red wine, one quart of new milk, a pound of double refined sugar, and the whites of two eggs well beat, mix them all together, and cover them close up two days, then run it through a jelly bag and bottle it for use.

To make WALNUT CATCHUP.

TAKE green walnuts before the shell is formed, and grind them in a crab mill, or pound them in a marble mortar, squeeze out the juice through a coarse cloth, put to every gallon of juice one pound of anchovies, one pound of bay salt, four ounces of Jamaica pepper, two of long, and two of black pepper, of mace, cloves, and ginger, each one ounce, and a stick of horse- radish; boil all together till reduced to half the quantity, put it in a pot, and when cold bottle it ; it will be ready in three months.

To make WALNUT CATCHUP another Way.

PUT your walnuts in jars, cover them with cold strong ale allegar, tie them close for twelve months, then take the walnuts out from the allegar, and put to every gallon of the liquor two heads of garlick, half a pound of anchovies, one quart of red wine, one ounce of mace, one of cloves, one of long, one of black, and one of Jamaica pepper, with one of ginger, boil them all in the liquor till it is reduced to half the quantity, the next day bottle it for use; it is good in fish sauce, or stewed beef. In my opinion it is an excellent catchup, for the longer it is kept the better it is, I have kept it five years, and it was much better than when first made. N. B. You may find how to pickle the walnuts you have taken out, amongst the other pickles.

To make MUM CATCHUP.

TO a quart of old mum put four ounces of anchovies, of mace and nutmegs sliced one ounce, of cloves and black pepper half an ounce, boil it till it is reduced one third; when cold bottle it for use.

To make a CATCHUP *to keep seven Years.*

TAKE two quarts of the oldest strong beer you can get, put to it one quart of red wine, three quarters of a pound of anchovies, three ounces of shallots peeled, half an ounce of mace, the same of nutmegs; a quarter of an ounce of cloves, three large races of ginger cut in slices, boil all together over a moderate fire, till one third is wasted, the next day bottle it for use; it will carry to the East Indies.

To make MUSHROOM CATCHUP.

TAKE the full grown flaps of mushrooms, crush them with your hands, throw a handful of salt into every peck of mushrooms, and let them stand all night, then put them into stew-pans, and set them in a quick oven for twelve hours, and strain them through a hair sieve ; to every gallon of liquor, put of cloves, Jamaica, black pepper, and ginger, one ounce each, and half a pound of common salt, set it on a slow fire, and let it boil till half the liquor is wasted away; then put it in a clean pot, when cold bottle it for use.

To make MUSHROOM POWDER.

TAKE the thickest large buttons you can get, peel them, cut off the root end, but do not wash them, spread them separately on pewter dimes, and set them in a flow oven to dry, let the liquor dry up into the mushrooms, it makes the powder stronger, and let them continue in the oven till you find they will powder, then beat them in a marble mortar, and lift them through a fine sieve, with a little Chyan pepper, and pounded mace; bottle it, and keep it in a dry closet.

To make TARRAGON VINEGAR.

TAKE tarragon just as it is going into bloom, strip off the leaves, and to every pound of leaves put a gallon of strong white wine vinegar in a stone jug to ferment for a fortnight, then run it through a flannel bag; to every four gallons of vinegar put half an ounce of isinglass dissolved in cyder, mix it well with vinegar, then put it into large bottles, and let it stand one month to fine, then rack it off, and put it into pint bottles for use.

To make ELDER FLOWER VINEGAR.

TO every peck of the peeps of elder flowers put two gallons of strong ale allegar ; and set it in the sun in a stone jug for a fortnight, then filter it through a flannel bag; when you bottle it, put it in small bottles, it keeps the flavour much better than large ones. Be careful you do not drop any stalks among the peeps. It makes a pretty mixture on a side table, with tarragon vinegar, lemon pickle, &c.

To make GOOSEBERRY VINEGAR.

TAKE the ripest gooseberries you can get, crush them with your hand in a tub, to every peck of gooseberries put two gallons of water, mix them well together, and let them work for three weeks, stir them up three or four times a day, then strain the liquor through a hair sieve, and put to every gallon a pound of brown sugar, a pound of treacle, a spoonful of fresh barm, and let it work three or four days in the same tub well washed, run it into iron-hooped barrels, and let it stand twelve months, then draw it into bottles for use. — This far exceeds any white wine vinegar.

To make SUGAR VINEGAR.

PUT nine pounds of brown sugar to every six gallons of water, boil it for a quarter of an hour, then put it into a tub lukewarm, put to it a pint of new harm, let it work for four or five days, stir it up three or four times a day, then tun it into a clean barrel iron-hooped, and set it full in the sun; if you make it in February it will be fit for use in August; you may use it for most sorts of pickles, except mushrooms and walnuts.

CHAP. XVI

Observations on PICKLING.

PICKLING is a very useful thing in a family, but is often ill managed, or at least made to please the eye by pernicious things, which is the only thing that ought to be avoided, for nothing is more common than to green pickles in a brass pan for the sake of having them a good green, when at the same time they will green as well by heating the liquor, and keeping them on a proper heat upon the hearth, without the help of brass, or verdegrease of any kind, for it is poison to a great degree, and no thing ought to be avoided more than using brass or copper that is not well tinned ; but the best way, and the only caution I can give, is to be very particular in keeping the pickles from any thing of that kind, and follow strictly the direction of your receipts, as you will find receipts for any kind of pickles, without being put in salt and water at all, and greened only by pouring your vinegar hot upon them, and it will keep them a long time.

To pickle CUCUMBERS.

TAKE the smallest cucumbers you can get, and as free from spots as possible, put them into a strong salt and water for nine or ten days or till they are quite yellow, and stir them twice a day at least, or they will scum over, and grow soft ; when they are thoroughly yellow pour the water from them, and cover them with plenty of vine leaves, set your water over the fire, when it boils pour it upon them, and set them on the hearth to keep warm, when the water grows cool, make it boiling hot again, and pour it upon them, keep doing so till you see they are a fine green, which will be in four or five times ; be sure you keep them well covered with vine leaves, a cloth and dish over the top to keep in the steam, it helps to green them sooner; when they are greened, put them into hair sieve to drain, then make a pickle for them ; to every two quarts of white wine vinegar, put half an ounce of mace, and ten or twelve cloves, one ounce of ginger cut in slices, the same of black pepper, and a handful of salt, boil them all together five minutes, then pour it hot upon your pickles, and tie them down with a bladder for use. — N. B. You may pickle them with ale allegar, or distilled vinegar; if you use vinegar, it must not be boiled; you may add three or four cloves of garlic or shalots, they are very good for keeping the pickle from caning.

To pickle CUCUMBERS a second Way.

GATHER your cucumbers on a dry day, and put them into a narrow-topped pitcher, put to them a head of garlick, a few white mustard feeds, and a few blades of mace, half an ounce of black pepper, the same of long pepper, and ginger, and a good handful of salt into your vinegar; pour it upon your cucumbers boiling hot, set them by the fire, and keep them warm for three days, and boil your allegar once every day, and keep them close covered till they are a good green, and then tie them down with a leather, and keep them for use.

To pickle CUCUMBERS in Slices.

GET your cucumbers large before the seeds are ripe, slice them a quarter of an inch thick, then lay them on a hair sieve, and betwixt every lay put a shalot or two, throw on a little salt, let them stand four or five hours to drain, then put them in a stone jar, take as much strong ale allegar as will cover them, boil it five minutes, with a blade or two of mace, a few white pepper corns, a little ginger sliced, and some horse- radish scraped, then pour it boiling hot upon your cucumbers, let them stand till they are cold, do so for three times more: let it grow cold betwixt every time, then tie them down with a bladder for use.

To pickle MANGOES.

TAKE the largest cucumbers you can get, before they are too ripe, or yellow at the ends, then cut a piece out of the side, and take out the seeds with an apple scraper, or a tea-spoon, and put them in a very strong salt and water for eight or nine days, or till they are very yellow, stir them well two or three times each day, then put them into a brass pan, with a large quantity of vine leaves both under and over them, beat a little roach alum very fine, and put it in the salt and water that they came out of, pour it upon your cucumbers, and set it upon a very slow fire, for four or five hours, till they are a pretty green, then take them out and drain them on a hair sieve, when they are cold, put to them a little horse-radish, then mustard seed, two or three heads of garlick, a few pepper corns, slice a few green cucumbers in small pieces, then horse-radish, and the same as before mentioned, till you have filled them, then take the piece you cut out, and sew it on with a large needle and thread, and do all the rest the same way, have ready your pickle ; to every gallon of allegar put one ounce of mace, the same of cloves, two ounces of ginger sliced, the same of long pepper, black pepper, Jamaica pepper, three ounces of mustard seed, tied up in a bag, four ounces of garlick, and a stick of horse radish cut in slices, boil them five minutes in the allegar, then pour it upon your pickles, tie them down and keep them for use.

To pickle CODLINGS.

GET your codlings when they are the size of a large French walnut, put a good deal of vine leaves in the bottom of a brass pan, then put in your codlings, cover them very well with vine leaves, and set them over a very slow fire till you can peel the skins off, then take them carefully up in a hair sieve, and peel them with a pen knife, and put them into the same pan again with the vine leaves and water as before, cover them close, and set them over a slow fire till they are a fine green, then drain them through a hair sieve, and when they are cold put them into distilled vinegar, pour a little meat oil on the top, and tie them down with a bladder.

To pickle KIDNEY BEANS.

GET your beans when they are young and small, then put them into a strong salt and water for three days, stir them up two or three times each day, then put them into a brass pan, with vine leaves both under and over them, pour on the same water as they came out of, cover them close, and set them over a very slow fire till they are a fine green, then put them into a hair sieve to drain, and make a pickle for them of white wine vinegar, or fine ale allegar, boil it five or six minutes, with a little mace, Jamaica pepper, long pepper, and a race or two of ginger sliced, then pour it hot upon the kidney beans, and tie them down with a bladder.

To pickle SAMPHIRE.

WASH your samphire very well in sour small beer, then put it into a large brass pan, dissolve a little bay salt, and twice the quantity of common salt in sour beer, then fill up your pan with it, cover it close, and set it over a slow fire till it is a fine green, then drain it through a sieve, and put it into jars, boil as much sugar vinegar or white wine vinegar, with a race or two of ginger, and a few pepper corns, as will cover it; then pour it hot upon your samphire, and tie it well down.

To pickle WALNUTS *black.*

GATHER. your walnuts when the sun is hot upon them, and before the shell is hard, which you may know by running a pin into them, then put them in a strong salt and water for nine days, then stir them twice a day, and change the salt and water every three days, then put them in a hair sieve, and let them stand in the air till they turn black ; then put them into strong stone jars, and pour boiling allegar over them, cover them up, and let them stand till they are cold, then boil the allegar three times more, and let it stand till it is cold betwixt every time ; tie them down with paper and a bladder over them, and let them stand two months, then take them out of the allegar, and make a pickle for them; to every two quarts of allegar put half an ounce of mace, the same of cloves, one ounce of black pepper, the same of Jamaica pepper, ginger, and long pepper, and two ounces of common salt, boil it ten minutes, and pour it hot upon your walnuts, and tie them down with a bladder and paper over it.

A second Way to pickle WALNUTS *black.*

WHEN you have got your walnuts as before, put them into a cold strong allegar, with a good deal of salt in it, let them stand three months, then pour off the allegar, and boil it with a little more salt in it, then pour it upon your walnuts, and let them stand till they are cold, make it hot again, and pour it upon your walnuts, and do so till they are black, then put them into a. hair sieve, and make a pickle for them the same way as above, keep them in strong stone jars, and they will be fit for use in a month or six weeks time.

To pickle WALNUTS *an olive colour.*

GATHER your walnuts, and put them in a strong ale allegar, and tie them down with a bladder and a paper over it, to keep out the air, and let them stand twelve months, then take them out of that allegar, and make a pickle for them of strong allegar, and to every quart put half an ounce of Jamaica pepper, the same of long pepper, a quarter of an ounce of mace, the same of cloves, one head of garlick, and a little salt, boil them all together five or six minutes, then pour it upon your walnuts when it is cold,' heat it again three times, then tie them down with a bladder, and paper over it; they will keep several years, without either turning colour, or growing soft if your allegar be good. — N.B. You may make exceeding good catchup of the allegar that comes from the walnuts, by adding a pound of anchovies, one ounce of cloves, the same of long and black pepper, one head of garlick, and half a pound of common salt to every gallon of your allegar; boil it till it is half reduced away, and scum it very well, then bottle it for use, and it will keep a long time.

To pickle WALNUTS.

TAKE the largest French walnuts, pare them till you can see the white appear, but take great care you do not cut it too deep, it will make them full of holes, put them into salt and water as you pare them, or they will turn black, when you have pared them all, have ready a saucepan well tinned, full of boiling water, with a little salt, then put in your walnuts, and let them boil five minutes very quick, then take them out, and spread them betwixt two clean cloths, when they are cold put them into wide mouthed bottles, and fill them up with distilled vinegar, and put a blade or two of mace, and a large tea spoonful of eating oil into every bottle; the next day cork them well, and keep them in a dry place.

To pickle WALNUTS green

TAKE the large double, or French walnuts, before the shells are hard, wrap them singly in vine leaves, put a few vine leaves in the bottom of your jar, fill it near full with your walnuts, take care that they do not touch one another, put a good many leaves over them, then fill your jar with good allegar, cover them close that the air cannot get in, let them stand for three weeks, then pour the allegar from them, put fresh leaves in the bottom of another jar, take out your walnuts, and wrap them separately in fresh leaves as quick as possibly you can, put them into your jar with a good many leaves over them, then fill it with white wine vinegar, let them stand three weeks, pour off your vinegar, and wrap them as before with fresh leaves at the bottom and top of your jar, take fresh white wine vinegar, put salt in it till it will bear an egg, add to it mace, cloves, nutmeg, and garlick if you choose it, boil it about eight minutes, then pour it on your walnuts, tie them close with paper and a bladder, and set them by for use. Be sure to keep them always covered; when you take any out for use, what is left must not be put in again, but have ready a fresh jar with boiled vinegar and salt to put them in.

To pickle BARBERRIES.

GET your barberries before they are too ripe, pick out the leaves, and dead stalks, then put them into jars, with a large quantity of strong salt and water, and tie them down with a bladder. N. B. When you see your barberries scum over put them into fresh salt and water, they need no vinegar, their own sharpness is sufficient enough to keep them.

To pickle PARSLEY green.

TAKE a large quantity of curled parsley, make a strong salt and water to bear an egg, put in your parsley, let it stand a week, then take it out to drain, make a fresh salt and water as before, let it stand another week, then drain it very well, put it in spring water, and change it every day for three days, and scald it in hard water, till it becomes green, take it out and drain it quite dry, boil a quart of distilled vinegar a few minutes, with two or three blades of mace, a nutmeg sliced, and a shallot or two ; when it is quite cold, pour it on your parsley, with two or three slices of horse-radish, and keep it for use.

To pickle NASTURTIANS.

GATHER the nasturtian berries soon after the blossoms are gone off, put them in cold salt and water, change the water once a day for three days, make your pickle of white wine vinegar, mace, nutmeg sliced, pepper corns, salt, shalots, and horse-radish; it requires to be made pretty strong, as your pickle is not to be boiled; when you have drained them, put them into a jar, and pour the pickle over them.

To pickle RADISH PODS.

GATHER your radish pods when they are quite young, and put them in salt and water all night, then boil the salt and water they were laid in, and pour it upon your pods, and cover your jars close to keep in the steam; when it grows cold, make it boiling hot, and pour it on again ; keep doing so till your pods are quite green, then put them on a sieve to drain, and make a pickle for them of white wine vinegar, with a little mace, ginger, long pepper, and horse-radish, pour it boiling hot upon your pods, when it is almost cold, make your vinegar twice hot as before, and pour it upon them, and tie them down with a bladder.

To pickle ELDER SHOOTS.

GATHER your elder shoots when they are the thickness of a pipe shank, put them into salt and water all night, then put them into stone jars in layers, and betwixt every layer strew a little mustard seed, and scraped horse radish, a few shallots, a little white beet root, and cauliflower pulled in small pieces, then pour boiling allegar upon it, and scald it three times, and it will be like piccalillo, or Indian pickle; tie a leather over it, and keep it in a dry place.

To pickle ELDER BUDS.

GET your elder buds when they are the are of hop buds, and put them into a strong salt and water for nine days, and stir them two or three times a day, then put them into a brass pan, cover them with vine leaves, and pour the water on them that they came out of, and set them over a slow fire till they are quite green, then make a pickle for them of allegar, a little mace, a few shalots, and some ginger sliced, boil them two or three minutes, and pour it upon your buds; tie them down, and keep them in a dry place for use.

To pickle BEET ROOTS.

TAKE red beet roots and boil them till they are tender, then take the skins off, and cut them in slices, and gimp them in the shape of wheels, flowers, or what form you please, and put them into a jar, then take as much vinegar as you think will cover them, and boil it with a little mace, a race of ginger sliced, and a few slices of horse-radish, pour it hot upon your roots, and tie them down. — They are a very pretty garnish for made dishes.

To pickle CAULYFLOWERS.

TAKE the closest and whitest caulyflowers your can get, and pull them in bunches, and spread them on an earthen dish, and lay salt all over them, let them stand for three days to bring out all the water, then put them in earthen jars, and pour boiling salt and water upon them, and let them stand all night, then drain them on a hair sieve, and put them into glass jars, and fill up your jars with distilled vinegar, and tie them close down with leather.

A second Way to pickle CAULYFLOWERS.

PULL your caulyflowers in bunches as be fore, and give them just a scald in salt and water, spread them on a cloth, and sprinkle a little salt over them, and throw another cloth upon them till they are drained, then lay them on sieves, and dry them in the sun-till they are quite dry like scraps of leather, put them into jars about half full, and pour hot vinegar with spice boiled in it to your taste) upon them; tie them down with a bladder, and a leather quite close, — N B. White cabbage is done the same way.

To pickle RED CABBAGE.

GET the finest and closest red cabbage you can, and cut it as thin as possible, then take some cold ale allegar, and put to it two or three blades of mace, a few white pepper corns, and make it pretty strong with salt, put your cabbage into the allegar as you cut it; tie it close down with a bladder, and a paper over it, and it will be fit for use in a day or two.

To pickle RED CABBAGE a second Way.

CUT the cabbage as before, and throw some salt upon it, and let it lie two or three days, till it grows a fine purple, then drain it from the salt, and put it into a pan with beer allegar, and spice to your liking, and give it a scald; when it is cold, put it into your jars, and tie it close up.

To pickle GRAPES.

GET your grapes when they are pretty large, but not too ripe, then put a layer into a stone jar, then a layer of vine leaves, then grapes and vine leaves as before, till your jar is full ; then take two quarts of water, half a pound of bay salt, the same of common salt, boil it half an hour, skim it well, and take it off to settle, when it is milk warm, pour the clean liquor upon the grapes, and lay a good deal of vine leaves upon the top, and cover it close up with a cloth, and set it upon the hearth for two days, then take your grapes out of the jar, and lay them upon a cloth to drain, and cover them with a flannel till they are quite dry; then lay them in flat bottomed stone jars, in layers, and put fresh vine leaves betwixt every layer, and a large handful on the top of the grapes, then boil a quart of hard water, and one pound of loaf sugar, a quarter of an hour, skim it well, and put to it three blades of mace, a large nutmeg sliced, and two quarts of white wine vinegar, give them all a boil together, then take it off, and when it is quite cold, pour it upon your grapes, and cover them very well with it ; put a bladder upon the top, and tie a leather over it, and keep them in a dry place for use, — N. B. You may pickle them in cold distilled vinegar.

To pickle young ARTICHOKES.

GET your artichokes as soon as they are formed, and boil them in a strong salt and water for two or three minutes, and lay them upon a hair sieve to drain, when they are cold put them into narrow topped jars, then take as much white wine vinegar as will cover your artichokes, boil with it a blade or two of mace, a few slices of ginger, and a nutmeg cut thin, pour it on hot and tie them down.

To pickle MUSHROOMS.

GATHER the smallest mushrooms you can get, and put them into spring water, then rub them with a piece of new flannel, dipped in salt, and throw them into cold spring water as you do them to keep their colour, then put them into a well tinned saucepan, and throw a handful of salt over them, cover them close, and set them over the fire four or five minutes, or till you see they are thoroughly hot, and the liquor is drawn out of them, then lay them between two clean cloths till they are cold, then put them into glass bottles, and fill them up with distilled vinegar, and put a blade or two of mace, and a tea-spoonful of eating oil in every bottle, cork them close up, and set them in a cool place N. B. If you have not any distilled vinegar, you may use white wine vinegar, or ale allegar will do, but it must be boiled with a little mace, salt, and a few slices of ginger, it must be cold before you pour it on your mushrooms; if your vinegar or allegar be too sharp it will soften your mushrooms, neither will they keep so long, nor be so white.

To pickle MUSHROOMS brown.

TAKE a quart of large mushroom buttons, wash them in allegar with a flannel, take three anchovies and chop them small, a few blades of mace, a little pepper and ginger, a spoonful of salt, and three cloves of shalots, put them into a saucepan with as much allegar as will half cover them, set them on the fire, and let them stew till they shrink pretty much ; when cold put them in small bottles with the allegar poured upon them, cork and tie them up close. N. B. This pickle will make a great addition in brown sauce.

To pickle ONIONS.

PEEL the smallest onions you can get, and put them into salt and water for nine days, and change the water every day, then put them into jars, and pour fresh boiling salt and water over them, let them stand close covered until they are cold; then make some more salt and water, and pour it boiling hot upon them, and when it is cold, put your onions into a hair sieve to drain, then put them into wide mouthed bottles, and fill them up with distilled vinegar, and put into every bottle a slice or two of ginger, one blade of mace, and a large tea-spoonful of eating oils it will keep the onions white ; then cork them well up. — N. B. If you like the taste of a bay leaf, put one or two into every bottle, and as much bay salt as will lie on a six-pence.

To make INDIAN PICKLE or PICCALILLO.

GET a white cabbage, one caulyflower, & few small cucumbers, radish-pods, kidney-beans, and a little beet root, or any other thing you commonly pickle; then put them on a hair sieve, and throws large handful of salt over them, and set them in the sun-shine, or before the fire, for three days to dry; when all the water is run out of them, put them into a large earthen pot in layers, and betwixt every layer, put a handful of brown mustard seed, then take as much ale allegar as you think will cover it, and to every four quarts of allegar, put an ounce of turmerick, boil them together, and pour it hot upon your pickle, and let it stand- twelve days upon the hearth, or till the pickles are all of a bright yellow, colour, and most of the allegar sucked up ; then take two quarts of strong ale allegar, one ounce of mace, the same of white pepper, a quarter of an ounce of cloves, the same of long pepper and nutmeg; beat them all together, and boil them ten minutes in your allegar, then pour it upon your pickles with four ounces of garlick peeled; tie it close down, and keep it for use, — N B. You may put in fresh pickles, as the things come in season, and keep them covered with vinegar, &c.

A pickle in Imitation of INDIAN BAMBOE.

TAKE the young shoots of elder, about the beginning or middle of May take the middle of the stalk, the top is not worth doing, peel off the out-rind, and lay them in a strong brine of salt and, beer one night, dry them in a cloth single, in the mean time make a pickle, of half gooseberry vinegar, and half ale allegar ; to every quart of pickle put one ounce of long pepper, one ounce of sliced ginger, a few corns of Jamaica pepper, a little mace, boil it, and pour it hot upon the shoots and stop the jar close up, and set it by the fire twenty-four hours, stirring it very often.

CHAP. XVII

Observations on keeping GARDEN-STUFF *and* FRUIT.

THE art of keeping garden-stuff is to keep it in dry places, for damp will not only make them mould, and give again, but take off the flavour, so it will likewise spoil any kind of bottled fruit, and set them on working; the best caution I can give, is to keep them as dry as possible, but not warm, and when you boil any dried stuff have plenty of water, and follow strictly the directions of your receipts.

To keep GREEN PEAS.

SHELL any quantity of green peas, and just give them a boil in as much spring water as will cover them, then put them in a sieve to drain, pound the pods with a little of the water that the peas were boiled in, and strain what juice you can from them, and; boil it a quarter of an hour, with a little salt, and as much of the water as you think will cover the peas in the bottles, fill your bottles with peas, and pour in your water, when cold put rendered suet over, and tie them down close with a bladder, and leather over it, and keep your bottles in a dry place.

To keep GREEN PEAS *another Way.*

GATHER your peas in the afternoon, on a dry day; shell them, and put them into dry clean bottles, cork them close, and tie them over with a bladder keep them in a cool dry place as before.

To keep FRENCH BEAMS.

LET your beans be gathered quite dry, and not too old, lay a layer of salt in the bottom of an earthen jar, then a layer of beans, then salt, then beans, till you have filled you jar: let the salt be at the top, tie a piece of leather over them, and lay a flag on the top, and set them in a dry cellar for use.

To keep FRENCH BEANS *a second Way.*

MAKE a strong salt and water that will bear an egg, and when it boils put in your French beans for five or six minutes, then lay them on a sieve, and put to your salt and water a little bay salt, and boil it ten minutes, skim it well, and pour it into an earthen jar to cool and settle, put your French beans into narrow topped-jars, and pour your clean liquor over them ; tie them close down, that no air can get in, and keep them in a dry place. — N. B. Steep them in plenty of spring water the night before you use them, and boil them in hard water.

To keep MUSHROOMS *to eat like fresh ones.*

WASH large buttons as you would for stewing, lay them on sieves, with the stalk up wards, throw over them some salt to fetch out the water; when they are drained, put them in a pot, and set them in a cool oven for an hour, then take them carefully out, and lay them to cool and drain ; boil the liquor that comes out of them with a blade or two of mace, and boil it half away ; put your mushrooms into a clean jar well dried, and when the liquor is cold, cover your mushrooms in the jar with it, and pour over it rendered suet ; tie a bladder over it, set them in a dry closet, and they will keep very well most of the winter. — When you use them, take them out of the liquor, pour over them boiling milk, and let them stand an hour, then stew them in the milk a quarter of an hour, thicken them with flour, and a large quantity of butter, and be careful you do not oil it, then beat the yolks-of two eggs with a little cream, and put it in, but do not let it boil after the eggs are in; lay untoasted sippets round the inside of the dish and serve them up; they well eat near as good as fresh gathered mushrooms; if they do not taste strong enough, put in a little of the liquor: this is a valuable liquor, and it will give all made dishes a flavour like fresh mushrooms.

To keep MUSHROOMS another Way.

SCRAPE large flaps, peel them, take out the inside, and boil them in their own liquor and a little salt, then lay them in tins, and set them in a cool oven, and repeat it till they are dry ; put them in clean jars, tie them close down, and they will eat very good.

To dry ARTICHOKE BOTTOMS.

PLUCK the artichokes from the stalks (just before they come to their full growth) it will draw out all the strings from the bottoms, and boil them so that you can just pull off the leaves, lay them on tins, and set them in a cool oven, and repeat it till they are dry, which you may know by holding them up against the light, and if you can see through them, they are dry enough; put them in paper bags, and hang them in a dry place.

To bottle DAMSONS to eat as good as fresh ones.

GET your damsons carefully when they are just turned colour, and put them into wide- mouthed bottles, cork them up loosely, and let them stand a fortnight, then look them over, and if you see any of them mould or spot, take them out and cork the rest close down ; set the bottles in sand, and they will keep till spring, and be as good as fresh ones.

Another Way to bottle DAMSONS.

TAKE your damsons when full grown and coloured, but not soft, have them gathered in dry weather, get your wide-mouth bottles clean warned, and very dry before your damsons are got, have them fitted with corks that your damsons may be done as soon as they are gathered, when they are pricked put them into your bottles as soon as you can ; when the bottle is half full put in two table spoonfuls of Lisbon sugar, then fill the bottles up with damsons, have the corks well beat in and cut close, then have a bladder soaked in cold water, and well wiped, which must be tied close over the corks, have the boiler or copper that you intend to do them in ready, and lay a little straw very thin, at the bottom of your copper, to keep them from breaking, put a little straw between each bottle, you may lay another row of bottles over the first, if your copper is deep enough, but mind they do not rub against each other, there must be a full inch of water over your bottles, and straw strewed thin over the top, over which you must get the cover of a hamper, and have it cut to fit the copper, that your bottles may not rise to the top of your water, there must be a proper weight over the cover of the hamper, to keep the bottles in their places ; when that is done, you must have as much cold water put over them as will cover them, have your fire lighted, and stand by them till you see them have one boil, then, as quick as you can, have the fire drawn out, and water thrown under the copper to cool it, as too much boiling spoils the fruit, let them stand in the water three hours in the copper, then have them taken out and wiped dry, but not shook, let your bottles stand in a cool and very dry place, they will keep two years; they must not be covered with any close cover : this is a very good way to do gooseberries, but leave out the sugar.

To bottle GOOSEBERRIES.

PICK green walnut gooseberries, bottle them, and fill the bottles with spring water up to the neck, cork them loosely, and let them in a cop per of hot water till they are hot quite through, then take them out, and when they are cold, cork them close, and tie a bladder over, and set them in a dry cool place.

To bottle GOOSEBERRIES a second Way.

PUT one ounce of roach alum beat fine, into a large pan of boiling hard water, pick your gooseberries, and put a few in the bottom of a hair sieve, and hold them in the boiling water till they turn white; then take out the five, and spread the gooseberries betwixt two clean cloths, put more gooseberries in your sieve, and repeat it till you have done all your berries, put the water into a glazed pot till next day, then put your gooseberries into wide-mouthed bottles, and pick out all the cracked and broken ones, pour your water clear out of the pot, and fill up your bottles with it; then put in the corks loosely, and let them stand for a fortnight, and if they rise to the corks, draw them out, and let them stand for two or three days uncorked, then cork them close, and they will keep two years.

To bottle CRANBERRIES.

GET your cranberries when they are quite dry, put them into dry clear bottles, cork them up close, and set them in a dry cool place,

To bottle GREEN CURRANTS.

GATHER your currants when the sun is hot upon them, strip them from the stalks, and put them into glass bottles, and cork them close, set them over head in dry sand, and they will keep till spring,

To keep GRAPES.

CUT your bunches of grapes, with a joint of the vine to them, hang them up in a dry room, that the bunches do not touch one another, and the air pass freely betwixt them, or they will grow mouldy and rot; they will keep till the latter end of January, or longer. N. B. The Frontiniac grape is the best.

CHAP. XVIII

Observations on DISTILLING.

IF your still be a limbeck, when you set it on, fill the top with cold water, and make a little paste of flour and water, and close the bottom of your still well with it, and take great care that your fire is not too hot to make it boil over, for that will weaken the strength of your water; you must change the water on the top of your still often, and never let it be scalding hot, and your still will drop gradually off; if you use a hot still, when you put on the top, dip a cloth in white lead and oil, and lay it well over the edges of your still, and a coarse wet cloth over the top : it requires a little fire under it, but you must take care that you keep it very clear ; when your cloth is dry, dip it in cold water and lay it on again, and if your still be very hot, wet another cloth, and lay it round the very top, and keep it of a moderate heat, so that your water is cold when it comes off the still.— If you use a worm-still, keep your water in the tub full to the top, and change the water often, to prevent it from growing hot; observe to let all simple waters stand two or three days before you work it, to take off the fiery taste of the still.

To distill CAUDLE WATER.

TAKE wormwood, horehound, feathers, few, and lavendar-cotton, of each three handfuls, rue, peppermint, and Seville orange peel, of each a handful, steep them in red wine, or the bottoms of strong beer, all night ; then distill them in a hot still pretty quick, and it will be a fine caudle to take as bitters.

To distill MILK WATER.

TAKE two handful s of spear or peppermint, the same of balm, one handful of cards, the same of wormwood, and one of angelico, cut them into lengths a quarter long, and steep them in three quarts of skimmed milk twelve hours, then distill it in a cold still, with a slow fire under it; keep a cloth always wet over the top of your still, to keep the liquor from boiling over, the next day bottle it, cork it well, and keep it for use.

To make HEPHNATICK WATER for the Gravel.

GATHER your thorn flowers in May, when they are in full bloom, and pick them from the stems and leaves, and to every half peck of flowers, take three quarts of Lisbon wine, and put into it a quarter of a pound of nutmegs sliced, and let them sleep in it all night, then put it into your still with the peeps, and keep a moderate even fire under it, for if you let it boil over, it will lose its strength.

To distill PEPPER-MINT WATER.

GET your pepper-mint when it is full grown, and before it seeds, cut it in short lengths, fill your still with it, and put it half full of water, then make a good fire under it, and when it is nigh boiling, and the still begins to drop, if your fire be too hot, draw a little out from under it, as you see it requires, to keep it from boiling over, or your water will be muddy, the slower your still drops, the water will be the clearer and stronger, but do not spend it too far, the next day bottle it, and let it stand three or four days, to take the fire off the still, then cork it well, and it will keep a long time.

To distill ELDER-FLOWER WATER.

GET your elder-flowers when they are in full bloom, shake the blossoms off, and to every peck of flowers put one quart of water, and let them sleep in it all night; then put them in a cold still, and take care that your water comes cold off the still, and it will be very clear, and draw it no longer than your liquor is good, then put it into bottles, and cork it in two or three days, and it will keep a year.

To distill ROSE WATER.

GATHER your red roses when they are dry and full blown, pick off the leaves, and to every peck put one quart of water, then put them into a cold still, and make a slow fire under it, the slower you distill it the better it is, then bottle it, and cork it in two or three days time, and keep it for use. N. B. You may distill bean-flower the same way.

To distill PENNY-ROYAL WATER.

GET your penny-royal when it is full grown, and before it is in blossom, then fill your cold still with it, and put it half full of water, make a moderate fire under it, and distill it off cold, then put it into bottles, and cork it in two or three days time, and keep it for use.

To distill LAVENDAR WATER.

TO every twelve pounds of lavendar-neps, put one quart of water, put them into a cold still, and make a slow fire under it, and distill it off very slow, and put it into a pot till you have distilled all your water, then clean your still well out, and put your lavendar water into it, and distill it off as slow as before, then put it into bottles, and cork it well.

To distill SPIRITS of WINE.

TAKE the bottoms of strong beer, and any kind of wines, put them into a hot still about three parts full, then make a very slow fire under, and if you do not take great care to keep it moderate, it will boil over, for the body is so strong, that it will rise to the top of the still; the slower you distill it the stronger your spirit will be, put it into an earthen pot till you have done distilling, then clean your still well out, and put the spirit into it, and distill it slow as before, and make it as strong as to burn in your lamp, then bottle it, and cork it well, and keep it for use.

A Correct LIST of every Thing in Season in every Month of the YEAR.

JANUARY.

FISH

CARP	Soles	Smelts
Tench	Flounders	Whitings
Perch	Plaice	Lobsters
Lampreys	Turbot	Crabs
Eels	Thornback	Prawns
Craw-fish	Skate	Oysters
Cod	Sturgeon	

MEAT.

Beef	Veal	Pork
Mutton	House- Lamb	

POULTRY, &c.

Pheasant	Woodcocks	Fowls
)Game	Snipes	Chickens
Partridge)	Turkeys	Tame Pigeons
Hares	Capons	
Rabbits	Pullets	

ROOTS

Cabbage	Thyme	Endive
Savoys	Savory	Sage
Coleworts	Pot-Marjoram	Parsnips
Sprouts	Hysop	Carrots
Brocoli purple	Cardoons	Turnips
and white	Beets	Potatoes
Spinage	Parsley	Scorzonera
Mint	Sorrel	Skirrets
Cucumbers in	Chervil	Lettuces
hot-houses	Celery	Cresses

Mustard
Rape
Radish
Turnips
Tarragon

Salsifie
To be had though not in season
Jerusalem

Artichokes
Asparagus
Mushrooms

FRUIT

Apples
Pears

Nuts
Almonds
Services

Medlars
Grapes

FEBRUARY.

FISH

Cod
Soles
Sturgeons
Plaice
Flounders
Turbot
Thornback

Skate
Whitings
Smelts
Lobsters
Crabs
Oysters
Prawns

Tench
Perch
Carp
Eels
Lampreys
Craw-fish

MEAT.

Beef
Mutton
Pork

Veal
House- Lamb

POULTRY &c

Turkeys
Capons
Pullets
Fowls

Chickens
Pigeons
Pheasants
Partridges

Woodcocks
Snipes
Hares
Tame Rabbits

ROOTS

Cabbage
Savoys

Coleworts
Sprouts

Brocoli, purple and white

Cardoons	Mint	Parsnips
Beets	Burnet	Potatoes
Parsley	Tansey	Onions
Chervil	Thyme	Leeks,
Endive	Savory	Shalots
Sorrel	Marjoram	Garlick
Celery	*Also may be*	Rocombole
Chardbeets	*had*	Salsifie
Lettuces	Forced	Skirret
Cresses	Radishes	Scorzonera
Mustard	Cucumbers	Jerusalem
Rape	Asparagus	Artichokes
Radishes	Kidney-Beans	
Turnips	Carrots	
Tarragons	Turnips	

FRUIT

Pears Grapes
Apples

MARCH.

MEAT.

Beef	Veal	Pork
Mutton	House-Lamb	

POULTRY, &c.

Turkeys	Fowls	Pigeons
Pullets	Chickens	
Capons	Ducklings	
Tame Rabbits		

ROOTS, &c.

Carrots	Turnips	Parsnips

315

Jerusalem	Parsley	Tarragon
Artichokes	Fennel	Mint
Onions	Celery	Burnet
Garlick	Endive	Thyme
Shalots	Tansey	Winter- Savory
Coleworts	Mushrooms	Pot- Marjoram
Borecole	Lettuces	Hysop
Cabbages	Chives	Fennel
Savoys	Cresses	Cucumbers
Spinage	Mustard	Kidney-Beans
Brocoli	Rape	
Cardoons	Radishes	
Beets	Turnips	

FRUIT.

Pears
Apples
Forced Strawberries

APRIL.

MEAT.

Beef Veal
Mutton Lamb

FISH.

Carp	Turbot	Crabs
Chub	Soles	Lobsters
Tench	Skate	Prawns
Trout	Mullets	
Craw-fish	Smelts	
Salmon	Herrings	

POULTRY &c.

Pullets	Chickens	Pigeons
Fowls	Ducklings	Rabbits

Leverets

ROOTS &C
Coleworts	Celery	All sorts of
Sprouts	Endive	small
Brocoli	Sorrel	salad
Spinage	Burnet	Thyme
Fennel	Tarragon	All sorts of Pot,
Parsley	Radishes	Herbs
Chervil	Lettuces	
Young Onions		

FRUIT
Apples	Forced	Apricots for
Pears	Cherries	Tarts

MAY.

FISH.
Carp	Salmon	Lobsters
Tench	Soles,	Craw-fish
Eels	Turbot	Crabs
Trout	Herrings	Prawns
Chub	Smelts	

MEAT.
Beef	Veal
Mutton	Lamb

POULTRY, &c,
Pullets	Green Geese,	Rabbits
Fowls	Ducklings	Leverets
Chickens	Turkey Poults	

ROOTS, &c

Early Potatoes	Balm	Savory
Carrots	Mint	All other sweet Herbs
Turnips	Purslane	
Radishes	Fennel	Peas
Early Cabbages	Lettuces	Beans
Cauliflowers	Cresses	Kidney Beans
Artichokes	Mustard	
Spinage	All sorts of small Sallad Herbs	Asparagus
Parsley		Tragopogon
Sorrel		Cucumbers, &c.
	Thyme	

FRUIT.

Pears	And Melons With Green Apricots	And Currants for Tarts
Apples		
Strawberries		
Cherries	Gooseberries	

JUNE.

MEAT

Beef	Lamb
Mutton	Buck
Veal	Venison &c –

POULTRY,

Fowls	Green Geese	Plovers.
Pullets	Ducklings	Wheat-Ears
Chickens	Turkey Poults	Leverets

Rabbits

FISH

Trout	Soles	Lobsters
Carp	Turbot	Craw-fish
Tench	Mullets	Prawns
Pike	Mackarel	
Eels	Herrings	
Salmon	Smelts	

ROOTS, &c

	Asparagus	Cresses
Carrots	Kidney-Beans	All other small
Turnips	Artichokes	Sallading
Potatoes	Cucumbers	Thyme
Parsnips	Lettuce	All sorts of Pot-
Radishes	Spinage	Herbs
Onions	Parsley	
Beans	Purslane	
Peas	Rape	

FRUIT.

Cherries	Apricots	Nectarines
Strawberries	Apples	Grapes
Gooseberries	Pears	Melons
Currants	Some	Pine Apples
Masculine	Peaches	

JULY.

MEAT

Beef	Veal	Buck
Mutton	Lamb	Venison, &c

POULTRY,

Pullets	Turkey Poults	Plovers
Fowls	Ducks	Leverets
Chickens	Young	Rabbits
Pigeons	Partridges	
Green Geese	Pheasants	
Ducklings	Wheat-Ears-	

FISH.

Cod	Plaice	Tench
Haddocks	Flounders.	Eels
Mullets	Skate	Prawns
Mackarel	Thornback	Pike
Herrings	Salmon	Lobsters
Soles	Carp	
Craw-fish		

ROOTS, &c.

Carrots	Sprouts	All sorts of small Sallad Herbs
Turnips	Artichokes	
Potatoes	Celery	
Radishes	Endive	Mint
Onions	Finocha	Balm
Garlick	Chervil	Thyme
Rocombole	Sorrel	All other Pot Herbs
Scorzonera	Purslane	
Salfifie	Lettuce	Peas
Mushrooms	Cresses	Beans
Cauliflowers		Kidney Beans
Cabbages		

FRUIT.

Pears	Peaches	Apricots
Apples	Nectarines	Gooseberries
Cherries	Plums	Strawberries

Raspberries		Melons		Pine Apples

AUGUST.

MEAT.

Beef
Mutton
Veal

Lamb
Buck Venison
&c

POULTRY,

Pullets
Fowls
Chickens
Green Geese
Turkey Poults

Ducklings
Leverets
Rabbits
Pigeons.
Pheasants

Wild Ducks
Wheat-Ears
Plovers

FISH.

Cod
Haddock
Flounders
Plaice
Skate
Thornback

Mullets
Mackarel
Herrings
Pike
Carp
Eels

Lobsters
Craw-fish
Prawns
Oysters

ROOTS, &c

Carrots
Turnips
Potatoes
Radishes
Onions

Garlick
Shalots
Scorzonera
Salsifie
Peas

Beans
Kidney-Beans
Mushrooms
Artichokes
Cabbages

Cauliflowers	Parsley	Savory
Sprouts	Lettuce	Marjoram
Beets	All sorts of small Sallads	All sorts of sweet Herbs
Celery		
Endive		
Finocha	Thyme	

FRUIT.

Peaches	Pears	Strawberries
Nectarines	Grapes	Gooseberries,
Plums	Figs	Currants
Cherries	Filberts	Melons
Apples	Mulberries	PineApples

SEPTEMBER.

MEAT.

Beef	Lamb
Veal	Pork
Mutton	Buck Venison

POULTRY, &c

Geese	Pullets	Ducks
Turkies	Fowls	Pheasants
Teals	Hares	Partridges
Pigeons	Rabbits	
Larks	Chickens	

FISH

Cod	Skate	Tench
Haddock	Soles	Pike
Flounders	Smelts	Lobsters
Plaice	Salmon	Oysterrs
Thornbacks	Carp	

ROOTS, &c.

Carrots	Kidney-Beans	Lettuce,
Turnips	Mushrooms	and all forts of
Potatoes	Artichokes	small Sallads
Shalots	Cabbages	Chervil
Onions	Sprouts	Sorrel
Leeks	Cauliflowers	Beets
Garlick	Cardoons	Thyme,
Scorzonera	Endive	and all sorts of
Salsifie	Celery	soup herbs.
Peas	Parsley	
Beans	Finocha	

FRUIT

	Peaches	
Plums	Hazel Nuts	Morello
Apples	Medlars	Cherries
Pears	Quinces	Melons
Grapes	Lazaroles	Pine Apples
Walnuts	Currants	
Filberts		

OCTOBER.

MEAT.

Beef	Lamb	Pork
Mutton	Veal	Doe Venison

POULTRY &c

Geese,	Fowls	Teals
Turkies	Chickens	Widgeons
Pigeons	Rabbits	Woodcocks
Pullets	Wild Ducks	Snipes

Larks	Hares	Partridges
Dotterels	Pheasants	

FISH

Dorees	Gudgeons	Salmon Trout
Holobert	Pike	Lobsters
Bearbet	Carp	Cockles
Smelts	Tench	Muscles
Brills	Perch	Oysters

ROOTS, &c.

Cabbages	Leeks	Sallad
Sprouts	Shalots	Lettuce
Cauliflowers	Garlick	All sorts of
Artichokes	Rocombole	young Sallad
Carrots	Celery	Thyme
Parsnips	Endive	Savory
Turnips	Cardoons	All sorts of Pot-
Potatoes	Chervil	herbs
Skirrets	Finocha	
Salsifie	Chardbeets	
Scorzonera	Corn	

FRUIT.

Peaches	Quinces	Filberts
Grapes	Black and	Hazel Nuts
Figs	white	Pears
Medlars	Bullace	Apples
Services	Walnuts	

NOVEMBER.

MEAT

Beef	Mutton	Veal

House Lamb   Doe Venison

POULTRY.

Geese	Wild Ducks	Dotterels
Turkies	Teals	Hares
Fowl	Widgeons	Rabbits
Chickens	Woodcocks	Partridges
Pullets	Snipes	Pheasants
Pigeons	Larks	

FISH.

Gurnets	Salmon Trout	Gudgeons
Dorees	Smelts	Lobsters
Holoberts	Carp	Oysters
Bearbet	Pike	Cockles
Salmon	Tench	Muscles

ROOTS, &

Carrots	Jerusalem	Cresses
Turnips	Artichokes	Endive
Parsnips	Cabbages	Chervil
Potatoes	Cauliflowers	Lettuces
Skirret	Savoys	Cresses
Salsifie	Sprouts	All sorts of
Scorzonera	Coleworts	small Sallad
Onions	Spinage	Herbs
Leeks	Chardbeets	Thyme,
Shalot .	Cardoons	And all other
Rocombole	Parsley	Pot- Herbs

FRUIT.

Pears   Apples   Bullace

Chestnuts   Walnuts   Grapes
Hazel-   Medlars
Nuts   Services

DECEMBER

MEAT.

Beef	Lamb	
Mutton	Pork	
Veal	Doe	
House	Venison	

FISH.

Turbot	Smelts	Eels
Gurnets	Cod	Cockles
Sturgeon	Codlings	Muscles
Dorees	Soles	Oysters
Holoberts	Carp	
Bearbet	Gudgeons	

POULTRY, etc.

Geese	Chickens	Wild Ducks
Turkies	Hares	Teals
Pullets	Rabbits	Widgeons
Pigeons	Woodcocks	Dotterels
Capons	Snipes	Partridges
Fowls	Larks	Pheasants

ROOTS, &c.

Cabbages	Parsnips	small
Savoys	Turnips	Sallad
Brocoli, purple	Lettuces	Potatoes
and white	Cresses	Skirrets
Carrots	All sorts of	Scorzonera

Salsifie	Asparagus	Spinage
Leeks	Garlick	Parsley
Onions	Rocombole	Thyme
Shalots	Celery	All sorts of
Cardoons	Endive	Pot-herbs
Forced	Beets	

FRUIT.

Apples	Services	Hazel-nuts
Pears	Chestnuts	Grapes
Medlars	Walnuts	

Directions for a GRAND TABLE.

JANUARY being a month when entertainments are most used, and most wanted, from that motive I have drawn my dinner at that season of the year, and hope it will be of service to my worthy friends; not that I have the least pretension to confine any Lady to such a particular number or dishes, but to choose out of them what number they please; being all in season, and most of them to be got without much difficulty; as I from long experience can tell what a troublesome task it is to make a bill of fare to be in propriety, and not to have two things of the same kind; and being desirous of rendering it easy for the future, have made it my study to set out the dinner in as elegant a manner as lies in my power, and in the modern taste; but finding I could not express myself to be understood by young house-keepers, in placing the dishes upon the table, obliged me to have two copper-plates; as I am very unwilling to leave even the weakest capacity in the dark, being my greatest study to render my whole work both plain and easy. As to French cooks and old experienced house-keepers, they have no occasion for my assistance, it is not from them I look for any applause. I have not engraved a copper-plate for a third course, or a cold collation, for that generally consists of things extravagant; but I have endeavoured to set out a dessert of sweetmeats, which the industrious house-keeper may lay up in summer at a small expence, and when added to what little fruit is then in season, will make a pretty appearance after the cloth is drawn, and be entertaining to the company. Before you draw your cloth, have all your sweetmeats and fruit dished up in china dishes or fruit baskets; and as many dishes as you have in one course, so many baskets or plates your dessert must have; and as my bill of fare is twenty-five in each course, so must your dessert be of the same number, and set out in the same manner, and as ice is very often plentiful at that time, it will be easy to make five different ices for the middle, either to be served upon a frame or without, with four plates of dried fruit round them; apricots, green gages, grapes, and pears — the four outward corners, pistachio nuts, prunelloes, oranges, and olives— the four squares, nonpareils, pears, walnuts, and filberts — the two in the centre, betwixt the top and bottom, chestnuts and Portugal plums — for six long dishes, pineapples, French plums, and the four brandy fruits, which are peaches, nectarines, apricots, and cherries.

1st Course — Fish Remove

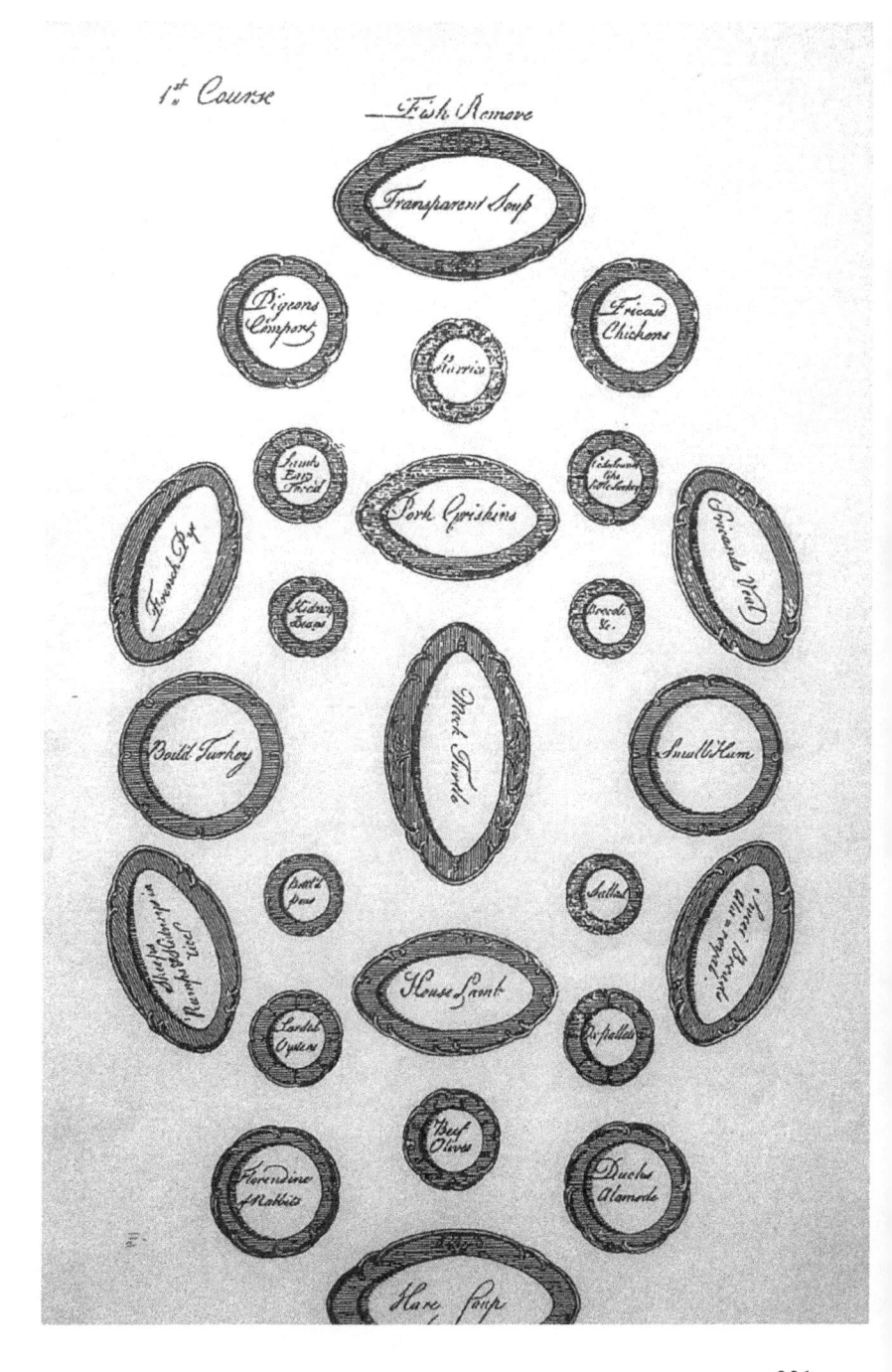

- Transparent Soup
- Pigeons Comport
- Curries
- Fricas'd Chickens
- Lambs Ears Fric'd
- Pork Griskins
- Calvs head hashed
- French Pye
- Kidney Beans
- Brocoli &c.
- Fricand Veal
- Boil'd Turkey
- Mock Turtle
- Small Ham
- Beef Collops in Ramkin Veal
- Boil'd Peas
- Sallet
- Hare Roast
- Larded Oysters
- House Lamb
- Vi'salles
- Florendine Rabbits
- Beef Olives
- Ducks Alamode
- Hare Soup

2d Course

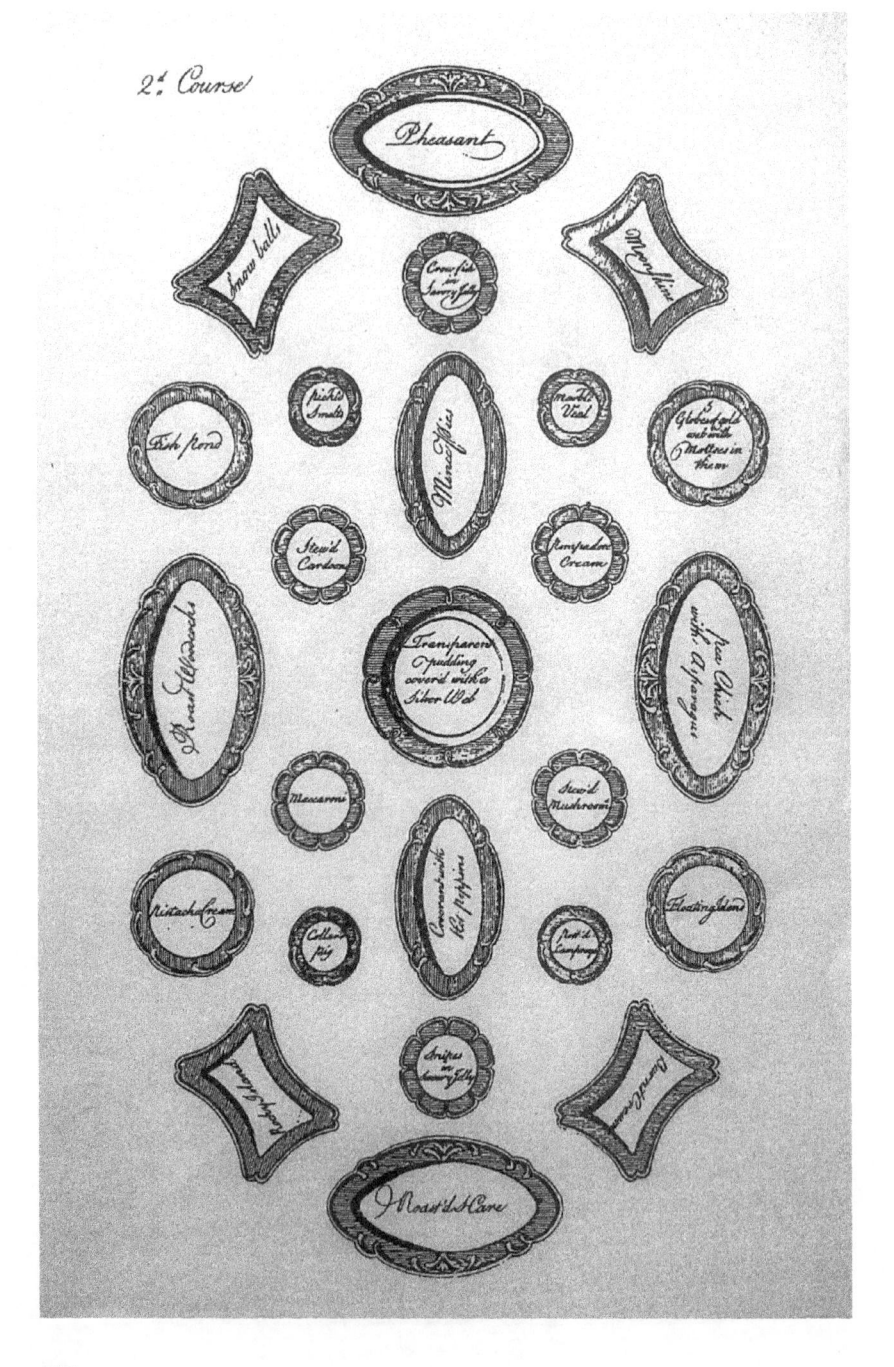

I N D E X.

A.   Page
ACID for Punch 334
Ale to mull 31 1
Almonds to burn 242
Almond Icing for Bride Cakes 265
Amulet to make 291
  of Asparagus 291
Angelica to candy 246
Apple-Sauce 59
Apple floating Island 258
Apple Tarts 145
Apricots to dry 244
Apricot Marmalade 225
  Paste 238
  to preserve 231
Asparagus to boil 78
Artichokes to boil 77
Artichoke Bottoms,
   to dress with eggs. 290
  Bottoms, to boil white 289
  Bottoms to dry 361
Artichokes to pickle 355

B.
Bacon,
  a Gammon to roast 112
  to salt , 307
Bances French 164
Barbadoes Jumballs 274
Beans French to dress 78
Beans French to keep . 359

a second way • 360
  Windsor to dress 78
Beef a la- mode 116
  Brisket a-la- royal 117
Beef to collar flat Ribs 87
  to force Inside Surloin 1 13
  Inside of Surloin to dress
  Bouille 113
  Fricando 115
  To hash 72
  Heart larded 1 18
  Heart Mock Hare 118
  Olives to make 117
  Porcupine flat Ribbs 116
  Porcupine to eat cold 299
  Round to force 304
  Rump to stew 105
  a second way 105
  Steaks to broil 70
  Steaks a good way to fry 71
  Steaks to dress
    a common way 71
  To hang a Sirloin 305
  to roast 305
  Tea 312
  to pickle 308
Biscuits common to make 276
  Drops 276
  Lemon to make 276
  Spanish to make 275
  Sponge to make 275
Blancmange 195

333

a second way 196
a third way 196
Brandy Cherry 336
   Orange 337
   Raspberry 336
Brawn Mock 302
Bread French 278
   to make white 279
Brocoli to boil 4 77
   and Eggs 289
Browning for made Dishes 81
Bullace Cheese 236
Butter to clarify 37
   Fairy 258

C.
Cabbage to boil 76
Cakes Apricot to make 242
   Bath 271
   Bride 264
   without Butter 273
   Cream 272
   Currant clear 239
   Currant 272
   Lemon 268
   Lemon a second way 269
   Orange 268
   Good Plum 266
   Little Plum 268
   White Plum, 267
   Prussian 267
   Queen 271
   Ratafia 269
   Ratafia a second way 269
   Rice 269
   Common Seed 272
   Rich Seed 267
   Shrewsbury 270

   Shrewsbury a second way 270
   Violet 240
Calf Head roasted 281
Calf's-Head Hash 85
   to dress 86
   to collar 88
   to grill 88
   Mock-Turtle 82
   A second way 87
   Surprise 83
Calf's Feet to fricassee 281
Candy Angelica 246
   Ginger 243
   Lemon, Orange- Peel 246
Caps black to make 206
   green to make 206
Carp to stew brown 29
   to stew white 26
   to dress 26
   Sauces 27
Catchup to keep seven years Mum 339
   Mushroom 339
   Walnut 338
   Walnut a 2d Way 338
Cauliflowers to boil 76
Celery to fry 286
   to ragoo 286
   to stew 285
Chardoons to fry 286
   to stew 286
Cheese-Cakes, Almond 258
   Bread 259
   Citron 259
   Common 260
Cheesecake Curd 260
   Rice 259

Bullace to make 236
Egg 261
Cheese Ramaquin 292
  Sloe 236
Cheese to stew 285
  to stew with light Wigs 285
Cherry Brandy 336
  to dry 240
  to dry a second way 241
Chicken-broth to make 312
Chickens to boil 64
  to force 126
  to fricassee 125
  to roast 65
  in savoury jelly 282
  Water to make 313
Chickens artificial 126
  and Pullets to stew 114
Chocolate to make 316
Chops to salt 306
Cockles to stew 38
Cod's Head and Shoulders to dress - 20
  a second way 22
Cod salt to dress 22
Codlings to dress like Salt fish 22
Codsounds to dress 23
  like little Turkies 23
Collar Beef 303
  Flat Ribs of Beef 303
  Calf's Head 300
  Eels 46
  Mackarel 43 a
  A Breast of Mutton 301
  A Pig 301
  A Swine's Face 302
  Breast of Veal to eat hot 90

Breast of Veal to! eat cold 300
Collops Scotch brown 96
  French Way 97
Cowslip Mead 332
Cracknells 274
Cranberries to bottle 364
Crawfish in savory Jelly 284
  in Jelly 284
Cream Cheese 255
  burnt 253
  Chocolate 248
  Clotted 250
  Hartshorn 250
  Ice 249
  King William's 254
  Lemon 25
  Lemon With Peel 252
  Orange 252
  Pistachio 248
  Pompadore 253
  Raspberry 251
  Ribband 250
  Snow and 254
  Spanish 249
  Steeple with Wine Sours 250
  Tea 253
Crumpets Orange to make 260
  a second way 260
  Tea 279
Cucumbers to stew 291
  with Eggs to dress 142
Currant clear Cake 239
  Drops 245
  Green to bottle 364
  to dry in Bunches 244
  Black Rob 237
Custard Almond 256

Beest 257
Common 257
Lemon 256
Orange 256

D
Damsons to bottle 362
  to dry 243
Desert Island to make 199
  of spun Sugar 193
Directions for setting out a grand Table 383
Distill Bean FlowerWater 367
  To distill Caudle Water 366
Distill ElderFlower Water 367
  Hephnatick Water 366
  Lavender Water 368
  Milk Water 366
  Peppermint Water 367
  Pennyroyal Water 368
  Rose Water 368
  Spirits of Win© 368
Ducks a-la braise 128
  a-la mode 129
  to boil with Onion sauce 59
  wild hash 75
  wild to roast 66
  tame to roast 59
  to stew 127
  to stew with green Peas 128
Drops Peppermint 245
  Lemon 245
  Raspberry 245
  Currant 245
Dumplings Apple to make 174
  Barm of Yest 184
  Damson 183
  Raspberry 183

Sparrow 184

E
Eels to boil 37
  to broil 37
  to collar 46
  to pitchccck 37
  to roaft 30
Eggs to dress with Artichoke Bottoms 289
  and Brocoli 289
  Cheese to make 2fci
  to fricassee 290
  Sauce to make 64
  And Spinage to dress 289
  to poach with Toasts 289
Elder Rob 236

F.-
Fish Pond to make 194
  to caveach 50
  to preserve 50
  to stew a good way 32
Flounders to boil, and all Kinds of Flat Fish to stew 38
Flummery to make 195
  Colouring for 194
  Cribbage Cards 205
  Green 197
  Eggs and Bacon in 203
  Melon in 197
  Oatmeal 204
  Solomon's Temple in Yellow 196
Forcemeat for Breast of Veal Porcupine 89
  for Hare Florentine 136
Fowls a-la-braise 123

to boil 63
to dress cold 75
to force 124
to hash 74
large to roast 64
Fritters Apple to make 161
  common ditto 161
  clary ditto 16
  Plumb with Rice ditto 5 3
  Raspberry ditto 162
  Tansey ditto 162
  Water 163
Fruit in Jelly 197

G
Giblets to stew 57
Ginger to candy 243
Good Green to make 197
Gofers to make 165
Goose to boil 57
  to marinate 126
  Stubble to roast 51
  Green to roast 58
Gooseberries to bottle 363
  to bottle a second way 364
Gooseberry paste 239
Grapes to keep 365
Gravy to draw 1
  to make 5
Green Gages to dry 241
Gruel Barley to make 315
  Groat 314
  Sago 315
  Water 316

H.
Haddocks to broil 35
  a second way 35

Ham to boil 69
to roast 112
to salt 306
to smoke 307
Hare Florendine 136
to hash 76
to jug 135
to roast 69
to stew 135
Hodge Podge 137
Harrico by way of Soup 140
  of Mutton or Lamb 140
  Neck of Mutton 141
Herrings to bake 34
  to boil 33
  to fry 33

J
Jam Apricots to make 212
  Black Currant 214
  Green Gooseberry 218
  Red Raspberry 212
  Strawberry- 213
Iceing for Tarts 144
  a second way 144
  Almond for Bride Cake 265
  Sugar for Bride Cake 265
Jelly Calf's Foot to make 191 -
  Savory for cold meat 192
  Colouring for J 14
  Craw-fish in Savory 284
  Birds in Savory 283
  Chickens in Savory 282
  Black Currant to make 211
  Red Currant 211
  White Currant 214
  Fish Pond in 194
  Gilded Fish in 198

Fruit in 197
Hartshorn to make 210
a second way 192
Hen and Chickens in 198
Hen's Nest 195
floating Island in 200
Ditto a second way 201
Rockey Island in 201
Moon and Stars in 203
Pigeons in Savory
Smelts in Savory
Transparent Pudding
Moonshine - .202
Orange 210

L
Lamb Bits to dress 282
   Head and Purtenance to dress 109
   Leg boiled, And Loin fryed 108
   a Quarter of, forced 109
   Stones fricasseed 110
Lampreys to pot 48
   a second way 48
   to roast 30
   to stew 31
Larks to toast 07
Lemonade -to make 333
   a second way 333
Lemon Drops 245
   Pickle 80
   Peel to candy 246
Loaf Drunken to make *202
   Oysters 40
   Princes 262
   Royal 262
Lobsters to boil 40
   to roast 40
   to stew 41
Lobster Patties to garnish fish 41
   to pot 49
   Sauce 28
   Pie 156

M
Macaroni, with Parmesan Cheese to dress 285
Maccaroons 275
Mackarel to boil 32
Malt Liquors to refine 330
Marmalade Apricot to rnakc 225
   Orange 223
   Quince 2.24
   Transparent 224
Mead Cowslip to make 331
   Sack 331
   Walnut 332
Midcalf to dress 101
Mince Pie without Meat 152
Mock Brawn to make 302
   Turtle 82.
   Turtle a second way 83
Moonshine to make 202
Moor Game to pot 52, 298
Muscles to stew 38
Mushroom Loaves 287
   to keep to eat like fresh 360
   Ditto a second way 361
   Powder to make 340
   to ragoo 288
   to stew 287
   another way 287
   to pickle brown 356

to fricassee 1 43
Mulled Ale 311
   Wine 311
   Ditto a second way 312
Mutton a Basque to make 107
   a Breast to collar 301,
   a Breast to grill 105
   Broth to make 313
   to hash 73
   to harrico 140
   Hodge Podge 141
   Kebob'd to make 105
Leg to force 100
   Leg to dress, called Oxford John 108
   Leg to salt 308
   Leg split, and Onion Sauce 105
Mutton Leg to dress, to eat like Venison 107
   neck to harrico 102,141
   Neck to make French Steaks of 103
   Neck to eat like Venison 1 102
   Shoulder boiled, Celery Sauce 140
   Shoulder boiled, called Hen and Chickens 104
   Shoulder boiled Onion Sauce 104
   Shoulder surprised 104
   Steaks to broil 71

O
Observations on boiling and roasting Beef, Mutton, Veal, and Lamb 52

on Cakes 264
on Creams, Custards, etc. 247
on Decorations for a Table, 1S5
on Distilling 365
on dressing Fish 14
on drying and candying J
on made dishes 79
on Pies and Paste 143
on Possets, Gruels &c. 308
on potting and collaring
on roasting wild and tame Fowls 14
on roasting Pig, Hare, &c. 55
on pickling 342
on preserving 209
on Puddings 167
on Wines, Catchup, &c. 317
on Soups I
on keeping Garden Stuff and Fruit 358
Orange Brandy to make 337
   Chips to candy 243
   Jelly to make 210
   Juice 334
   Marmalade 223
   Peel to candy 246
Ox Pallates to fricando 119
   to fricassee 120
   to stew 119
Oyster sauce to make 60
   Soup 13
Oysters to fry 39
   to pickle 42
   to scollop 39

to stew & all Kinds of Shell
Fish 221 33
Ozyat to make 332
 a second way 333

P
Panada savoury 292
 sweet 316
Pancakes batter 166
 Clary 166
 Cream 165
 Fine 166
 Pink coloured 167
 Tansey 166
 Wafer165
Parsnips to boil 79
Partridge to hash 75
 in Panes 133
 to stew 134
 to stew a second way 134
 to roast 65
Paste for Desert Baskets for Covers 188
 a Chinese Temple or Obelisk 189
 Apricot to make 228
 Cold for Dish Pies 146
 Red & white Currants 239
 for Custards 146
 for Goose Pie 145
 Gooseberry 239
 Crisp for Tarts 144
 Light for Tarts 144
 Raspberry Pasty 238
Pasty a Venison145
Patties common to make 160
 to fry 159
 Lobster to garnish Fish 41

 Fine 160
 Fried 150
 Savory 158
 Sweet , 160
Peaches to dry
Pears to stew
Peas Green to boil
 to keep
 to keep a second way 359
 to stew 142
 to stew with Lettuce 289
Peppermint Drops 345
Perch to fry 36
 in Water Soaky 37
Pheasant to roast 65
Pickle Indian to make 357
 In Imitation of Bamboe 358
 Artichokes 355
 Barberries 350
 Red Beet Root 362
 Red Cabbage 354
 Red Cabbage, a second way 354
 White Cabbage 353
 Cauliflowers 353
 Cauliflowers, a second way 353
 Cockles 46
 Codlings 325
 Cucumbers 342
 Cucumber, a second way 1
 Cucumbers in Slices 344
 ElderBuds 352
 Elder Shoots 352
 Grapes 354
 Kidney Beans 346
 Mangoes 344
 Mackarel 44

Mushrooms 355
Nasturtians 351
Onions 356
Oysters 42
Parsley 35
Pork 308
Radish Buds 351
Salmon, Newcastle way 42
Samphire 346
Shrimps 51
Smelts or Sparlings 45
Walnuts Black 347
Ditto, a second way 347
Ditto green 349
Ditto Olive Colour 348
Ditto white 349
Pigs Chops to salt 302
Pig to barbecue 111
   to dress in Imitation of Lamb 110
   Feet and Ears to ragoo 280
   Feet and Ears to souse 305
   Petty toes to dress 56
   to roast 55
Pigeons artificial 156
   to boil 67
   to boil with Bacon 33
   to boil in Rice 131
   to broil 131
   to compote 129
   to fricando 132
   to fricassee 133
   in a Hole 130
   jugged 132
   to roast 67
   in savoury Jelly 283
   to transmogrify 130

Pike to boil, with a Pudding in the Belly 25
Pikelets to make 278
Pippins to stew whole 237
Plaice to stew 31
Pork to barbecue 111
   Chine to stuff 112
   to pickle 308
   to salt 308
   Steaks to broil 72
Possets Ale to make 311
   Almond to make 310
   Brandy 309
   Lemon 309
   Orange 310
   Sack 309
   Wine 310
Potatoes to scallop 287
Pot, Beef to 293
   Beef to eat like Venison 294
   all kinds of small Birds 299
   Chars 47
   Eels 47
   Ham with Chickens 297
   Hare 297
   Lampreys 48
   Lobsters 4S
   Moor Game 52, 298
   Ox Cheek 294.
   Pigeons 298
   Salmon 44
   Ditto, a second way 45
   Shrimps 50
   Smelts or Sparlings 45
   Tongues 296
   Woodcocks 297
   Veal 295
   Marble Veal 296

Venison 295
Preserve Apricots 221
  Apricots green 218
  Barberries in Bunches 222
  Barberries for Tarts 229
  Bullace Cheese 236
  Cherries in Brandy 336
  Morello Cherries 228
  Codlings to keep all the year 217
  Cucumbers 215
  Currants red in Bunches 214
  Currants white in Bunches 2I4
  Black Currant Rob 237
  Currants for Tarts 215
  Damsons 229
  Elder Rob 236
  Grapes in Brandy 216
  Green Gage Plums 220
  GreenGooseberries 218
  Red Gooseberries 226
  Gooseberries in Imitation of hops
  Lemons carved 233
  Ditto in Jelly 234-
  Magnum Bonum Plums 232
  Oranges 232
  Ditto carved 232
  Ditto in Jelly 232
  Ditto with Marmalade
  Peaches 231
  Golden Pippins 217
  Kentish Pippins 217
  Plums GreenGage 220
  Plums Bonum Magnum 230
  Pine Apples 225
  Quinces whole 230

Ditto in Quarters 232
Red Raspberries ' 228
White ditto 227
Sloe Cheese 236
Sprigs Green 220
Strawberries whole 227
Wine Sours 230
Walnuts Black 221
Ditto Green 222
Ditto white 225
Puddings, Almond 168
  Apple 169
  Apricot 174
  Bread 173
  Bread, a second Way 73
  Calf's Feet 172
  Little Citron 177
  Green Codling 178
  Boiled Custard 169
  Gooseberry 182
  Hanover 184
  Herb 182
  Hunting 168
  Lemon 170
  Lemon, a 2d way 170
  Lemon a third way 170
  Marrow 179
  Marrow, a second way
  Marrow, a third way 180
  Boiled Milk 182
  Nice 173
  Orange 171
  Orange, a second Way
  Plain 174
  Quaking 180
  Quaking, a second Way 161
  Rice Common 171
  Ditto boiled 172

Ditto ground 179
Red Sago 175 Sago,
another way 177
to scollop 287
Sippet 174
Tansey with Almonds
Tansey baked 177
Tansey boiled 176
Tansey with ground Rice
Transparent 175
Ditto, a second way 199
Vermicelli J 75
White in Skins 189
Yam 182
Yorkshire under Meat
Puffs, Almond 2?8
  Chocolate 277
  Curd 261
  German 164
  Lemon 277
Pies, Beef-steak 150
  Bride 155
  Calf's-head 151
  Codling 153
  Chicken a savoury 151
  Eel 155
  Egg and Bacon
  to eat cold X5X
  French 146
  Hare 149
  Herb for Lent 153
  Hottentot 154
  Lobster 156
  Mince 152
  Olive 157
  Rook 157
  Salmon 149
  Thatched House 150

Veal savory 158
Veal sweet 157
Venison 154
Yorkshire Goose 148
Yorkshire Giblet 156

Q
Quince Marmalade 224
  preserved whole 231

R
Rabbits to boil 68
  Florendine 137
  Fricassee brown 139
  Fricassee White 139
  to roast 68
  surprised 138
Raspberry Brandy 336
  Cream 251
  Red Jam 212
  White Jam 213
  Paste 238
  Drops 245
Ray, or Scate to boil 34
Ruffs and Rees to roast 60

S
Sago to make with Milk 315
Salmon to boil Crimp 23 3
  to pot 44
  to pot a second way 45
  rolled 24
Sauce Apple for Goose 59
  Bread for roast Turkey 62
  For   Cod's   Head   and Shoulders 21
  For Cod's Head a second way 22

Celery 103
Egg for Salt Cod 24
Egg for roasted fowls 68
Lobster 28
  for Green Goose 59
  for Stubble Goose 59
  for most Sorts of Fish 28
Onion 59
Onion for boiled Goose 57
Oyster for boiled Turkey 60
  for roasted Pig 56
  for roasted Pig a second way 56
  for Salmon 24
Shrimp 21
  for boiled Turkey a second way 61
White for Fish 27
White for Fowls 63
White for boiled breast of Veal 91
Sausages to fry 290
Scate or Ray to boil 34
Scotch Collops brown 96
  Collops French way 97
  Collops white 96
  Collops to warm 73
Sheeps rumps and Kidneys 106
Sherbet to make 335
  to make a second way 335
Shrimps to stew 41
Shrub Almond 337
  Currant 337
  another way 336
Smelts or Sparling to fry 36
Snipes to roast 66
Snow balls to make 236
  a Dish of 305

Soles to caveach 50
  to fry 35
  to marinate 35
Solomon gundy to make 280
  a second way 281
Soup Almond to make 6
  a-la-Reine 7
  Common Peas 10
  Oyster 13
  Craw- fish 13
  Gravy with yellow Peas 11
  Green Peas 9
  Green Peas without Meat 12
  White Peas 11
  Hare 3
  Onion 8
  Brown Onion 9
  White Onion 8
  Ox Cheek 5
  Partridge 14
  Peas for Lent 10
  Portable for Travellers 2
  Rich Vermicelli 4
  Transparent 3
  White 12 and 13
Spinage to 'stew 77
Sprats to bake 34
Stew Cheese with light wigs 285
  Carp 29
  Ducks 127
  Ducks and Green Peas 128
  Hare 135
  Oysters all sorts of Shell Fish 38
  Partridge 134
  Ditto a second way 134
  Pears 206

Peas 142
Peas with Lettuces 288
Rump of Beef 115
Tench 29
Turkey brown 121
Ditto with Celery Sauce 120
Strawberry Jam to make 213
   to preserve whole 227
Stum to make 329
   To preserve whole
Stuffing for a marinate Goose 127
Sturgeon to dress 30
   to pickle 41
Sugar to boil Candyheight 247
Sugar to spin Gold Colour 189
   Silver Colour 188
Spun Sugar, a Dessert of 190
Sweetbreads a-la-daub 98
   to fricassee brown 99
   to fricassee white 99
   forced 98
   to ragoo 99
Syllabubs Lemon to make 207
   Lemon a second way
   Solid 207
   under the Cow 208
   Whip 207

T
Teale to roast 66
Tench to stew brown 29
   to stew 307
Toast fried to make
Tongue to boil
   to salt
Trifle to make
Tripe soused

Trout to fry
Turbot to boil
Turkey boiled, Oyster Sauce 60
   a-la-daub, hot 122
   cold 122
   to hash 74
   to roast 62
   soused 304
   stewed and Celery sauce 120
   stewed brown 121
Turtle to dress 100 lb. Weight 15
   to dress a second way 19
   artificial to make 84
   Forcemeat for ditto 85
   Mock to dress 82
   a second way 83

V
Veal a breast to boil 91
   a Breast to collar 90
   Ditto to porcupine 89
   Ditto to ragoo 90
   a Fillet bombarded 93
   to ragoo a Fillett 100
   to stew a Fillet 100
   to fricando 9
   to hash 73
   to disguise a Leg 101
   to mince 73
   to a-la royal a Neck of 92
   Neck of Cutlets 92
   Olives 94-
   Ditto a second way 35
Venison Pasty 194
   to hash 72
   Haunch roasted 70
Vinegar Elder Flower 340

Gooseberry 341,
Sugar 341
Tarragon 340
Violet Cakes 240

W
Wafers to make 277
Wafer Pancakes 265
Water Imperial 31
  Barley 314
Web Silver to spin
  Gold to spin 188
Whet before Dinner 139
Whey Cream of Tartar 314
  Scurvy Grass 314
  Wine 313
Whitings to broil 35
  a second way 35
Wigs light to make 274
Wine
  Balm 327
  Blackberry 322
  Birch 324
  Birch a second way 325
  Clary 327

  Cowslip 325
  Ditto a second way 326
  Red currant 323
  Ditto a second way 32
  Elder-Flower 32
  Elder Raisin 319
  Ginger 320
  Pearl Gooseberry 321
  Gooseberry, a second way 321
  Lemon to drink like Citron Water 317
  a second way 318
  Orange 318
  a second way 318
  a third way 319
  Acid Raisin to cure 327
  Smyrna Raisin 319
  Raisin, another way 320
  Raspberry 322
  Sycamore 324
  Walnut 325
Woodcock to hash 75
  Ditto to roast. 66

FINIS.